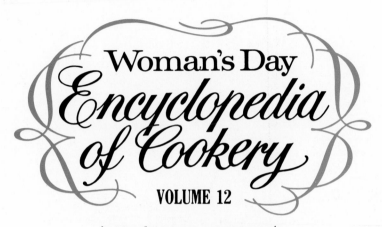

Woman's Day
Encyclopedia of Cookery
VOLUME 12

*in 12 volumes—over 2,000 pages—
with more than 1,500 illustrations in color,
1,000 entries and 8,500 recipes
1,200 menus, 50 specialty cook books
and a host of delightful features by distinguished food writers.*

Prepared and edited by the Editors of Woman's Day
Editor: EILEEN TIGHE
Managing Editor: EVELYN GRANT   *Food Editor:* GLENNA MCGINNIS
Art Consultant: HAROLD SITTERLE   *Photographic Editor:* BEN CALVO
Associates: OLIVIA RISBERG, CHARLOTTE SCRIPTURE,
CAROLYN STORM, JOHANNA BAFARO

SPECIAL PROJECT STAFF
Editor: NIKA STANDEN HAZELTON   *Art Director:* LEONARD A. ROMAGNA
Associates: L. GERALDINE MARSTELLER, HELEN FEINGOLD,
SUSAN J. KNOX, INEZ M. KRECH

FAWCETT PUBLICATIONS, INC.   NEW YORK

PRINTED AND BOUND BY
FAWCETT-HAYNES PRINTING CORPORATION
ROCKVILLE, MARYLAND

Table of Contents

VOLUME 12

TOPPING TO ZWIEBACK
plus
150 WAYS TO BE A BETTER COOK

Definitions and 440 Recipes
How to buy, store, prepare, cook, and serve ·
Nutritive Food Values · Caloric Values

To help you plan more varied meals
with the recipes in this volume

Foreword

To the best of our knowledge, no work of this magnitude ever has been undertaken by any author, editor, or publisher in America. The editors of Woman's Day, with a special staff of experts, present to you this Encyclopedia of Cookery, a comprehensive and colorful library on all culinary matters. The twelve-volume encyclopedia contains in its 2,000 pages over 8,500 recipes from all over the world, 1,500 food illustrations in color, 1,200 menus, 50 special cook books and over 1,000 food definitions. In addition, there are full details about all foods, their nutritive and caloric values, how to buy, serve, prepare, and cook them. There is a history of food and cooking, articles on nutrition, diet, entertaining, menu planning, herbs and spices. Every topic of culinary interest is covered. Five years of intensive work have gone into its preparation, backed by twenty-five years of food and cookery experience in the publication of Woman's Day.

We think you will find this Encyclopedia of Cookery the most complete and authoritative work ever published on the subject. It is a library for everyone who cares about good food and the fine art of preparing it.

The Editors

=≪ **VOLUME 12** ≫=

TOPPING—A covering or garnish for foods. Toppings are also used to add to the flavor of many dishes. Some toppings are thin and glazy while others are puffy and light. Whipped cream, fudge sauce, sugar glazes, hard sauce, honey caramel toppings, buttered crumbs, mashed potatoes, cheese, and melted chocolate are all used for toppings.

WHIPPED-CREAM TOPPING

Whip 1 cup heavy cream with 2 tablespoons cocoa and 2 teaspoons sugar until almost stiff. Serve on plain cake. Makes about 2 cups.

TORTE—A rich cake or pastry, made with eggs, sugar, jam, liqueur, and little or no flour, with nuts or dry bread crumbs often used instead of flour. Tortes can be baked in layers put together with luscious fillings, such as buttercream. They may be frosted in an elegant manner with rich icings and/or whipped cream or meringues. Tortes can also be decorated to the nth degree with glacé fruits, nuts, or candied flowers; in short, anything that will dress up a cake.

ALMOND BRANDY TORTE

3 eggs
1 cup sugar
1 teaspoon ground mace
  Grated rind of 2 lemons
1 cup fine dry bread crumbs
1 cup good-quality brandy
1¾ cups finely ground blanched almonds
  (about ½ pound)
  Simple Lemon Icing
  Toasted almonds, cut into halves

Beat eggs and sugar until light. Add mace and lemon rind. Stir in bread crumbs and brandy alternately. Blend in almonds. Pour into greased and floured deep 8-inch cake pan. Bake in preheated moderate oven (350°F.) for 30 to 35 minutes, or until cake tests done. Cool. Ice with Simple Lemon Icing. Decorate top with toasted almond halves. Makes 12 servings.

Simple Lemon Icing

Sift 2 cups confectioners' sugar into bowl. Gradually beat in 2 tablespoons fresh lemon juice. Beat to spreading consistency. If necessary, add a little more sifted confectioners' sugar or lemon juice.

VIENNESE TORTE

1½ cups sugar (use fine granulated)
⅔ cup sifted all-purpose flour
1 tablespoon Dutch-type cocoa
1 cup finely ground hazelnuts
9 egg whites
1 cup heavy cream, whipped and
  sweetened to taste
1 tablespoon rum
12 marrons glacés
  Candied violets

Sift together sugar, flour, and cocoa; add hazelnuts. Beat egg whites until very stiff. Fold into sugar mixture. Grease and flour 3 cookie sheets. Pipe mixture from pastry bag or spread in 9-inch layers on cookie sheets. There should be 3 layers. Bake in preheated slow oven (300°F.) for 30 minutes, or until layers are barely golden. Cool. Combine whipped cream and rum. Fill layers with whipped cream and put together. Spread a thin layer of whipped cream on top. Arrange *marrons glacés* in a circle on the top, 1 inch from edge. Fill spaces between them with candied violets. Pipe a decorative whipped-cream border around top.

FRENCH CHOCOLATE TORTE

4 ounces (4 squares) unsweetened
  chocolate
¼ cup water
½ cup sweet butter, cut into pieces
½ cup sugar
3 large or 4 small eggs, separated
½ cup ground unblanched almonds
2 teaspoons rum or brandy
⅓ cup all-purpose flour
  Sour-cherry jam
  Chocolate Icing

Melt chocolate in water over low heat, stirring constantly. Remove from heat. Stir in butter and stir until completely melted. Blend in sugar. Cool. Beat in egg yolks, one at a time. Blend in nuts and flavoring. Stir in flour and blend well. Fold in stiffly beaten egg whites. Grease and flour two 8-inch layer-cake pans. Divide batter between pans. Bake in preheated moderate oven (350°F.) for about 25 minutes, or until cakes test done. Cool. Put sour-cherry jam between the layers and spread a thin layer of jam over top. Frost top and sides of cake thickly with Chocolate Icing. Makes 12 to 16 servings.

Chocolate Icing

1½ cups sugar
1½ cups hot water
2 ounces (2 squares) unsweetened
  chocolate
⅓ cup cornstarch
¼ cup cold water
1 tablespoon rum or brandy extract

Combine sugar, hot water, and chocolate in heavy saucepan. Over medium heat, bring to a boil. Lower heat and cook for

5 minutes, stirring constantly. Mix cornstarch and cold water to a smooth paste. Stir mixture into chocolate syrup. Cook for 3 or 4 minutes, stirring constantly to avoid lumping. Remove from heat. Blend in extract. Beat until cool enough to spread. Makes enough for top and sides of two 8-inch layers, about 2 cups.

Note: This icing should be flavored in the same manner as the French Chocolate Torte, to match flavors.

JAEGERTORTE
(Hunter's Torte)

1 cup fine dry bread crumbs
3 tablespoons sherry
2 tablespoons fresh lemon juice
5 eggs, separated
1¼ cups sugar
1 cup almonds, blanched and shredded
1 teaspoon baking powder
½ teaspoon salt
⅔ cup apricot jam or currant jelly
4 egg whites

Soak bread crumbs in sherry and lemon juice. Beat egg yolks until light. Gradually beat in 1 cup sugar; beat until mixture is thick and lemon-colored. Beat in bread crumbs, ¾ cup of the almonds, and the baking powder. Beat the 5 egg whites with salt until stiff. Fold lightly into batter. Put batter into greased and floured 9-inch shallow baking dish suitable for serving. Bake in preheated moderate oven (350°F.) for 20 to 25 minutes, or until cake tests done. Reduce oven heat to slow (300°F.). Remove torte from oven. Cool slightly in dish. Spread with apricot jam. Beat the 4 egg whites until frothy. Add ¼ cup sugar, 1 tablespoon at a time, beating well after each addition. Meringue should be stiff and glossy. Spread meringue evenly over torte. Sprinkle with remaining almonds. Bake for 10 to 15 minutes, or until top is honey-colored. Cool, and serve from baking dish. Makes 10 to 12 servings.

MOCHA TORTE

8 eggs, separated
1 cup sugar
1½ cups cake flour
½ cup butter, melted and cooled
5 cups Mocha Buttercream
1 cup slivered toasted almonds
Whole coffee beans

Beat egg yolks and sugar until light and fluffy. Gradually beat in flour, 2 tablespoons at a time. Beat egg whites until stiff. Gently fold into mixture. Stir in butter, stirring just sufficiently to blend. Grease and flour four 8-inch layer-cake pans. Divide batter among pans. Bake in preheated moderate oven (350°F.) for about 15 minutes, or until layers test done. Remove from pans and let cool. Reserve 1 cup Mocha Buttercream. Spread remaining Mocha Buttercream between layers, over sides, and on top. Stick almonds on sides of torte. Put remaining cup of Mocha Buttercream into pastry bag with fluted tube. Pipe a row of large rosettes around edge of torte. Pipe more rows of rosettes on top of torte until it is completely covered. Top each rosette with a coffee bean. Chill before serving. Makes 16 servings.

Mocha Buttercream

1 cup sugar
⅔ cup strong or espresso-type coffee, cold
12 egg yolks, well beaten
2½ cups sweet butter, softened
¼ cup triple-strength coffee, cold

In heavy saucepan cook sugar and ⅔ cup coffee to thread stage (234°F. on a candy thermometer). Pour syrup slowly over egg yolks, stirring constantly. Beat mixture until cold and foamy. Gradually beat in butter, a little at a time, alternately with ¼ cup coffee. Beat only until mixture is smooth. If cream separates, keep beating until smooth. Chill to spreading consistency before using. Makes about 5 cups.

SWEDISH VARMLANDSTARTA

3 egg whites
½ cup granulated sugar
¼ cup finely chopped hazelnuts
2 tablespoons cocoa
Buttercream
Slivered toasted almonds

Beat egg whites until very stiff. Gradually beat in sugar. Beat until stiff and glossy. Beat in nuts and cocoa. Grease 2 cookie sheets and mark 8-inch circles on each sheet. Spread the meringue mixture out into 8-inch circles and bake in preheated slow oven (300°F.) for 30 to 35 minutes. Lower heat to very slow (275°F.) for the last 5 to 10 minutes. Loosen the layers while they are still warm and let them cool before the Buttercream is spread on them. Spread Buttercream on the tops of layers. Put layers together and sprinkle cake with slivered toasted almonds. Makes 8 to 10 servings.

Buttercream

3 egg yolks
2 tablespoons sugar
⅓ cup light cream
⅓ cup butter

Put egg yolks, sugar, and cream in a saucepan and let simmer while whipping firmly until the cream thickens. Let cool. Cream butter until light and fluffy. Gradually beat in the cooled cream mixture, 1 teaspoon at a time. Beat until well blended and fluffy.

CHERRY TORTE WITH CREAM

1½ cups sifted all-purpose flour
2 egg yolks
9 tablespoons sugar
Grated rind of 1 lemon
½ cup butter, softened and cut into small pieces
¼ cup finely grated hazelnuts or filberts
6 cups pitted fresh bing cherries (about)
½ teaspoon ground nutmeg
½ cup heavy cream
½ cup slivered blanched almonds

Put flour in a bowl. Make a well in the center. Add 1 egg yolk, 1 tablespoon of the sugar, the grated lemon rind, and butter. Stir with a fork until mixture blends and forms a dough. Knead with the hands on a lightly floured board until dough is smooth. Pat dough with the fingers into the bottom and sides of a 9-inch pie pan, pressing the dough into a high edge on the side of the pan. Sprinkle dough with grated hazelnuts. Chill for 2 hours. Put pitted cherries on top of dough in overlapping circles, making 2 layers. Sprinkle with remaining sugar and nutmeg. Bake in preheated moderate oven (350°F.) for 15 minutes. Beat remaining egg yolk with cream and pour mixture over cherries. Sprinkle top with slivered almonds. Continue baking in moderate oven (350°F.) for 30 minutes, or until dough is golden brown and cherries are tender. Serve warm. Makes 6 to 8 servings.

APRICOT TORTE

4 eggs
1 cup sugar
½ teaspoon salt
⅔ cup sifted all-purpose flour
⅔ cup cornstarch
1 package (11 ounces) dried apricots
¾ cup dark corn syrup
¼ cup cold water
½ cup chopped almonds or walnuts

Beat eggs in large mixing bowl until fluffy. Gradually add ⅔ cup sugar and salt, beating until mixture doubles in bulk and mounds slightly when dropped from spoon. Sift flour and ½ cup cornstarch over egg mixture; fold in. Pour into 2 greased and floured 9-inch layer-cake pans. Bake in preheated moderate oven (350°F.) for about 25 minutes, until top springs back when lightly touched. Cool slightly. Remove from pan. Cool completely on a rack; then cut each cake into 2 layers with a sharp thin knife.

Put apricots in saucepan, cover with water, and bring to a boil. Simmer, uncovered, for 30 minutes, stirring occasionally. Add ½ cup corn syrup and remaining ⅓ cup sugar; stir until sugar is melted. Purée mixture, using an electric blender or a strainer. Reserve ¾ cup. Stack cake layers, using all but ¾ cup purée as filling; use about ½ cup between each layer.

Blend remaining 2 tablespoons cornstarch and water in saucepan. Stir in reserved ¾ cup purée and remaining corn syrup. Stirring constantly, bring to boil, and simmer for 1 minute. Cool slightly. Pour over cake. Spread evenly over top and sides with spatula. Cover sides with chopped nuts. Serve with whipped cream, if desired. Makes 8 servings.

Viennese Torte

SWEDISH SANS RIVAL TORTE
5 egg whites, at room temperature
½ teaspoon cream of tartar
2 cups sifted confectioners' sugar
1½ cups blanched almonds
1 cup sweet butter
¼ cup water
1 cup granulated sugar
3 egg yolks
1 teaspoon vanilla extract
24 slightly toasted blanched almonds, halved

Beat egg whites with cream of tartar until foamy throughout. Using an egg beater or electric mixer, beat in confectioners' sugar, 2 tablespoons at a time, beating after each addition until sugar is thoroughly blended. (Do not beat in sugar any faster or meringue will not stand up.) Grind 1 cup of the almonds. Carefully fold almonds into meringue. Cut out three 8-inch squares from wax paper or plain brown paper such as packing paper. Place on greased cookie sheets. With spatula, spread meringue on squares. Bake in preheated very slow oven (275° F.) for about 20 minutes or until light golden and firm to the touch. Remove from cookie sheet. When cooled, carefully peel off paper from meringue squares.

■ Meanwhile make buttercream. Beat butter until light and fluffy. Boil water and ⅓ cup of the sugar until syrup spins a 2-inch thread when dropped from spoon (232°F. on candy thermometer). Beat egg yolks until well blended. Pour sugar syrup over egg yolks, a little at a time, beating constantly. Beat until cooled. Add butter very carefully, a little at a time, to prevent curdling. Stir in vanilla. (If cream curdles, place over hot water and beat until smooth.)

■ To make praline powder, melt remaining ⅔ cup sugar over lowest possible heat. Add remaining ½ cup whole blanched almonds and stir until almonds are coated with sugar. Pour mixture onto buttered cookie sheet. Cool thoroughly until hard. Break praline into very small pieces with rolling pin or grind coarsely in meat grinder.

■ To assemble torte, stir half of ground praline into buttercream. Spread ⅔ of this mixture on the 3 meringue layers and sandwich them together. Spread remaining ⅓ on sides. Sprinkle sides with remaining praline. Decorate top with toasted almond halves in a decorative pattern. Makes 10 to 12 servings.

OPERA TORTE
Cake:
2 cups sifted confectioners' sugar
1⅓ cups sifted cornstarch
6 eggs, separated
¼ teaspoon cream of tartar
¼ cup water
1 teaspoon vanilla extract

Filling:
1 tablespoon unflavored gelatin
¼ cup cold water
4 egg yolks
6 tablespoons sugar
3 tablespoons cornstarch
2 cups milk
1 tablespoon vanilla extract
1 cup heavy cream, whipped
3 tablespoons brandy (optional)

Almond Paste:
1 cup blanched almonds
2 cups confectioners' sugar
1 teaspoon almond extract
2 egg whites, slightly beaten
Green food coloring

Topping:
½ cup sifted confectioners' sugar

Grease four 8-inch layer-cake pans and line the bottoms with wax paper.

■ To make the cake, sift together 3 times 1 cup confectioners' sugar and the cornstarch. Beat the egg whites, cream of tartar, and water in a large bowl until the mixture forms soft peaks. Gradually beat in remaining 1 cup confectioners' sugar, a little at a time. Continue beating until stiff peaks form when beater is raised. Add egg yolks and vanilla; beat in just until well blended. Fold in sugar-cornstarch mixture, a little at a time, and blend thoroughly. Divide batter among pans and bake in a preheated moderate oven (350°F.) for 30 minutes, or until top of cake springs back when touched lightly with finger. Cool before removing from pans.

■ Meanwhile, make the filling. Soften gelatin in cold water. Combine egg yolks, sugar, cornstarch, and milk in top part of double boiler. Cook over simmering, not boiling, water until mixture is smooth and thick. Stir constantly. Remove from heat and beat in gelatin and vanilla. Cool, beating occasionally to keep smooth. Fold in whipped cream and brandy. Chill before using.

■ While filling chills, make almond paste. Put almonds through nut grinder twice, or grind fine in electric blender. Combine with sugar, almond extract, and egg whites. Work with spoon until smooth. Stir in a few drops of green food coloring to color the paste light green. Knead almond paste with hands until it is very smooth and the sugar has been completely absorbed. This may take from 5 to 10 minutes. Roll out on wax paper into an 8-inch circle.

■ To assemble the Torte, neatly spread filling on cake layers; the top layer should also be spread with filling. Put layers together. Place almond paste over filling on top layer. Sift confectioners' sugar through a paper lace doily onto almond paste to form decorative pattern. Remove doily carefully. Makes 10 to 12 servings.

Note: This handsome delicate cake is at its best if served very cold, almost frozen.

TORTILLA—The daily bread of Mexico, made since time immemorial by the Indians and later by the Mexicans, in the shape of a round, flat, thin cake resembling a pancake. Tortillas are cooked on a griddle until done, but not browned. They are eaten as is, or stuffed and rolled with meat, cheese, etc., in which case they are called *tacos*.

The word tortilla means "little cake." True tortillas are made with a lime-treated cornmeal dough called *masa*, but they are also made with wheat flour. The *masa* needed for them can be bought fresh in the Mexican-American border districts, and dried in all stores catering to people of Mexican and Central American origin. Tortillas are also sold canned.

Tortillas should be served hot. The Mexicans put them in a hot dish and cover them with a napkin to keep them hot. If cooled, they can be reheated in preheated moderate oven (350°F.). Before putting in the oven, brush them with water, or rub with dampened hands to moisten them.

WHITE CORN TORTILLAS
Boiling water
2 cups masa
1 teaspoon salt

Stir boiling water into *masa* to make a stiff dough. Add salt. Let stand for 1 hour. With damp hands, pat dough into 5-inch round cakes. They should be as thin as possible. Bake on greased griddle, turning frequently to cook through thoroughly. Makes about 12.
Note: The dough may also be rolled out between 2 sheets of clear plastic or wax paper, and trimmed to size.

TORTILLA DE HARINA DE TRIGO
(Wheat Tortillas)
2 cups all-purpose flour
1 teaspoon baking powder
1 teaspoon salt
½ cup lard
¾ cup water (about)

Sift dry ingredients together into mixing bowl. Cut in lard as when making pie dough. Add enough water to make a soft dough. Roll out thinly on floured board. Cut into 5-inch rounds. Bake on lightly greased griddle, turning frequently to cook through. Makes about 16.

CHILI-FILLED TORTILLAS
Fry tortillas in small amount of cooking oil until crisp. Spread heated canned chili con carne on each tortilla. Cover with shredded lettuce. Sprinkle with a little French dressing and some grated Parmesan cheese. Fold over; garnish with black olives, green onions, and tomato wedges.

Tortilla de Harinha de Trigo   *Chili-Filled Tortillas*

CHICKEN-FILLED TORTILLAS WITH TOMATO SAUCE

- 12 tortillas
- 2 tablespoons cooking oil
- 1 green onion, minced
- 1 cup (one 8¼-ounce can) tomatoes, drained and chopped
- 2 cups chopped cooked chicken
  Salt
- 1 cup (8-ounce can) tomato sauce
- 1 hot dried red pepper
  Dash of oregano

Fry tortillas in 1 tablespoon of the oil until crisp. Cook onion in remaining oil for 2 minutes. Add tomatoes; cook for 5 minutes. Add chicken, heat, and add salt to taste. Spread on tortillas and fold over. Top with remaining ingredients, heated together. Makes 12.

TOSTADAS

Cut canned tortillas into 6 or 8 wedge-shape pieces. Fry in deep fat (375°F. on a frying thermometer) for 2 to 3 minutes, until golden brown. Drain on ab-sorbent paper and sprinkle with salt. These will stay crisp for several weeks if kept in an airtight container, or they may be frozen for longer storage.

TORTONI—An Italian dessert in which whipped cream is flavored with sherry, rum, or other liquor, combined with macaroon crumbs, put into little paper cups, sprinkled with more crumbs or with almonds, and frozen. The classic is Biscuit Tortoni.

BISCUIT TORTONI

- ½ cup coarsely ground dried almond macaroons
- 1 cup light cream
- ⅓ cup sugar
- ¼ cup sherry
- 1 cup heavy cream, whipped
- ½ cup blanched almonds, minced and toasted

Soak the ground macaroons in the light cream for 30 minutes. Add sugar and sherry; freeze until mushy. Fold in whipped cream and pack into eight ¼-cup paper or foil cups. Sprinkle with the almonds and freeze until firm. Makes 8 servings.

COFFEE TORTONI

- 1 egg white
- 1 tablespoon instant coffee powder
- ⅛ teaspoon salt
- 6 tablespoons sugar
- 1 cup heavy cream
- 1 teaspoon vanilla extract
- ⅛ teaspoon almond extract
- ¼ cup toasted blanched almonds, finely chopped

Turn refrigerator control to coldest setting. In small bowl mix egg white, coffee, and salt. Beat with rotary beater until almost stiff. Gradually beat in 2 table-spoons of the sugar and beat until stiff. Whip cream and fold in remaining sugar and the flavorings. Fold in meringue and nuts. Spoon into ¼-cup paper or foil cups and freeze in freezing compartment of refrigerator until firm. Makes 8 servings.

SHERRY TORTONI

Melt ½ pound marshmallows in ⅔ cup sherry in top part of double boiler; cool to room temperature. Whip 2 cups heavy cream; fold into marshmallow mixture. Spoon into 8 individual soufflé cups or double thickness of paper baking cups which have been set in muffin pans. Sprinkle with very finely chopped almonds or cake or cookie crumbs. Freeze; wrap individually in foil or plastic wrap and return to freezer. Makes 8 servings.

TOSS, TO—In culinary usage the phrase means to mix a food lightly, usually with a fork and spoon. Tossing is done in order to allow all parts of the food to come into contact with other ingredients; a salad, for instance, is tossed so that the ingredients will be well coated with the dressing.

TOURNEDOS—A meat cut, consisting of small filets of beef taken from the tip of the tenderloin. They are also known as filet steaks. Since the meat of the filet is very lean, the tournedos are circled with a strip of pork fat secured with string; the string, and usually the fat, is removed before serving. Tournedos are sautéed in butter or broiled. They are served, usually on bread rounds so that the delicious meat juices will not be wasted, with different accompaniments and sauces, such as mushrooms, artichokes, etc.

TRIFLE—A dessert of English origin made from jam-covered, spirit-soaked spongecake, over which a rich custard is poured. The trifle is then covered with whipped cream and handsomely decorated with glacé fruit and almonds. Another name for it is tipsy cake. But trifle need not be so elaborate. It may be simple spongecake soaked with fruit juice, covered with fresh or canned fruit, and decorated with whipped cream.

Trifles can also be varied in other ways. Instead of using spongecake, macaroons may be the base. Cake crumbs too have been used to advantage. Instead of covering the cake with whipped cream, it may be covered with a sugared meringue and quickly baked in the oven, as in a meringue pie.

The name trifle is also given to fruit desserts served with custard and whipped cream.

A TRUE ENGLISH TRIFLE

2 layers of plain spongecake
1 dozen ladyfingers, split
1 cup apricot, strawberry, raspberry, or any other jam
1 cup good-quality sherry or Madeira
½ cup brandy
8 egg yolks
½ cup sugar
4 cups light cream, scalded
1 teaspoon vanilla extract
½ teaspoon almond extract
1 cup heavy cream, whipped
  Angelica strips and candied cherries
  Blanched almonds and tiny macaroons

Line silver or crystal dish with one of the spongecake layers. Make a border with the ladyfingers, allowing them to protrude ½ inch over edge of the dish. Spread spongecake layer with jam and sprinkle with half of sherry. Top with second cake layer. Combine remaining sherry and the brandy and pour over cakes. Let stand until cake has absorbed the liquid. In top part of a double boiler beat egg yolks with sugar until thick. Slowly stir in scalded cream. Cook over simmering, not boiling, water, stirring constantly, until thickened. Remove from heat and stir in vanilla and almond extracts. Cool. Pour custard over cake layers. Chill. Spread top of trifle with whipped cream or pipe ornamental swirls of whipped cream through pastry tube. Cut angelica into strips and cut candied cherries into halves and quarters. Decorate trifle with glacé fruit in any fancy pattern. Arrange almonds and tiny macaroons around border. Chill before serving. Makes 16 servings.

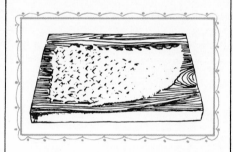

TRIPE—The inner lining of the stomach of beef. There are three kinds: honeycomb, pocket, and plain or smooth. Honeycomb tripe is considered the most desirable.

Availability and Purchasing Guide—Honeycomb, pocket, and plain tripe are all available fresh, pickled, and canned. The fresh and canned tripe are widely available; pickled tripe is not often found outside the New England area.

Tripes à la mode de Caen, the most famous of French tripe dishes, is available canned.

Storage—Refrigerate fresh and pickled tripe.

☐ Fresh, refrigerator shelf: 1 day
☐ Pickled, refrigerator shelf: 2 to 3 days
☐ Canned, kitchen shelf: 1 year

Nutritive Food Values—A good source of protein.

☐ Fresh, 3½ ounces = 100 calories
☐ Pickled, 3½ ounces = 62 calories

Basic Preparation—Fresh tripe, although it has been cooked before it is sold, requires additional cooking. Pickled tripe is usually sold thoroughly cooked, but should be parboiled before using. Canned tripe is ready to heat and serve.

☐ **To Cook Fresh Tripe**—Put in kettle and cover with water. Add 1 tablespoon salt. Simmer, covered, for 1½ hours, or until tender. Drain and dry between paper towels. Cut into serving pieces and serve with hot tomato sauce, or use in recipes.

☐ **To Sauté Fresh Tripe**—Dip serving pieces of cooked fresh tripe into 1 beaten egg mixed with 2 tablespoons water; then into fine dry bread crumbs. Sauté tripe in small amount of hot fat in skillet until golden-brown on both sides. Serve with hot tomato sauce or lemon wedges.

☐ **To Broil Fresh Tripe**—Brush serving pieces of cooked fresh tripe with melted butter or margarine. Broil about 3 inches from heat for 5 minutes. Turn and brush with butter. Broil for 5 minutes longer, or until golden brown. Brush again with butter and season with salt, pepper, and paprika.

☐ **To Parboil Pickled Tripe**—Put tripe in saucepan and cover with cold water. Bring to boil, cover, and simmer for about 15 minutes. Drain, and dry between paper towels. Cut into serving pieces.

☐ **To Panfry Pickled Tripe**—Roll pieces of parboiled pickled tripe in a mixture of half flour and half cornmeal. Fry in ⅛ inch of hot bacon fat or lard until well browned on both sides and crisp. Put on a hot platter and put a small pat of butter or margarine on each piece.

BATTER-FRIED TRIPE

1 pound fresh tripe, cooked
1 cup all-purpose flour
¼ teaspoon salt
1 teaspoon baking powder
1 egg, beaten
½ cup milk
1 teaspoon cooking oil
  Bacon fat or lard
  Chili sauce or ketchup

Cut tripe into 1½-inch squares. Mix dry ingredients. Add next 3 ingredients and beat until smooth. Dip pieces of tripe in the batter and fry in hot bacon fat in skillet until browned on both sides. Serve with chili sauce. Makes 4 servings.

TRIPES À LA MODE DE CAEN
The most famous tripe recipe in French cookery

2 pounds fresh tripe
3 carrots, scraped and cut into rounds

6 whole cloves
3 garlic cloves, chopped
3 ounces salt pork, diced
8 peppercorns
1 calf's foot, cut into 3 pieces, or
1 veal knuckle, cracked
  Large bouquet garni (1 celery stalk with tops, ¼ leek, 1 bay leaf, 3 parsley sprigs, ¼ teaspoon ground thyme
6 slices of bacon
¾ cup water
1½ cups dry white wine

Wipe tripe and cut into cubes. Put in a large earthenware pot a layer of carrots and half of cloves, garlic, salt pork, and peppercorns. Add a layer of tripe. Repeat the process. Put calf's foot and *bouquet garni* in the center of the pot. Cover the last layer of tripe with slices of bacon. Fill casserole three-fourths full with water mixed with white wine. Cover tightly and bake in preheated moderate oven (350° F.) for 5 hours, or until tripe is tender. Add boiling water if needed. Remove calf's foot and *bouquet garni*. Thicken sauce with cornstarch before serving if desired. Makes 6 to 8 servings.

TRIPES À LA LYONNAISE

2 pounds fresh tripe, cooked
¼ cup butter or cooking oil
4 large onions, thinly sliced
  Salt and pepper to taste
¼ teaspoon ground nutmeg

Cut tripe into squares. Heat 2 tablespoons of the butter, add onion slices and sauté until pale yellow. Remove onions. Add tripe and remaining butter. Brown tripe on both sides. Add sautéed onions. Cook over medium heat, stirring, for 8 minutes. Season with salt and pepper and stir in nutmeg. Serve very hot. Makes 6 large servings.

CRISP BREADED TRIPE

1 pound fresh tripe
1 egg
⅓ cup undiluted evaporated milk
1 teaspoon salt
⅛ teaspoon pepper
½ teaspoon crumbled dried sage
1 small onion, grated
1¼ cups fine dry bread crumbs

Wash tripe; cover with seasoned water and simmer for about 1½ hours, or until tender. Drain, and cool. Cut into 16 pieces. Combine beaten egg, evaporated milk, salt, pepper, sage, and onion. Dip tripe into mixture, then coat with crumbs. Arrange pieces 1 inch apart on greased cookie sheet. Let stand for 30 minutes. Bake in preheated hot oven (400°F.) for 20 minutes, or until browned. Makes 4 servings.

STEWED TRIPE WITH VEGETABLES

1 pound fresh tripe
2 cups water
2 cups (one 1-pound can) tomatoes
1 bay leaf
2 whole cloves
4 peppercorns
½ green pepper, chopped
1 onion, chopped
1½ teaspoons salt
⅛ teaspoon pepper
½ teaspoon Worcestershire
4 medium potatoes
  All-purpose flour
  About 2 cups (one 1-pound can) whole green beans, drained

Cut tripe into 1-inch squares. Add water and all ingredients except last 3. Simmer, covered, for 2 hours. Add potatoes and simmer for 1 hour longer. Thicken with flour mixed with a little cold water. Add beans, and heat. Makes 4 servings.

TRIPE CREOLE

Cut 1 pound cooked fresh tripe into strips. Simmer for 30 minutes with 1 tablespoon cooking oil, 1 sliced onion, 2⅓ cups (one 1-pound, 3-ounce can) tomatoes, 1 minced garlic clove, and salt, pepper, ground nutmeg, and herbs to taste. Makes 4 servings.

TROUT—The name given to a large group of fishes of the family *Salmonidae*. Although most varieties are fresh-water fish and favor clear cool waters, a few, such as the sea trout and some of the rainbow trout, live in the sea and ascend rivers to breed. Trout vary greatly in size and coloration according to their environment, but they all have one thing in common: they are a fine sporting fish. They are also one of the most delicious fish to eat; their flesh is lean and delicate.

Among the most widely known are the rainbow trout, *Salmo gairdnerii,* native to the streams of California, but now found in other parts of the United States and throughout the world; the brook, or speckled, trout, *Salvelinus fontenalis,* of the eastern United States; the steelhead, or salmon-trout, which is a variety of the rainbow trout; the cutthroat trout, *Salmo clarkii,* and the Dolly Varden, *Salvelinus malma,* both found in cold waters from California to Alaska.

Trout can be broiled, baked, poached, or panfried, usually whole.

Availability—Trout are available whole, fresh and frozen. Trout are also available canned. Smoked or kippered trout are available.

Storage

☐ Fresh, refrigerator shelf, raw: 1 to 2 days

☐ Fresh, refrigerator shelf, cooked: 4 to 5 days

☐ Frozen, refrigerator frozen-food compartment, prepared for freezing: 2 months

☐ Frozen, freezer, prepared for freezing: 4 to 6 months

Caloric Values

☐ Brook trout, 3½ ounces, raw = 101 calories

☐ Rainbow trout, 3½ ounces, raw = 195 calories

Basic Preparation

☐ **To Poach**—Put cleaned trout in a flat pan and barely cover with hot Court Bouillon. Cover and simmer for 4 to 6 minutes, or until fish flakes easily with a fork. Serve with béarnaise or other sauce.

Court Bouillon

Combine 1 quart water, 3 tablespoons fresh lemon juice or 1 tablespoon vinegar, and 1½ teaspoons salt. Bring to a boil and cook for 3 minutes before using for poaching fish.

☐ **To Panfry**—Dip cleaned trout into milk and roll in flour. Fry in hot butter or margarine in skillet until well browned on both sides and fish flakes easily with a fork. Season with salt and pepper.

☐ **To Bake**—Put cleaned trout in a well-greased shallow baking pan. Sprinkle with salt and pepper and brush with melted butter or margarine. Bake in preheated hot oven (400°F.) for 15 to 20 minutes, or until fish flakes easily with a fork. Season with salt and pepper.

☐ **To Broil**—Put cleaned trout on broiler rack and brush with melted butter or margarine. Broil about 3 inches from the heat for 3 to 5 minutes, depending on the thickness of the fish. Turn and brush again with butter. Broil for 5 to 8 minutes longer, brushing once or twice with butter. Season with salt and pepper.

☐ **To Fry Brook Trout**—Clean and wash fish, allowing 2 or 3 per person. Dry thoroughly. Dip each fish into undiluted evaporated milk, then into seasoned cornmeal. Fry in shallow fat until golden-brown on both sides.

☐ **To Freeze**—Eviscerate fish and leave whole or remove head. Wash thoroughly and drain. Wrap in moisture- vapor-proof wrapping, excluding as much air as possible. Seal.

TROUT EN PAPILLOTE

1 steelhead trout (4 to 5 pounds)
  Salt and pepper
½ cup butter or margarine
1 tablespoon chopped fresh mint

Have trout cleaned but do not remove head. Sprinkle lightly inside and out with salt and pepper. Arrange a large sheet of foil in bottom of shallow baking dish.

Truite au Bleu

Spread butter on foil. Put fish on foil and sprinkle with mint. Roll up and twist ends of foil. Bake fish in preheated hot oven (400°F.) for about 50 minutes. Put, still wrapped, on hot platter. Cut portions through bones and all. Serve with cream sauce or other preferred sauce. Makes 4 to 6 servings.

RAINBOW TROUT, ROCKY MOUNTAIN STYLE

    4 rainbow trout, about 1 pound each
1½ teaspoons salt
    ¼ teaspoon pepper
      Yellow cornmeal
      Butter or margarine

Sprinkle cleaned trout inside and out with salt and pepper, mixed together. Roll in cornmeal and panfry in hot butter for 5 minutes on each side, or until golden-brown and fish flakes easily with a fork. Makes 4 servings.

BROOK TROUT MEUNIÈRE

    4 brook trout
      All-purpose flour seasoned with salt and pepper
    ½ cup clarified butter

    ⅓ cup chopped parsley
      Lemon wedges

Wash trout and drain, leaving head and tail on. Dip fish into flour. Melt ¼ cup butter and sauté trout until firm and brown. Put trout on a serving platter and cover with chopped parsley. Add remaining butter to pan drippings. Cook over medium heat until butter becomes golden-brown. Spoon butter over fish. Serve with lemon wedges. Makes 4 servings.

TRUITE AU BLEU

    3 cups water
    1 cup vinegar
    6 peppercorns
    1 small bay leaf
    1 teaspoon salt
    4 trout, freshly dressed
      Melted butter
      Hot boiled potatoes

Bring first 5 ingredients to a boil. Drop in trout and simmer just long enough to cook fish through, about 4 minutes for the average fish. Serve hot with melted butter and boiled potatoes, and asparagus, if desired. Makes 4 servings.

TROUT, ENGLISH STYLE

    6 trout
    3 tablespoons butter or margarine
    2 tablespoons olive oil
      All-purpose flour
      Salt and pepper
    1 egg, slightly beaten
    1 cup fine dry bread crumbs

Wash and dry trout. Heat butter and olive oil in a large skillet. Dredge fish with flour, and sprinkle with salt and pepper. Dip in egg, then in the crumbs, and sauté quickly in the hot fat. Serve with tartare sauce. Makes 6 servings.

COMMANDER'S PALACE TROUT ALEXANDER

    3 pounds speckled trout
      Milk and water
      Salt and pepper
    3 bay leaves
    ½ cup butter
    ¾ pound mushrooms, sliced
    1 garlic clove, minced
    4 scallions with green tops, minced
    ¼ pound each of cooked shrimps and lobster
    2 tablespoons all-purpose flour
    1 cup heavy cream

Skin and bone trout. Place pieces side by side in a buttered shallow saucepan. Add milk to cover fish halfway and add about half as much water as milk. Sprinkle lightly with salt, add bay leaves, and cover the pan. Bring liquid to a boil. Reduce heat and simmer slowly for about 15 minutes, or until the fish flakes readily at the touch of a fork. Reduce the broth in which the fish was poached to ½ cup and reserve it for use in the sauce. Melt butter, add mushrooms and garlic, and sauté for 5 minutes, stirring occasionally. Add scallions and simmer for 5 minutes longer. Add shrimps and lobster. Heat thoroughly. Sprinkle with flour and cook, stirring, for 2 more minutes. Gradually stir in 1 cup milk, the cream, and reserved fish broth. Simmer the sauce for 10 minutes, stirring, over low heat until smooth and thickened. Season to taste with salt and pepper. Pour sauce around the fish on the platter and serve at once. Makes 4 servings.

TRUFFLE by Lucy Kavaler

—"Sensual men of fashion consume them to whet their appetite for lovemaking." With these words an Italian writer of the 1470's expresses the age-old belief about the aphrodisiac qualities of truffles.

Modern science does not back up this legend, but the popularity of the truffle, which is a fungus growing beneath the ground, does not depend upon lovers alone. Adding its incomparable flavor to the best *pâté de foie gras,* the truffle is appreciated by the true gourmet. Anthelme Brillat-Savarin, 19th-century French expert on the art of dining, recommended stuffing turkeys with truffles, and lyrically declared this "a luxury only for the tables of the great or . . . homes of kept women." Some cooks cut truffles into fancy shapes and use them to decorate platters of cold chicken or meats, while others stretch the expensive delicacy by chopping it very fine and adding it to a cream sauce flavored with Madeira. One inspired chef some years back created truffled ice cream. Ward McAllister, social arbiter of the extravagant gilded age of the 1890's, beseeched such friends as *the* Mrs. Astor to serve *filet de boeuf* with truffles rather than mushrooms.

But neither McAllister nor the modern gourmet would be likely to recognize the truffle in its natural state. Unlike the appealing mushroom, the truffle is an extremely ugly fungus. Belonging to the *Ascomycetes* class of fungi, the truffle is a roundish dark-brown ball with a thick, warty, rindlike surface. Within lies a series of elaborate folds, which contain the spores or seeds. In the Middle Ages its appearance gave rise to the legend that truffles were formed from witches' spit, which was believed to be dark in color, rather than the white of normal humans. Although the average truffle weighs but a few ounces, every so often a king-size specimen tipping the scales at two-and-a-half pounds is found.

Finding the truffle at all is quite a feat, as no part of it ever appears above ground. The fungus grows in the woods on the roots of oaks or beeches, taking nourishment from the trees and giving them back water and minerals from the soil in a perfect example of the harmony of nature. The only giveaway of the whereabouts of a truffle is its odor, and the human sense of smell is not keen enough to detect that. Animals love truffles just as much as people do, which has turned out to be very fortunate for those of us who appreciate good food. The Russians tried to use bear cubs and the Sardinians employed goats, but dogs and pigs have proved to be the best hunters.

It takes several years to teach a pig to hunt, and a trained animal is worth its weight in truffles. Tenderly treated by its master, it is trundled to the forest in a wheelbarrow. The pig snuffles along the ground until attracted by the delectable smell. It digs up the truffle, and then comes the critical moment: the owner must prevent the animal from eating the fungus without discouraging it to the point where it will not go on to find more truffles. An acorn or other tidbit is, therefore, substituted, while the truffle is whisked away.

Many different kinds of truffle lie hidden beneath the soil, but not all of them are edible. Unfortunately, none of the forty varieties growing in the United States is good, so gourmets must rely on imports, primarily from southern France and northern Italy. Of the Italian truffles, the Piedmont is the most renowned. But the reputation for best flavor belongs to the *Tuber melanosporum,* which grows in the oak forests of Périgord in France.

It is possible, but by no means easy, to increase truffle production by planting groves of oaks or beeches, putting bits of truffle in the soil nearby, and waiting. The first harvest appears from six to ten years later. It is easy to see why truffles remain such a luxury.

In the desert, however, truffles can be a lifesaving, rather than a luxury food. The desert truffle, known scientifically as *Terfezia,* is different from the species eaten in America or Europe and does not require a tree partner. Hungry nomads traveling over the burning wastes of the Sahara watch for the telltale sign that reveals the hidden fungus. A truffle pushes the sand up an infinitesimal amount, just enough to cast a shadow at sunset or sunrise. The Arabs roast the truffles in the hot ashes of the fire and then dip them into salt. Any leftover truffles are dried and taken along to provide sustenance on the weary journey to the oasis.

Availability and Purchasing Guide—Fresh truffles are not available in the United States.

Canned truffles are available in most gourmet food stores. They are put up in several sizes of cans or jars, some being very small, and all being very expensive: a seven-ounce can costs about $20.

Storage—If only a part of a can is used, it should be tightly covered and refrigerated since the full flavor and aroma are quickly lost after a can is opened. If the opened can must be kept for some time, pour bacon or poultry drippings over the remaining truffles, cover, and store in the refrigerator.

Nutritive Food Values—Truffles, like mushrooms, are low in calories and have very little nutritive value. They are served for the delicate flavor and aroma they give to foods.

Basic Preparation—Canned truffles have already been cooked so they are added to the food they are to accompany just long enough to heat them through.

☐ **To Use in Salads**—Truffles are mixed with diced boiled potatoes or artichoke hearts and the salad seasoned with a dressing made of salad oil, lemon juice, salt, and pepper. Never use other herbs as they will mask the delicate flavor of the truffles.

Truffles are diced and inserted into pieces of meat. They are sometimes minced and added to dressing for fowl or game.

TRUSS, TO

—To tie a bird with string, holding the wings and legs tightly to the body. This is done before cooking so that the bird will not loose its shape.

To truss a bird, fold wing tips back under. With a long piece of clean string, tie the leg tips together tightly and make a taut loop around the tail. Have the two ends of the string of reasonably even length. Cross the string over the back of the bird. Take it across the wings to hold them closely to the body. Finally, tie the string securely to what is left of the bird's neck. Remove string after bird is cooked.

All types of poultry and game bird may be trussed, but it is not absolutely necessary to truss a duck since its legs are short and close to the body. In barbecueing, a bird is trussed to keep the bird well balanced on the roasting rod so that the bird will cook evenly. Let roasted or barbecued birds stand for twenty minutes before removing cord, and then carve.

═══════ 🐦 ═══════

TRY OUT, TO—To render, that is, to heat fat or fat meat, such as salt pork or bacon or kidney fat, until the fat melts and can be separated from the remaining tissue. The tried-out fat is then used for cooking, or stored in solid form for future use.

TUNA—This salt-water game fish belongs to the mackerel family. It is also called tunny fish or horse mackerel. Tuna is found in almost all the seas of the temperate and warm zones of Asia, Africa, and America. In some parts of the world tuna can be enormous, reaching weights of 1500 pounds.

There are several varieties, including the albacore, bluefin, skipjack, and yellowfin.

Tuna is one of the best sporting fish and a fine food fish, fresh or canned.

Availability and Purchasing Guide—Because of its size fresh tuna is usually sold in steaks. Bluefin steaks are available from July to October; albacore from May to September. Frozen tuna steaks are available year round.

Canned tuna is sold packed in water or oil or seasoned oil, chunk style or solid pack. The all-white meat tuna comes from the albacore. A tuna-and-noodles dish is available canned.

Storage

☐ Fresh, refrigerator shelf, raw: 1 to 2 days
☐ Fresh, cooked; and canned, opened, refrigerator shelf: 3 to 4 days
☐ Fresh, prepared for freezing; or frozen, refrigerator frozen-food compartment: 2 to 3 weeks
☐ Fresh, prepared for freezing; or frozen, freezer: 3 to 4 months
☐ Canned, kitchen shelf: 1 year

Nutritive Food Values—A good source of protein.

☐ Fresh, 3½ ounces, raw = 145 calories
☐ Canned in oil, 3½ ounces, solids and liquid = 288 calories
☐ Canned in water, 3½ ounces, solids and liquid = 127 calories

Basic Preparation—Fresh tuna can be broiled, panfried, and baked. Canned tuna can be used in an endless variety of dishes. However, remember to drain and wash the oil or brine from canned tuna before using in cooked dishes.

☐ **To Broil Fresh Tuna**—Put steaks, cut into serving pieces, on broiler rack and brush with melted butter or margarine. Broil for 3 to 4 minutes on each side, depending on thickness of steak. Brush again with butter and season with salt and pepper. Serve with lemon wedges.

☐ **To Panfry Fresh Tuna**—Put steaks, cut into serving pieces, in hot butter or margarine in skillet and panfry for 3 to 5 minutes on each side, or until golden-brown. Serve with lemon wedges.

☐ **To Bake Fresh Tuna**—Put steaks, cut into serving pieces, in buttered shallow baking pan. Brush with melted butter or margarine. Bake in preheated hot oven (400°F.) for 8 to 10 minutes per pound, or until fish flakes easily with a fork. Time will depend on thickness of steak. Serve with lemon wedges.

TUNA COOK BOOK

FRESH TUNA

TUNA EN BROCHETTE

2 pounds fresh tuna steaks
1 slender loaf French bread
½ cup butter, melted
¼ cup olive oil
3 tablespoons fresh lemon juice
1 teaspoon salt
Bay leaves

Slice tuna ¾ inch thick, remove skin and dark meat, and cut into pieces slightly smaller than the diameter of the bread. Slice bread thin. Mix remaining ingredients except bay leaves and marinate fish in mixture for 1 hour. Impale a slice of bread on a skewer and add a slice of fish and a bay leaf; repeat until skewers contain 3 slices of fish and 4 of bread. Do not push too close together. Broil, basting with remaining marinade and turning until browned on all sides, for about 15 minutes. Makes 6 servings.

FRESH TUNA TARRAGON

2 pounds tuna steaks
White wine (about 1½ cups)
1 tablespoon crumbled dried tarragon
All-purpose flour
Salt
¼ cup butter or cooking oil

Marinate tuna steaks in white wine to cover for 2 hours. Drain. To the marinade add tarragon and let soak. Dry steaks, dust lightly with flour, sprinkle with salt, and sauté in butter on both sides until brown. Add the wine and tarragon mixture and cook at high heat until the wine is reduced to half. Remove fish to a hot platter, pour sauce over, and serve at once. Makes 4 to 6 servings.

CANNED TUNA: APPETIZERS AND SOUP

TUNA AND HORSERADISH CANAPÉS

1 can (about 7 ounces) tuna, drained and flaked
1 tablespoon minced celery
3 tablespoons mayonnaise
½ cup soft butter or margarine
3 tablespoons well-drained prepared horseradish
8 slices of toast, each cut into 4 triangles
Chopped parsley

Mix tuna, celery, and mayonnaise to a paste. Add butter and horseradish and mix well. Spread on toast and sprinkle with parsley. Makes 32 triangles.

TUNA DIP, FINES HERBES

1 can (about 7 ounces) tuna
1 package (3 ounces) cream cheese
¼ cup sherry
2 tablespoons minced parsley
2 tablespoons minced chives or 1 teaspoon dried chives
1 teaspoon minced tarragon or ¼ teaspoon dried tarragon
Dairy sour cream
Salt to taste

Combine all ingredients, adding enough sour cream to make of spreading or dunking consistency. Season with salt to taste and, if you wish, 1 or 2 tablespoons chopped capers or nuts. Makes about 1 cup.

TUNA APPETIZER

Here is a good first course, or a main dish for a light luncheon. It is very simple. Arrange large flakes of tuna (white preferred) on lettuce leaves on 4 individual plates. Whip ¼ cup heavy cream; fold in ½ cup mayonnaise, 2 teaspoons fresh lemon juice, and 1 teaspoon crushed dillseed (use a mortar and pestle, or a heavy bowl and wooden spoon). Spread sauce over tuna and top with a bit of pimiento or sliced stuffed olive. Makes 4 servings.

CABBAGE AND TUNA PIROG

1 package hot-roll mix
4 cups finely chopped cabbage

1 onion, chopped
¼ cup butter or margarine
1 or 2 cans (about 7 ounces each)
  tuna
2 tablespoons dillweed
  Salt and pepper
1 egg
1 tablespoon water

Make hot-roll mix according to directions on the box. Cook cabbage and onion in butter until wilted. Add tuna, flaked, and dillweed. Season to taste with salt and pepper. After dough has risen, divide into halves and roll each half into a rectangle about 9 x 11 inches. Put one rectangle in a shallow baking pan and spread with tuna-cabbage mixture. Moisten edges, top with second rectangle, and seal. Brush the top with egg beaten with water. Bake in preheated hot oven (400° F.) for 15 to 20 minutes, or until nicely browned. Cut into squares. Makes 12 servings.

TUNA TREAT

2 medium tomatoes, peeled and seeded
2 hard-cooked eggs, chopped
1 green pepper, chopped
¼ cup drained tuna fish
2 flat anchovy fillets, chopped
  Salt and pepper to taste
4 slices of white bread
  Butter
½ cup Russian dressing (about)
  Worcestershire

Chop tomatoes and drain well. Mix with next 4 ingredients. Season. Remove crusts from bread and toast slices. Cut toast into quarters and butter each piece. Spread with tuna mixture and cover with dressing. Sprinkle a drop of Worcestershire on each. Makes 16.

TUNA COCKTAIL

Combine 1 can tuna (white preferred) and ½ cup minced celery. Mix ½ cup mayonnaise, 2 teaspoons each of grated horseradish and grated onion, and 2 tablespoons fresh lemon juice. Combine tuna with sauce. Serve in cocktail glasses and garnish with slivered almonds, pimiento, or olives. Makes 4 servings.

TUNA FISH MOUND

2 cans (8 ounces each) tuna fish,
  drained
¼ cup minced chives
2 large sweet pickles, minced
2 teaspoons A-1 sauce
3 tablespoons ketchup
3 tablespoons grated Parmesan cheese
2 tablespoons mayonnaise

Combine the ingredients and mix well. Spoon into a round 3-cup mold or bowl. Refrigerate. When ready to use, turn out on a plate. Decorate with sliced stuffed olives. Surround with crackers. Makes 4 to 6 servings.

TUNA CHOWDER

¼ cup diced salt pork or bacon
1 onion, chopped
2 cans (about 7 ounces each) tuna
  in oil

2 cups hot water
1 cup diced potatoes
2 cups milk
  Salt and pepper
1 tablespoon minced parsley

Cook salt pork until crisp. Remove and reserve. To fat in pan add onion and oil drained from tuna. Cook until onion is wilted; then add the water and potatoes. When potatoes are almost tender, add tuna, milk, and salt and pepper to taste. Simmer until potatoes are done. Add salt pork. Top with parsley. Makes 4 servings.

CANNED TUNA: MAIN DISHES

TUNA-NOODLE CASSEROLE

½ pound noodles
1 garlic clove, minced
½ cup minced green onions
3 tablespoons butter or margarine
¼ cup all-purpose flour
2 cups milk
2 cans (about 7 ounces each) tuna
2 tablespoons sherry (optional)
  Salt and pepper
3 tablespoons bread crumbs
2 tablespoons minced parsley
2 tablespoons melted butter

Cook noodles in salted water, and drain. In the meantime, sauté garlic and onions in butter until wilted; add flour, blend over heat, and add milk. Cook, stirring constantly, until thickened and smooth; add tuna, sherry, and salt and pepper to taste. Other ingredients of your choice may be added with the tuna. Put in a 1½-quart casserole. Mix crumbs, parsley, and butter, and sprinkle on top. Reheat in preheated moderate oven (350°F.) for about 15 minutes. Makes 6 to 8 servings. Some suggestions for other ingredients: sliced cooked mushrooms, pimientos, sliced olives, nuts, tiny shrimps, hard-cooked eggs, some halved or quartered artichoke hearts, cooked peas, green beans, or Limas.

The seasonings may be varied, too: curry, chili powder, mustard, dill, tarragon, chives, basil, and thyme all blend happily with tuna; so does tomato, so a little tomato paste could be added.

TUNA FLORENTINE

1 pound spinach, cooked, chopped,
  and seasoned
2 tablespoons butter or margarine
3 tablespoons all-purpose flour
2 cups milk
¼ cup grated Swiss cheese
⅓ cup grated Parmesan cheese or
  ½ cup grated Cheddar
2 cans (about 7 ounces each) tuna

Put spinach in a large shallow baking dish and keep hot. Make a *roux* with the butter and flour; add milk, Swiss cheese, 2 tablespoons of the Parmesan, and the oil and juice from the tuna. Cook over hot

water for 20 minutes. Add tuna, flaked, and pour over spinach. Sprinkle top with remaining Parmesan and broil until brown and bubbly. Makes 6 servings.

CURRIED TUNA

2 cups chopped onions
1 cup chopped apples
½ cup butter or margarine
2 tablespoons curry powder
2 cups canned tomatoes
  Salt
2 cans (about 7 ounces each) tuna
  Hot cooked rice
  Chutney

Sauté onions and apples in butter until wilted. Add curry powder and tomatoes; cover and simmer for 30 minutes. Season with salt to taste. Separate tuna into flakes; add, and heat. Serve with rice, chutney, and any other desired condiments. Makes 4 servings.

SWEET-AND-SOUR TUNA

1 cup (one 7-ounce can) pineapple
  tidbits
½ cup vinegar
¼ cup sugar
1 tablespoon soy sauce
2 tablespoons cornstarch
4 green onions, sliced diagonally
1 green pepper, sliced thin
2 tomatoes, peeled, seeded, and cut
  into eighths
2 cans (about 7 ounces each) tuna

Drain syrup from pineapple and combine it with vinegar and sugar. Mix soy sauce with cornstarch, and add. Cook, stirring constantly, until clear and thickened. Add onions, green pepper, pineapple, and tomatoes, and simmer for 4 minutes. Add tuna, broken into large flakes, and cook just long enough to heat. Serve with chow-mein noodles if desired; or ¼ cup split almonds can be added to this dish. Makes 4 to 6 servings.

TUNA AND RICE

¼ cup butter or margarine
1 small onion, minced
1 cup uncooked rice
  Pinch of ground saffron
2¾ cups hot fish or chicken bouillon
½ cup grated Parmesan cheese
1 can (about 7 ounces) tuna, drained

Melt butter, add onion, and cook until lightly colored. Add rice and stir for 3 minutes. Put saffron in ½ cup of the bouillon; add remaining bouillon to the rice. Cook over low heat, stirring occasionally. When the liquid is absorbed, add saffron-flavored bouillon and cook until the rice is tender. Remove from heat and stir in cheese and tuna. Mix lightly. Makes 6 servings.

TUNA MARKA

2 cans (about 7 ounces each) tuna,
  white preferred
½ cup chopped green onions
1 tablespoon butter
½ cup sliced water chestnuts
2 teaspoons slivered fresh or candied
  gingerroot

2 cups dairy sour cream
Salt and pepper
Hot cooked rice

Drain tuna oil into pan, add onions and butter, and cook until wilted. Add tuna, broken into large flakes, water chestnuts, gingerroot, sour cream, and salt and pepper to taste. Heat gently. Serve with rice. Makes 6 servings.

TUNA AND POTATO TART

1 tablespoon chopped onion
1 tablespoon butter
1 can (about 7 ounces) tuna
2 cups seasoned mashed potatoes
2 tablespoons minced parsley
Salt and pepper if necessary
Pastry for 1-crust 10-inch pie, baked
6 eggs
1 tablespoon melted butter

Cook onion in butter until wilted. Add tuna, potatoes, parsley, and salt and pepper if needed. Spread in the pie shell; make 6 depressions in the potato mixture, drop a raw egg into each, and drizzle a little melted butter over each. Bake in preheated moderate oven (375°F.) until eggs are set. Makes 6 servings.

TUNA AND CHILI FONDUE

1 can (about 7 ounces) tuna
½ cup minced celery
2 tablespoons minced onion
¼ cup minced canned green chilies
¼ cup mayonnaise or salad dressing
1 teaspoon chili powder
¼ teaspoon salt
12 slices of bread
2 cups grated sharp Cheddar cheese
3 eggs, beaten
1 cup milk
¼ cup cream
¼ teaspoon salt
Dash of hot pepper sauce

Combine first 7 ingredients. Spread on half of the bread and make sandwiches. Cut each sandwich into quarters and arrange in a square baking dish, putting cheese between layers and on top. Combine remaining ingredients and pour over all. Bake in preheated slow oven (300° F.) for 50 minutes, or until set and nicely browned. Makes 6 servings.

TUNA PIZZA

1 package hot-roll mix
2 cans (about 7 ounces each) tuna chunks
¼ cup olive oil
1 garlic clove, crushed
Pitted ripe olives
2 cans tomato sauce
1 teaspoon crumbled dried oregano
Salt and pepper
½ pound Mozzarella cheese, sliced

Prepare hot-roll mix according to directions on package. Divide into two parts. Roll each portion into a large round about ¼ inch thick. Put on greased cookie sheet or two 12-inch pizza pans. Drain tuna, reserving liquid. Combine 3 tablespoons olive oil and the garlic, and paint surface of dough liberally. Separate tuna chunks, and divide between the two pizzas, arranging so that the surfaces are

fairly well covered. Arrange olives in spaces left. Combine oil drained from tuna, any garlic oil remaining, tomato sauce, oregano, and salt and pepper to taste, and spread over tuna. Divide Mozzarella cheese between the two, paint tops with remaining 1 tablespoon olive oil, and bake in preheated hot oven (425° F.) for 20 minutes, or until nicely browned around the edges. Makes 6 to 12 servings.

TUNA MORNAY IN RICE RING

5 cups hot cooked rice
½ cup slivered almonds
6 tablespoons melted butter
2 cans (about 7 ounces each) tuna, drained and washed
Mornay Sauce

Mix well rice, almonds, and butter. Pack in 8- or 9-inch ring mold and keep warm. Heat tuna in top part of a double boiler. Make Mornay Sauce and add 1 cup to hot tuna. Keep it and remaining sauce hot while you unmold rice. Fill center with tuna; top with remaining sauce. Makes 6 servings.

Mornay Sauce

¼ cup butter
¼ cup all-purpose flour
2 cups milk
2 tablespoons grated Parmesan cheese
¼ cup grated Swiss cheese
½ teaspoon powdered mustard
Salt and pepper

Cook butter and flour together for a minute; add milk and stir until thickened. Add cheeses, mustard, and salt and pepper to taste; then cook, stirring constantly, for 10 minutes. Makes about 2 cups.

BRANDADE DE THON

1 cup dried white beans, washed
4 garlic cloves
2 tablespoons heavy cream or olive oil
1 can (7 ounces) tuna, drained and washed
Salt
¼ cup each of grated Swiss and Parmesan cheese
2 tablespoons butter or margarine
½ cup soft stale-bread crumbs

Cook white beans and garlic in water until tender, usually about 2 hours. Drain and purée, or whirl in a blender until smooth, with cream, tuna, and a little of the bean liquid. When smooth, season to taste with salt, and add grated Swiss and grated Parmesan cheese. Put in a shallow baking dish, dot with butter, and sprinkle with bread crumbs. Bake in preheated moderate oven (375°F.) for about 20 minutes. Makes 6 servings.

TONNO CON PISELLI
(Tuna with Peas)

This is a very easy, very simple dish. Combine 1 can (about 7 ounces) of tuna, 1 tablespoon olive oil, 2 cups cooked peas, and salt and pepper to taste. Heat. Makes 4 servings.

TUNA GREEN-BEAN CASSEROLE

2 tablespoons minced onion
2 tablespoons butter or margarine
2 tablespoons all-purpose flour
1 cup milk
¼ cup chicken bouillon
1 tablespoon or more prepared mustard
½ pound green beans, cooked
2 hard-cooked eggs, chopped
1 can (about 7 ounces) tuna, flaked
1 tablespoon minced parsley
½ teaspoon crumbled dried tarragon (optional)
Salt and pepper
¼ cup fine dry bread crumbs
2 tablespoons melted butter or margarine

Cook onion in butter until wilted. Add flour, milk, and bouillon, and cook, stirring constantly, until thickened. Add mustard, beans, eggs, tuna, parsley, and tarragon. Taste, and add salt and pepper if necessary. Put in a 1-quart casserole and sprinkle with crumbs and melted butter, mixed. Bake in preheated hot oven (400° F.) for about 20 minutes. Makes 4 servings.

TUNA-MACARONI BAKE

8 ounces macaroni
1 can (10½ ounces) cream-of-mushroom or chicken soup
¾ cup milk
1 can (7 ounces) tuna, flaked
Grated rind of ½ lemon
¼ teaspoon pepper
¼ teaspoon seasoned salt
3 cups shredded sharp Cheddar cheese
1½ cups crushed potato chips

Cook macaroni in boiling salted water until tender; drain and add soup, milk, tuna, lemon rind, pepper, seasoned salt, and 2 cups cheese. Mix well. Put in shallow baking dish; cover with potato chips mixed with remaining cheese. Bake in preheated moderate oven (350°F.) for about 40 minutes. Makes 6 to 8 servings. Can be frozen.

TUNA MUSHROOM MACARONI

2 cups (8 ounces) elbow macaroni
1 medium onion, chopped
2 tablespoons butter or margarine
¼ cup all-purpose flour
1 teaspoon seasoned salt
1½ teaspoons paprika
½ teaspoon garlic salt
¼ teaspoon crumbled dried oregano
¼ teaspoon pepper
2½ cups milk
½ cup dairy sour cream
2 cans (6½ to 7 ounces each) tuna, drained
¼ pound mushrooms, sliced
2 tablespoons grated Parmesan cheese

Cook macaroni according to package directions. Drain and reserve. Cook onion in butter until tender. Stir in flour and seasonings. Gradually add milk and cook over low heat, stirring, until thickened. Mix in sour cream, tuna, and mushrooms; heat. Stir in cooked macaroni and turn into 2-quart casserole. Sprinkle with additional paprika and Parmesan cheese. Bake in preheated moderate oven (375° F.) for 30 minutes. Makes 6 servings.

Fresh Tuna Salad

Tuna Mornay in
Rice Ring

Fresh Tuna Tarragon

Sweet = and = Sour Tuna

INDIVIDUAL TUNA PIES

Pastry

    1 cup all-purpose flour
    ½ teaspoon salt
    ⅓ cup shortening
    Cold water

Sift flour with salt. Cut in shortening until mixture resembles coarse cornmeal. Add cold water and stir until dough cleans the bowl. Knead on lightly floured board until smooth. Roll dough into 12-inch square; cut into four 6-inch squares.

Tuna Filling

    1 can (7 ounces) tuna fish, drained
    2 tablespoons chopped onion
    1½ teaspoons Worcestershire
    ¼ cup mayonnaise
    ¼ teaspoon salt
    Dash of pepper

Combine tuna fish with remaining ingredients. Spread some of mixture over lower half of each pastry square; fold top half over mixture. Moisten edges with water. Seal with tines of fork. Put on oiled cookie sheet. Bake in preheated very hot oven (450°F.) for 12 to 15 minutes. Makes 4 pies.

TUNA VÉRONIQUE

    ¼ cup sliced onion
    ¼ cup butter or margarine
    ¼ cup all-purpose flour
    ¼ teaspoon each of salt, crumbled
      dried marjoram, and monosodium
      glutamate
      Dash of pepper
    1 cup vegetable bouillon
    2 cups milk
    1 egg, slightly beaten
    3 cans (6½ to 7 ounces each) tuna,
      drained and flaked
    1½ cups seedless grapes or 2 cans
      (8¾ ounces each), drained
      Toast points

Cook onion in butter until crisp-tender, about 3 minutes. Quickly stir in flour and seasonings. Gradually stir in bouillon and milk. Bring to boil, stirring constantly; boil for 1 minute. Beat some of hot sauce into egg; return to heat; cook and stir for 1 minute. Add tuna and grapes. Reheat until piping hot. Serve on toast points; garnish with paprika and parsley, if desired. Makes 6 servings.

DOUBLE-BOILER TUNA SOUFFLÉ

    2 tablespoons butter or margarine
    1 small onion, minced
    3 tablespoons all-purpose flour
    ¾ teaspoon salt
    ½ teaspoon celery salt
    ⅛ teaspoon pepper
    ¾ cup milk
    2 eggs, separated
    1 can (about 7 ounces) tuna, drained
      and flaked
      Juice of ½ small lemon

Melt butter in top part of double boiler. Add onion and cook over direct heat until golden. Blend in flour and seasonings. Put over boiling water and gradually add milk, stirring. Cook until thickened, stirring. Beat egg whites until stiff; set aside. Beat yolks until thick and lemon-colored. Add tuna and lemon juice to

yolks. Gradually beat in hot sauce. Return to top part of double boiler. Fold in egg whites. Cover and cook over simmering water for 45 minutes, or until firm. Makes 4 servings.

TUNA FRITTERS

    2 cups biscuit mix
    ¼ cup wheat germ
    1 egg, well beaten
    1 cup milk
    2 cans (7 ounces each) flaked tuna,
      drained

Mix biscuit mix with wheat germ. Add egg beaten with milk. Fold in tuna. Drop by tablespoonfuls into hot shallow fat (360°F. on frying thermometer) and fry until golden-brown, turning once. Serve with chili sauce if desired. Makes 12.

TUNA PASTRIES

Moisten flaked drained tuna fish with melted butter and dairy sour cream. Season to taste with salt, cayenne, and mustard. Fill bought 1-inch patty shells with mixture. Top with a little piece of pimiento.

TUNA TETRAZZINI

    1 can (4 ounces) sliced mushrooms
      Water
    1 cup evaporated milk, undiluted
    ¼ cup butter or margarine
    2 tablespoons all-purpose flour
    ½ teaspoon salt
    ⅛ teaspoon white pepper
    1 can (7 ounces) tuna, drained and
      flaked
    1½ cups, about (half of 8-ounce
      package) fine noodles, cooked
    1 cup soft bread cubes

Drain mushrooms; reserve liquid; add water to liquid to make 1 cup. Add to milk. Melt 2 tablespoons butter in a saucepan; blend in flour, salt, and pepper. Gradually stir in milk mixture and cook over low heat, stirring, until thickened. Add tuna, mushrooms, and noodles. Put in 1½-quart casserole. Melt remaining butter, mix in bread cubes, and toss. Arrange around edge of casserole. Bake, uncovered, in preheated moderate oven (375°F.) for about 20 minutes. Makes 4 servings.

TUNA CORNISH PIES

    1 package (10 ounces) piecrust mix
    2 tablespoons toasted sesame
      seeds (optional)
    ½ cup chopped celery
    ¼ cup chopped green pepper
    2 tablespoons chopped onion
    1 tablespoon butter or margarine
    1 can (10½ ounces) condensed
      cream-of-mushroom soup, undiluted
    2 tablespoons chopped pecans
    1 tablespoon fresh lemon juice
    1 teaspoon curry powder
    2 cans (6½ to 7 ounces each) tuna
      fish, drained and finely flaked
      Mushroom Cream Sauce

Combine dry piecrust mix and sesame seeds. Prepare according to package directions. Roll into six 7-inch pastry circles. Cook celery, green pepper, and

onion in butter until crisp-tender, about 3 minutes. Combine cooked vegetables, ½ cup soup (reserve remaining soup for sauce), pecans, lemon juice, and curry powder; blend. Stir in tuna. Place about ⅓ cup tuna mixture on each pastry circle; fold over and seal. Slash tops to allow steam to escape. Bake in preheated hot oven (425°F.) for 20 to 25 minutes, or until lightly browned. Serve with Mushroom Cream Sauce. Garnish with parsley and radish roses, as desired. Makes 6 servings.

Mushroom Cream Sauce

Cook 1 tablespoon chopped onion in 1 teaspoon butter. Stir in reserved undiluted soup, an additional 1 can (10½ ounces) undiluted condensed cream-of-mushroom soup, 1 can (6 ounces) sliced mushrooms, and ⅓ cup of the mushroom liquid. Heat to serving temperature. Makes about 2 cups.

CASHEW TUNA CASSEROLE

    2 cans (7 ounces each) tuna, flaked
    1½ cups chopped cashew nuts
    ½ pound fresh mushrooms
    ⅓ cup diced onion
    6 tablespoons butter or margarine
    3 tablespoons flour
    2½ cups milk
      Salt and pepper
    ½ cup crushed potato chips

Drain tuna and flake. Mix tuna with cashew nuts. Sauté mushrooms and onion in 3 tablespoons butter until onion is golden. Add to tuna mixture. Spoon mixture into shallow 1½-quart casserole. Melt 3 tablespoons butter. Stir in flour. Gradually stir in milk. Cook over low heat, stirring constantly, until smooth and thickened. Season with salt and pepper to taste. Pour sauce over tuna mixture. Sprinkle potato chips over top. Bake in preheated moderate oven (350°F.) for about 25 minutes. Makes 6 servings.

ITALIAN TUNA FRITTATA

    2 tablespoons olive oil
    1 green pepper, chopped
    1 onion, chopped
    8 eggs
    1 cup (6- or 7-ounce can) tuna, flaked
    ½ teaspoon salt
    ⅛ teaspoon white pepper

Heat olive oil. Sauté green pepper and onion for 5 minutes. Beat eggs; add tuna and seasonings. Mix well and pour into skillet with vegetables. Cook, lifting edges with spatula and tilting skillet to allow uncooked egg to run under. Divide into 4 portions and turn each to brown. Serve on toast spread with mayonnaise. Makes 4 servings.

CANNED TUNA: SALADS

TUNA-VEGETABLE MOLD

    1 box (3 ounces) lemon-flavored gelatin

1 cup hot water
1 cup cold water
2 tablespoons vinegar
2 tablespoons minced onion
½ teaspoon salt
1 can (about 7 ounces) tuna, drained
and flaked
¾ cup diced celery
¾ cup diced raw carrots
¼ cup diced sweet pickles
Salad greens
Mayonnaise

Dissolve gelatin in hot water. Add cold water, vinegar, onion, and salt. Chill until thickened but not firm. Fold in tuna, celery, carrots, and pickles. Pour into 1½-quart mold and chill until firm. Unmold on salad greens and serve with mayonnaise. Makes 4 to 6 servings.

MARINATED TUNA

2 cans (about 7 ounces each) tuna,
drained
2 tablespoons fresh lemon juice
2 teaspoons chopped chives
1 teaspoon instant minced onion
¼ teaspoon ground rosemary
¼ teaspoon cracked pepper
Dash of ground cloves
½ teaspoon salt
1 cup dairy sour cream

Separate tuna into bite-size chunks. Mix remaining ingredients, pour over tuna, and toss lightly with fork. Chill for at least 1 hour. Makes 4 servings.

HOT TUNA-POTATO SALAD

6 slices of bacon
¼ cup sugar
6 tablespoons vinegar
2 tablespoons water
1 teaspoon celery seeds
1 egg, beaten
4 medium potatoes, cooked and cut
into chunks
¾ cup diced celery
1 medium onion, chopped
1 can (about 7 ounces) tuna, drained
Seasoned salt
Salt and pepper

Cook bacon until crisp. Remove bacon and reserve ¼ cup fat. Add sugar, vinegar, water, and celery seeds to fat in skillet; bring to boil and simmer for 5 minutes. Stir small amount of mixture into egg. Put back in skillet, mix well, and remove from heat. Pour mixture over potatoes, celery, onion, and tuna and mix well; season to taste. Put in 1½-quart casserole and crumble bacon on top. Bake in preheated moderate oven (350° F.) for about 30 minutes. Makes 4 to 6 servings.

WEST COAST SALAD

1 large or 2 medium heads romaine
2 hard-cooked eggs, chopped
3 green onions, finely minced
1 can (about 7 ounces) tuna
6 slices of bacon
2 tablespoons or more wine vinegar
Pepper and salt

Wash romaine, dry, and chill; break into pieces and put in a large bowl. Add eggs, onions, and tuna broken into pieces. Cook bacon until crisp; drain and crumble into bowl, reserving fat. Add vinegar to bacon fat in same pan, also a few grindings of pepper. Heat and pour over salad, mixing gently. Add salt if necessary. Makes 6 servings.

TUNA, POTATO, AND BEAN SALAD, GENOA STYLE

1 can (about 7 ounces) tuna
1 cup cooked sliced potatoes
1 cup cooked cut green beans
1 tablespoon minced onion
½ cup minced celery
2 tablespoons each of olive oil and
vinegar
½ teaspoon salt
Pepper
½ cup mayonnaise

Drain tuna, reserving oil and liquid. Combine tuna, broken into large pieces, potatoes, beans, onion, and celery. Add tuna oil to olive oil, vinegar, salt, and a little pepper. Combine with mayonnaise, and mix carefully with salad. Chill. Makes 6 servings.

TUNA COLESLAW WITH GRAPES

2 cups finely sliced cabbage
1 cup seedless grapes or Tokays, Black
Ribiers, or Muscats, cut into halves
and seeded
2 tablespoons minced onion
¼ cup mayonnaise
⅓ cup dairy sour cream
1 teaspoon fresh lemon juice
Salt and pepper to taste
1 can (about 7 ounces) tuna

Combine all ingredients except tuna and mix thoroughly. Separate tuna chunks and fold in lightly but well. Makes 6 servings.

TUNA RADICCIO

1 quart curly endive, escarole, or
dandelion leaves
1 can (about 7 ounces) tuna
8 fillets of anchovies, chopped
¼ cup each of minced green olives,
parsley, and green onions
1 hard-cooked egg, chopped
½ cup sliced radishes
¼ cup each of sliced green pepper and
shredded salami
½ cup olive oil
1 garlic clove, pressed
2 to 3 tablespoons vinegar
Salt and pepper to taste

Wash greens very well, and shred. Combine with other ingredients; mix well. Makes 6 servings.

SALUBRIOUS TUNA SALAD

1 can (about 7 ounces) tuna, drained
and flaked
1 cup cottage cheese
2 tablespoons each of chopped celery,
green pepper, onion, and ripe olives
Salt and pepper
Dillweed, chili powder, or curry
powder
Lettuce leaves

Combine tuna with cottage cheese, celery, green pepper, onion, and ripe olives. Add salt and pepper to taste, and a little dillweed. Serve on lettuce leaves and accompany with crisp crackers. Makes 4 to 6 servings.

Note: If dietetic tuna is used, this is a good low-calorie, high-protein dish.

APPLE-TUNA SALAD

1 large red apple, cored and cut into
wedges
2 tablespoons fresh lemon juice
1 orange, peeled and sliced
½ cup red grapes, split and seeded
1 can (7 ounces) tuna, drained and
flaked
Salad greens
¼ cup mayonnaise
2 tablespoons orange juice

Mix apple wedges and lemon juice. Arrange fruits and tuna on greens. Mix mayonnaise and orange juice and pour over top. Makes 2 servings.

CANNED TUNA: SANDWICHES

TUNA-CAPER OPEN-FACE SANDWICHES

Mash 1 can (about 7 ounces) tuna with 2 tablespoons butter and 2 teaspoons capers. Spread on rounds of bread and decorate each with a thin slice of hard-cooked egg and a whole caper. Makes about ¾ cup.

WALNUT TUNA SPREAD

Flake 1 can (about 7 ounces) tuna well. Combine with 1 cup finely chopped or ground walnuts, 1 teaspoon fresh lemon juice, and enough mayonnaise to moisten (about ¼ cup if the tuna is drained, less if it isn't). Makes about 2 cups.

SAVORY TUNA SANDWICH SPREAD

1 can (about 7 ounces) tuna, drained
3 tablespoons mayonnaise
2 tablespoons minced celery
Dash of Worcestershire
1 tablespoon chili sauce or ketchup
1 or 2 tablespoons fresh lemon juice
1 cucumber
White toast or bread

Mix all ingredients except last 2. Peel and thinly slice cucumber. Cover half of toast slices with cucumber and spread with mixture; top with remaining toast to make sandwiches. Makes about 1¼ cups.

Note: Above mixture can be used for hot canapés if desired. Put each cucumber slice on a toast round of the same size, spread with mixture, and broil until hot.

TURBOT—A large European salt-water flatfish that belongs to the flounder family. The turbot, which is brown and speckled in color and weighs an average of ten pounds, is a highly prized food fish, since its flesh is most delicate and delicious. Its closest American relative is the halibut.

TURKEY—A native American game bird which is related to the pheasant. There are a number of varieties. Wild turkeys were once unbelievably numerous throughout the United States and Central America, living in the forests in small flocks and coming out to the clearings only to feed. They are fast on their feet and when pursued they run rather than fly, although when they must fly, they fly high and fast, at speeds estimated at fifty miles per hour or more.

The Indians domesticated turkeys long before the arrival of the early settlers. The Spanish *conquistadores* took birds domesticated by the Aztec Indians of southern Mexico back with them to Spain as early as 1519. Interestingly, some of these European turkeys were brought back to the New World later and crossed with the native wild varieties.

The turkey is a bird not only native to America, but, because of its associations with Thanksgiving, it is the most American of all food birds. So much so that Benjamin Franklin, in a letter to his daughter Sara Bache, wrote: "I wish the Bald Eagle had not been chosen as the Representation of our Country; he is a Bird of bad moral Character, like those among men who live by sharpening and robbing . . . The turkey is a much more respectable bird, and withal a true original Native of America."

Availability and Purchasing Guide—Turkeys are sold in two styles: oven-ready (sometimes called "ready-to-cook" or "eviscerated") and dressed. Oven-ready turkeys are drawn and cleaned, ready for roasting. This style comes fresh or frozen—

fresh and is often individually packaged. The neck and cleaned giblets are wrapped and put into the cavity of the bird. If you buy this style, you'll need about 1 pound per person.

Dressed turkeys have the head and feet on; the feathers are removed, but the birds are not drawn. The butcher will draw the bird for you. Have him pull the leg tendons and cut the neck off close to the body. Buy about 1¼ pounds per person, as you lose about ⅕ of the weight in drawing. To be sure of the final weight in order to time the roasting, ask the butcher to weigh the drawn bird. If bird is frozen, allow ample thawing time, 24 hours for each 6 pounds of turkey in the refrigerator. At room temperature, allow 1 hour per pound.

Frozen stuffed turkeys are available. Contrary to most unstuffed frozen turkeys, these are roasted without thawing. A roast-meat thermometer is necessary in cooking these birds.

Fresh or frozen turkey parts such as whole breasts and drumsticks are available, packaged separately. Frozen turkey dinners and frozen turkey slices in giblet gravy are available, as is turkey pie and frozen, boned rolled turkey roasts.

Smoked turkey, some of which is ready to eat, some requiring further cooking, is available.

Canned boned turkey, turkey à la king, turkey and noodles, and turkey soups, are available. Turkey dinners prepared as baby and junior foods are also available.

Storage

☐ Fresh, refrigerator shelf, raw: 6 to 8 days
☐ Fresh, refrigerator shelf, cooked, 4 to 5 days
☐ Fresh, prepared for freezing; or frozen, refrigerator frozen-food compartment, raw: 2 to 3 weeks
☐ Fresh, prepared for freezing; or frozen, freezer, raw: 6 months
☐ Fresh, refrigerator frozen-food compartment, prepared for freezing, cooked: 2 to 3 weeks
☐ Fresh, freezer, prepared for freezing, cooked: 3 months

To store leftover turkey, remove stuff-

ing from bird and put stuffing in a separate container. When cold, cover, and store in refrigerator. If there is a lot of meat left, cool the entire carcass, wrap in foil or wax paper, and store in the refrigerator. Otherwise, remove the meat from the bones and refrigerate meat. Or wrap and freeze it. If you plan to make soup, crack the bones, wrap, and refrigerate. If you have time, make, cool, and refrigerate the broth, so the bones can be discarded.

Nutritive Food Values—A good source of protein.

☐ 3½ ounces, raw = 218 calories
☐ 3½ ounces, roasted = 263 calories

Basic Preparation—If turkey is frozen, thaw in refrigerator in original wrapping. Put in shallow pan and allow 1 to 3 days for thawing. A thawed, fresh ready-to-cook turkey can be kept on the refrigerator shelf at 38°F. for 1 to 2 days. After thawing, it is important to remove the original wrapping and to rewrap very loosely. Do not refreeze.

☐ **To Roast**—When ready to prepare turkey, rinse bird inside and out with cold water, drain and pat dry. Rub skin and cavity lightly with salt. Insert stuffing and stuff neck cavity; fasten skin to back with a skewer. Stuff body cavity loosely and close with skewers or stitching. Fold wings and bring wing tips onto the back. (If bird is too big for this, let wings stay close to body of bird.) Push drumsticks under band of skin at tail or tie them to tail with string. Line a shallow roasting pan with foil to avoid messy clean-up. Place bird on a rack in the foil-lined pan. Brush all over with vegetable oil. Roast according to directions on foil package or in preheated slow oven (325°F.), according to the Timetable at left, basting several times with drippings in pan. When turkey breast is brown, cover with a loose tent of foil. To make tent, tear off a sheet of heavy foil 5 to 10 inches longer than turkey. Crease lengthwise through center. Place over the bird and press the foil gently at drumsticks and breast to anchor it. Differences in the shape and tenderness of individual birds may necessitate increasing or decreasing the cooking time slightly. Cut band of skin or string at drumstick 1 hour before bird is done. Remove from oven 30 minutes before serving.

A roast meat thermometer placed in the center of the inside thigh muscle or in the thickest part of the breast muscle should register approximately 185°F. when turkey is done. Turkey is done when thickest part of drumstick feels very soft when pressed between fingers.

When dinner is set for a definite hour, start the bird 20 to 30 minutes ahead of

TIMETABLE FOR ROASTING TURKEY

PURCHASED READY-TO-COOK WEIGHT	OVEN TEMPERATURE	INTERIOR TEMPERATURE	GUIDE TO TOTAL ROASTING TIME
6 to 8 lbs.	325°F.	185°F.	2 to 2½ hours
8 to 12 lbs.	325°F.	185°F.	2½ to 3 hours
12 to 16 lbs.	325°F.	185°F.	3 to 3¾ hours
16 to 20 lbs.	325°F.	185°F.	3¾ to 4½ hours
20 to 24 lbs.	325°F.	185°F.	4½ to 5½ hours

schedule to avoid delay should the turkey take longer to cook than was estimated.

☐ **To Stuff**—Stuff the bird just before you're ready to roast it. If desired, stuffing can be prepared ahead and refrigerated. Do not add liquid or eggs until ready to use. For Basic Bread Stuffing recipe plus variations see chart below. Extra stuffing can be put in a baking pan and baked in preheated hot oven (425°F.) until well browned after the turkey is removed from the oven. Spoon some of the drippings over the top before baking. If you have your own favorite recipe, allow about 1 cup of stuffing per pound of drawn bird.

☐ **To Prepare Giblets**—Wash giblets; cook neck, heart, and gizzard for about 2 hours in boiling salted water with a bay leaf, an onion, and a few celery leaves. Add liver during last 20 minutes. Drain, reserving broth for gravy. Remove meat from neck; grind or chop with the heart, gizzard, and liver. Giblets can be prepared a day ahead and refrigerated. Add to stuffing or gravy.

☐ **To Make Gravy**—For 6 cups gravy: pour drippings from roasting pan into bowl, skim off fat, and put ½ cup fat into saucepan. Blend in ½ cup flour. Measure skimmed drippings, and add water to make 6 cups. Cook fat and flour until bubbly. Add liquid all at once and cook until thickened, stirring constantly. Season to taste. Ground or chopped cooked giblets can be added.

☐ **To Bone Turkey**—Wash poultry and pat dry. Remove wings. With a sharp knife with a sharp point cut the bird down the center back downward to the tail. Remove the tail section. Using the point of the knife against the bones of the bird cut away the skin and flesh from the back and ribs. When the legs are reached cut the joint at the hip to remove the leg, bone and all. The bones will be removed from the legs later. Do the same with the wings, leaving the wing bone for later removal. Continue cutting the meat away from the bones until the breastbone is reached. Carefully cut the skin away from the top of the breastbone so that the skin remains in one piece. Now with the sharp knife cut and scrape away the meat from the leg and wing bones. In doing this the wing and leg will be turned inside out when the bone is removed. Turn legs and wings right side out. Now the bird is ready for stuffing or rolling. When preparing a turkey, if it is not to be stuffed and will only be rolled into a boneless roast, it may be cut into halves through the breastbone skin and then rolled and tied. This is done when a turkey is quite large.

☐ **To Freeze**—Clean and eviscerate turkey. Wash well and drain. Wrap giblets separately in moisture- vapor-proof material. Seal, and freeze. Tie turkey so that wings and legs lie close to body. Wrap in moisture- vapor-proof material, excluding as much air as possible. Seal, and freeze.

To freeze cooked turkey, remove meat from bones. If desired, use bones for making broth or soup which can be frozen in freezer jars or containers. Leftover gravy can also be frozen. Separate large slices from scraps, and package types and amounts of meat for the particular recipes in which you plan to use it. Tear off generous strips of heavy-duty foil, put meat in the center, and fold ends over tightly, making several double folds. Fold sides in the same way. Secure with string or freezer tape, and mark the contents with a freezer pencil (white-meat slices for pie; chopped light and dark for salads, mixed light and dark strips for turkey ragout). It's also a good idea to date packages. Frozen cooked turkey will retain its good quality for up to 3 months.

BASIC BREAD STUFFING, WITH SOME VARIATIONS

	(DRAWN WEIGHT)				
	8 to 11 lbs.	11 to 15 lbs.	15 to 19 lbs.	19 to 25 lbs.	Directions
Basic Bread Stuffing					
Butter or margarine, cups	½	⅔	1	1⅓	Cook all ingredients except
Medium onions, minced	2	3	4	5	crumbs in skillet for 5
*Poultry seasoning, tablespoons	1	1½	2	2½	minutes. Toss with crumbs.
Salt, teaspoons	1½	2	3	4	
Pepper, teaspoons	¾	1	1½	2	
Chopped parsley, cups	⅓	½	¾	1	
Chopped celery leaves, cups	¾	1	1½	2	
Soft stale-bread crumbs, quarts	2½	3½	4½	6	
Egg Stuffing					
Same as Basic Stuffing **plus** eggs	2	3	4	5	Beat slightly, and add with crumbs.
Oyster Stuffing					
Same as Basic Stuffing **plus** oysters, pints	1	1½	2	2½	Drain oysters, and chop. Cook with onion mixture.
Chestnut Stuffing					
Same as Basic Stuffing bread crumbs, quarts	½	¾	1	1½	Cook chestnuts in boiling water for 15 minutes. Remove shells and brown skins, and chop. Add with crumbs.
plus chestnuts, pounds	1	1½	2¼	3	
Nut Stuffing					
Same as Basic Stuffing **plus** chopped nuts, cups	1	1½	2	2½	Add with crumbs.
Corn-Bread Stuffing	Same as Basic Stuffing; but substitute crumbled unsweetened cornbread, made with eggs, for half of bread crumbs				
Rice Stuffing					
Same as Basic Stuffing, but **omit** crumbs; **add** raw rice, cups	2¼	3¼	4½	5½	Cook rice in boiling salted water until nearly tender. Drain.

Or use thyme and sage, or other herbs, to taste.

Turkey Cook Book

Roast stuffed turkey;
broiled, pot-roasted, and
barbecued turkey; and dozens
of ways to use cooked turkey.

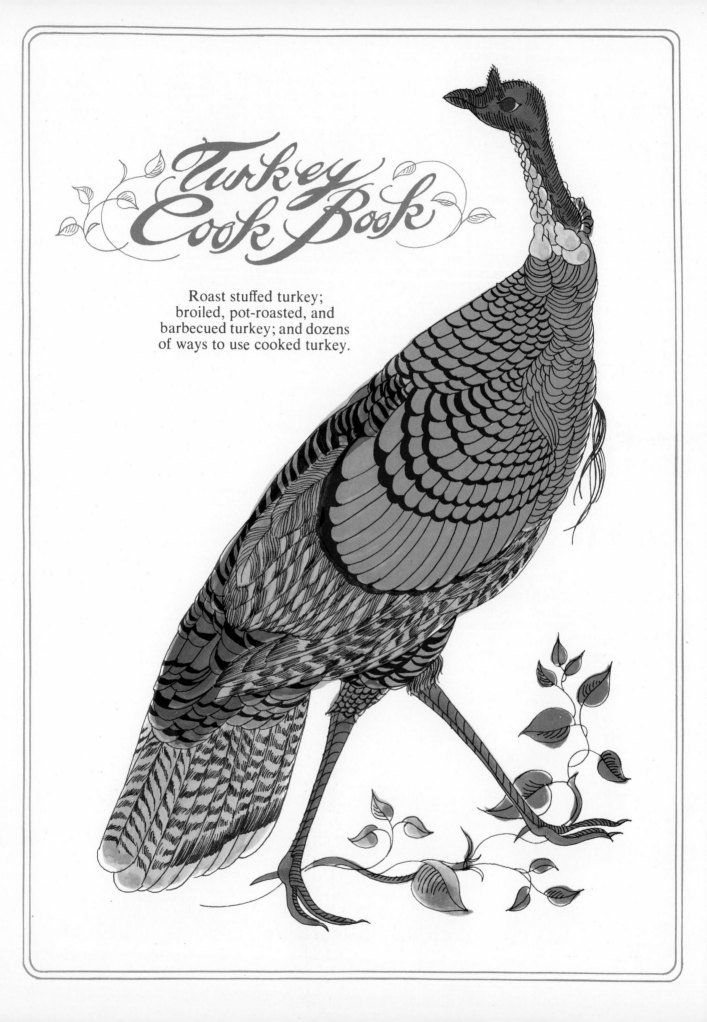

BROILED TURKEY

Have a 4- to 6-pound turkey split into halves lengthwise. Fold wing tips into back. Put, skin side down, in broiler pan without rack. Brush with cooking oil and season to taste with salt and pepper and a little sugar. Put pan about 9 inches from heat. Turkey should just begin to brown after 20 minutes of cooking. Broil slowly until well browned, about 40 minutes. Turn and baste with pan drippings. Broil until brown and done, for 40 to 50 minutes. Baste with pan drippings several times during broiling.

PANFRIED TURKEY

Dredge pieces of cut-up turkey with seasoned flour. Put turkey, meatiest pieces first, in about ½ inch of hot fat or cooking oil in a heavy skillet and fry until golden-brown. Reduce heat, add 2 tablespoons water; cover, and cook slowly for 45 to 60 minutes, or until tender. Turn pieces several times to assure even cooking. Uncover pan for the last 10 minutes to recrisp skin.

POT-ROASTED TURKEY, JAMAICA STYLE

1 ready-to-cook turkey, about 6 pounds
¼ cup butter or margarine
1½ cups chicken broth
¾ cup sliced celery
1 medium onion, chopped
½ teaspoon garlic salt
2 dried red peppers, crushed
1 tablespoon vinegar
¼ teaspoon ground allspice
½ cup sliced green olives
1 medium green pepper, sliced
2 tablespoons cornstarch
Salt and pepper

Brown turkey on all sides in the butter in Dutch oven. This should take 20 to 30 minutes. Put turkey on rack. Add next 7 ingredients. Cover and simmer for 2 to 2½ hours, or until tender. Add olives and green pepper and cook for 10 minutes longer. Remove turkey to a hot platter and thicken liquid in Dutch oven with cornstarch blended with a little cold water. Season to taste with salt and pepper and pour over turkey. Makes 8 servings.

ROAST BONELESS TURKEY ROLL

Thaw frozen roll in the refrigerator, allowing 1 to 2 days. When thawed, remove wrapper, leaving string on. Rinse roll in cold water. Drain and pat dry. If not preseasoned, sprinkle with salt and pepper. Put on rack in shallow roasting pan. Brush with melted butter or margarine. Insert roast-meat thermometer in center of roll. Roast as directed on package label. Or roast in preheated moderate oven (350°F.) for 2 to 2½ hours for a 3- to 5-pound roll. Meat thermometer should register 170°F. to 175°F. when roll is done. Brush occasionally with pan drippings or melted butter during the roasting. If roll is becoming too brown, cover loosely with a tent of foil.

BARBECUED TURKEY ROLL

One 5- to 7-pound turkey roll, thawed
1 cup bottled barbecue sauce

Place turkey roll in roasting pan. Add about ¼ inch water to pan and cover. Roast, covered, in preheated moderate oven (350°F.) to an internal temperature of 170°F. to 175°F. on meat thermometer. This will take 2½ to 3¼ hours. Half an hour before the roast is done, pour barbecue sauce over turkey. Baste several times with liquid in pan. Makes 10 to 12 servings.

BARBECUED TURKEY STEAKS

Have butcher cut 1-inch-thick steaks from a large frozen tom turkey. Some steaks will be all white meat, some part dark meat, and some all dark meat. Marinate for several hours in 1 part oil and 1 part white wine, herbed if desired. Broil for 10 minutes, basting with marinade.

BOILED TURKEY, VEGETABLE, AND DUMPLING DINNER

1 ready-to-cook turkey, about 6 pounds
5 cups water
1 onion, cut up
2 celery stalks, cut up
1 tablespoon salt
½ teaspoon pepper
¼ cup all-purpose flour
2 packages (10 ounces each) frozen mixed vegetables
Savory Dumpling Batter

Wash turkey. Simmer with water and next 4 ingredients for 2½ hours, or until very tender. Lift out turkey, and remove meat from bones; keep hot. Strain broth; thicken with flour mixed with a little cold water. Add mixed vegetables, and bring to boil. Drop in Savory Dumpling Batter by tablespoonfuls. Simmer, covered, for 15 minutes. Put turkey on platter; lift out dumplings and vegetables and arrange around turkey. Pour some of gravy over turkey, and serve remainder in bowl. Lefover small pieces of turkey can be used for salad. Makes 4 to 6 servings.

Savory Dumpling Batter

2 cups sifted all-purpose flour
2 teaspoons baking powder
1½ teaspoons salt
4 egg yolks
⅔ cup milk
½ cup chopped parsley
2 tablespoons chopped green-onion tops

Sift dry ingredients. Beat egg yolks with milk; add to dry ingredients together with the parsley and onion tops. Mix lightly until blended.

PUERTO RICAN TURKEY SAUSAGE

1 uncooked turkey (about 10 pounds)
½ pound boiled ham
9 eggs
1 can (2 ounces) truffles, sliced (optional)
1 can (4 ounces) sliced mushrooms, drained
2 teaspoons salt
1 teaspoon ground nutmeg
1½ teaspoons pepper
Cracker crumbs, about ½ cup
Chicken broth

Remove skin and meat from turkey bones. Grind turkey skin, meat, and ham twice through the finest blade of a meat grinder. Beat in 7 eggs, one at a time. Stir in truffles, mushrooms, salt, nutmeg, and pepper. Blend well. It may be necessary to add some cracker crumbs. Shape mixture into 5 rolls 2 to 3 inches in diameter and 6 to 8 inches long. Roll in 2 beaten eggs. Roll in cracker crumbs. Wrap roll in cheesecloth and tie ends to seal tightly. Put roll into a deep kettle. Add enough hot chicken broth just to cover. Cover kettle and simmer for 1 hour. Remove roll from broth and chill. Remove cheesecloth; cut roll into thin slices. Makes 15 to 20 servings.
Note: This is a large recipe; after cooking it can be cooled and refrigerated until needed.

SPIT-ROASTED TURKEY

Select a turkey weighing 10 to 12 pounds. Wash turkey and dry. Sprinkle cavity with salt and a little thyme or marjoram. Add a stalk of celery and a few slices of onion. Truss turkey securely, having both wings and legs close to body and neck skin skewered on at back. Drive spit from a point just in front of the tail, having it go through back and come out at about the top of the wishbone. Rub skin with cooking oil. Insert a meat thermometer in the thickest part of the thigh. Connect spit to the motor and roast over medium heat until meat thermometer registers 175°F., or until leg moves easily in joint. Allow about 15 minutes cooking time for each pound of bird. Baste frequently as it turns with melted margarine. Makes 6 to 8 servings.

COOKED TURKEY

TURKEY SOUP

1 roast-turkey carcass
2 quarts water
2 teaspoons salt
¼ teaspoon pepper
2 celery stalks, including leaves, diced
1 medium onion, peeled and sliced
Few parsley sprigs
1 bay leaf

Scrape any stuffing from turkey bones. Put carcass in kettle and add remaining ingredients. Bring to boil, cover, and simmer for 2 hours. Strain. Pick off any meat from bones and add to soup. Makes about 1½ quarts.

Note: If desired, add ¼ cup rice or ⅓ cup elbow macaroni or noodles to strained soup. Simmer, covered, for about 15 minutes.

TURKEY AND COCKTAIL SAUCE

Mix 1 cup chili sauce, 2 tablespoons each of prepared horseradish and fresh lemon juice, 1 teaspoon salt, and ¼ teaspoon pepper. Chill. Put in bowl in center of platter, and arrange diced cooked turkey around bowl. Serve with toothpicks for dipping turkey pieces into sauce. Good for buffet with deviled eggs, cheese, celery, green and ripe olives, hot garlic bread, marble cake, and grapes. Makes 1¼ cups sauce.

TURKEY PÂTÉ

2 cups lightly packed ground turkey meat and skin
1 onion, minced
2 hard-cooked eggs, minced
½ cup ground almonds
Salt and pepper to taste
A generous dash of hot pepper sauce
2 tablespoons brandy
Enough mayonnaise to bind

Combine all ingredients except mayonnaise. Then bind with mayonnaise until a just-stiff paste is formed. Place in a bowl or container. Decorate with aspic, truffles, or sliced olives, if desired. Chill. Serve as an hors-d'oeuvre or as a snack. Makes about 3 cups.

TURKEY PIE, BREADSTICK TOPPING

½ cup all-purpose flour
1 cup cold turkey or chicken broth
3 cups hot broth
1 package (10 ounces) frozen peas
2 cups (one 1-pound can) onions, drained
2 cups carrot chunks, cooked
2 cups diced cooked turkey
Salt and pepper

1 can ready-to-bake breadsticks
1 egg yolk
1 tablespoon water

Blend flour and cold broth; stir into hot broth and cook, stirring constantly, until thickened. Add peas and simmer for a few minutes. Add onions, carrots, and turkey; season to taste with salt and pepper and pour into 2-quart baking dish. Put in preheated very hot oven (450°F.). Separate breadsticks, and weave on a greased cookie sheet to fit top of baking dish, stretching slightly if necessary. Trim ends to fit. Brush with egg yolk mixed with water. Bake with casserole for about 10 minutes. Press topping down slightly on pie. Good with parsley potatoes, mixed green salad, and honeydew with berries. Makes 6 servings.

TURKEY HAWAIIAN

2 eggs, beaten
½ cup all-purpose flour
½ teaspoon salt
Water
2 cups cubed cooked turkey
Fat for frying
1 can (13½ ounces) pineapple chunks
2 tablespoons cornstarch
1 tablespoon butter
1 tablespoon chicken-stock base
1 each of green and red peppers, cut into eighths
1 tablespoon soy sauce
1 can (8 ounces) onions, drained

Combine first 3 ingredients and 3 tablespoons water; beat until smooth. Add turkey, and stir until all pieces are coated. Drop into hot shallow fat, and brown on all sides; keep warm. Drain pineapple juice into saucepan. Blend in cornstarch. Add butter, pineapple, and remaining ingredients. Simmer for 5 minutes, stirring frequently. Add turkey, and serve at once. Makes 4 servings.

TURKEY PAPRIKA

2 large onions, sliced
1 garlic clove, minced
¼ cup butter or margarine
1 can (10½ ounces) tomato purée
¼ cup paprika
Salt and pepper to taste
2 cups turkey broth or 2 chicken bouillon cubes dissolved in 2 cups water
3 cups cut-up leftover turkey
1 cup dairy sour cream

Brown onions and garlic slightly in butter. Add remaining ingredients except sour cream. Simmer for about 20 minutes. Just before serving, top with sour cream. Serve with noodles or rice. Makes 6 servings.

PRESSED TURKEY

Mix 1 cup turkey broth and 3 cups minced cooked turkey in saucepan. Simmer until broth is nearly evaporated. Season to taste with salt and pepper. Let stand until cold. Pour into a 3-cup bowl; weight with a plate. Chill overnight. Then unmold, and cut into slices. Garnish with parsley and serve with mayonnaise. Makes 4 to 6 servings.

Note: Prepare this a day ahead.

TURKEY AND BROCCOLI AMANDINE

4 ounces (about 2 cups) medium noodles
1 package (10 ounces) frozen broccoli, cooked
2 tablespoons butter or margarine
2 tablespoons all-purpose flour
1 cup each of undiluted evaporated milk and turkey or chicken broth
1 cup diced Cheddar cheese
½ teaspoon monosodium glutamate
1 teaspoon Worcestershire
¼ teaspoon pepper
2 cups diced cooked turkey
Salt
¼ cup toasted slivered blanched almonds

Cook and drain noodles; put in shallow baking dish. Cut broccoli into 1-inch pieces, and reserve blossoms. Arrange stems on noodles. Make a sauce with butter, flour, and liquids. Add cheese, monosodium glutamate, Worcestershire, and pepper; stir until cheese is melted. Add turkey and salt to taste; pour over ingredients in dish. Arrange broccoli blossoms on top, and sprinkle with almonds. Bake in preheated moderate oven (350°F.) for about 30 minutes. Good with tomato juice, peas, and fudge cake. Makes 4 servings.

TURKEY RAGOUT

To 2 cups leftover turkey gravy add ¼ cup sherry, 1 teaspoon Worcestershire, ½ teaspoon monosodium glutamate, 1 tablespoon currant jelly, and salt and pepper to taste. Heat, stirring to blend jelly. Add 2 cups cooked turkey cut into strips. Heat. Good with mashed potatoes, snap beans and mushrooms, radishes, green onions, and cheesecake. Makes 4 servings.

TURKEY CURRY

1 onion, minced
1 tart apple, peeled and chopped
¼ cup butter or margarine
⅓ cup all-purpose flour
1 to 2 tablespoons curry powder
1½ teaspoons salt
⅛ teaspoon pepper
¼ teaspoon ground ginger
1 cup turkey broth
1 cup milk
½ cup heavy cream
Juice of ½ lemon
3 cups diced cooked turkey

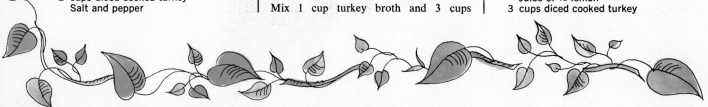

Spit-Roasted Turkey

Cook onion and apple in butter in top part of a double boiler over direct heat until onion is golden. Blend in flour and seasonings. Add broth, milk, and cream; cook over boiling water, stirring constantly, until thickened. Cook, covered, for 10 minutes longer. Add lemon juice and turkey. Heat thoroughly. Good with fluffy rice, sautéed bananas, cashews, chutney, raisins, and lemon bread pudding. Makes 4 servings.

TURKEY CHOW MEIN

- 1 large onion, sliced
- 2 cups sliced celery
- 2 tablespoons cooking oil
- 2⅓ cups (one 1-pound, 3-ounce can) bean sprouts, drained
- 1½ cups chopped cooked turkey
- 2 chicken bouillon cubes
- 1½ cups hot water
- 2 tablespoons soy sauce
- 2 tablespoons cornstarch
- ¼ cup cold water
  Salt and pepper
  Chow-mein noodles

Cook onion and celery in oil for 10 minutes. Add bean sprouts, turkey, and bouillon cubes dissolved in hot water. Bring to boil and simmer for 5 minutes. Add soy sauce. Stir in cornstarch blended with cold water. Cook, stirring constantly, until thickened. Season to taste with salt and pepper. Serve over noodles, with additional soy sauce if desired. Makes 4 servings. Good with broccoli, jellied tomato salad, and apple cobbler.

Turkey Chop Suey

Use recipe above. Omit noodles; serve on hot cooked rice.

BAKED TURKEY AND RICE

- 1 cup uncooked rice
- ¼ cup butter or margarine
- ¼ cup all-purpose flour
- 1¼ cups turkey or chicken broth
- ½ cup sauterne or other dry white wine
- 1 can (3 ounces) sliced mushrooms, undrained
  Few parsley sprigs, chopped
- 1 teaspoon instant minced onion
- ⅛ teaspoon ground sage
- 1 cup grated sharp Cheddar cheese
- 2 cups diced cooked turkey
  Salt and pepper
  Paprika to taste

Cook and drain rice. Make a sauce with next 4 ingredients. Add mushrooms, parsley, onion, sage, and half of cheese. Stir until cheese is melted. Stir in rice and turkey; season to taste with salt and pepper. Put in shallow baking dish, and sprinkle with remaining cheese and the paprika. Bake in preheated moderate oven (375°F.) for about 30 minutes. Good

with zucchini, sliced tomatoes, and apple crunch (made from mix). Makes 6 servings.

TURKEY CREOLE IN RICE RING

- 1 onion, chopped
- ½ medium green pepper, chopped
- 1 can (3 ounces) sliced mushrooms, undrained
- 2 celery stalks, diced
- 2 tablespoons butter or margarine
- 2⅓ cups (one 1-pound, 3-ounce can) tomatoes
- 1 bay leaf
- 1 teaspoon seasoned salt
- ¼ teaspoon pepper
- ½ teaspoon monosodium glutamate
- 1 teaspoon Worcestershire
- 1 teaspoon sugar
- 1½ cups diced cooked turkey
- 1 tablespoon cornstarch
- 1 tablespoon water
- 2 cups uncooked long-grain rice
- ½ cup chopped parsley

Cook first 4 ingredients in butter for 5 minutes. Add tomatoes, seasonings, and sugar. Simmer, uncovered, for 10 minutes. Remove bay leaf; add turkey, and heat. Blend cornstarch and water. Stir into hot mixture and cook, stirring constantly, until slightly thickened. Cook and drain rice. Add parsley, and mix lightly. Pack into oiled 2-quart ring mold. Unmold on hot platter; fill with Turkey Creole. Good with frozen asparagus, cottage-cheese salad, and pineapple upside-down cake. Makes 6 servings.

SHERRIED TURKEY WITH POTATOES

- ¼ cup butter or margarine
- ¼ cup all-purpose flour
- 2 tablespoons chicken-stock base
- 1¼ cups water
- ½ cup heavy cream
- ¼ cup sherry
  Salt and pepper to taste
- 1 can (3 ounces) mushrooms, undrained
- 2 envelopes instant mashed potatoes
- 6 large slices of cooked turkey or 2 cup pieces of turkey
- 3 tablespoons grated Parmesan cheese
  Paprika

Make a sauce with first 6 ingredients. Add seasonings and mushrooms. Prepare potatoes as directed on label, and put in shallow baking dish. Arrange turkey on potatoes. Cover with the sauce. Sprinkle with cheese and paprika. Bake in preheated hot oven (425°F.) for about 20 minutes; or put under broiler until golden-brown and bubbly. Good with Brussels sprouts with almonds, fresh-pear and orange salad, and poundcake. Makes 6 servings.

TURKEY WITH WELSH-RABBIT SAUCE

- 3 tablespoons butter or margarine
- 3 tablespoons all-purpose flour

- 1 teaspoon salt
  Dash of cayenne
- ⅛ teaspoon pepper
- 1 teaspoon prepared mustard
- 1 teaspoon Worcestershire
- 2 cups milk
- 2 cups (½ pound) sharp Cheddar cheese, shredded
- 4 to 6 large slices cooked turkey
  Hot toast

Melt butter; blend in flour and seasonings. Add milk and cook, stirring constantly, until thickened. Add cheese and cook until cheese is melted. Arrange turkey on broilerproof platter or baking dish; cover with the sauce. Put under broiler until bubbly. Serve on toast. Good with frozen mixed vegetables, sliced cucumbers with French dressing, and fresh plums. Makes 4 to 6 servings.

SAVORY TURKEY SQUARES WITH MUSHROOM SAUCE

- 3 cups coarsely chopped or ground cooked turkey
- 2 cups soft bread crumbs
- 1 cup turkey broth or 1 chicken bouillon cube and 1 cup water
- ⅔ cup minced celery
- 2 tablespoons minced parsley
- 1 teaspoon monosodium glutamate
- 3 eggs, slightly beaten
- 1 tablespoon fresh lemon juice
- 2 tablespoons instant minced onion
- 1 pimiento, chopped
- ⅔ cup light cream
  Salt and pepper
  Mushroom Sauce

Mix all ingredients except last three. Season to taste with salt and pepper. Pour into baking dish (12 x 7 x 2 inches) and put in pan of hot water. Bake in preheated moderate oven (350°F.) for 50 to 60 minutes. Cut into squares and serve with Mushroom Sauce. Makes 6 to 8 servings.

Mushroom Sauce

In saucepan blend ¼ cup soft turkey fat or butter and ¼ cup flour; heat until bubbly, stirring. Gradually stir in 2 cups turkey broth and cook, stirring, until thickened. Drain 1 can (3 ounces) chopped mushrooms and add to sauce. Season to taste with salt, pepper, and poultry seasoning.

CUCKOO'S EGGS

- 1 cup each of minced turkey and smoked ham
- ¾ cup Béchamel sauce
  Salt and pepper to taste
  Dash of ground nutmeg
  Fine dry bread crumbs
- 6 tablespoons cooking oil
  Chopped spinach, mashed turnip, or mashed potato

Mix turkey, ham, Béchamel sauce (medium white sauce made with half milk, half chicken broth), salt, pepper, nutmeg, and ½ cup fine dry bread crumbs. Shape into 8 balls; roll in bread crumbs and fry in very hot oil. Serve each egg in a nest of spinach. Makes 4 servings.

TURKEY PUDDING

¼ pound bacon, diced
1 cup minced cooked turkey
1½ cups cooked spaghetti or noodles
3 tablespoons grated cheese
3 to 4 tablespoons turkey gravy
   Salt and pepper
1 cup soft white bread crumbs
   Parsley
1 hard-cooked egg, chopped

Cook bacon. Drain fat, leaving 2 tablespoons in pan. Add turkey, spaghetti, cheese, gravy, and salt and pepper to taste. Heat well. Heavily grease a loaf pan (9 x 5 x 3 inches) and sprinkle soft bread crumbs over bottom and sides. Fill with turkey mixture, pressing with spoon to pack tightly. Bake in preheated very hot oven (450°F.) for 15 to 20 minutes. Garnish with parsley and chopped hard-cooked egg. Serve with additional hot turkey gravy. Makes 4 servings.

TURKEY PIE WITH CORN-BREAD TOPPING

1 can (10½ ounces) cream-of-mushroom soup
1 cup milk
1 cup cooked peas
1 pimiento, sliced
1½ cups cubed leftover turkey
¾ cup sifted all-purpose flour
¾ cup yellow cornmeal
2 teaspoons baking powder
¾ teaspoon salt
¼ cup shortening
1 egg, slightly beaten
¾ cup milk

In saucepan heat soup, milk, peas, pimiento, and turkey. Put in shallow 2-quart baking dish. Mix flour, cornmeal, baking powder, and salt. Cut in shortening. Mix egg and milk; add to dry ingredients; mix well. Pour over turkey mixture. Bake in preheated hot oven (425°F.) for about 25 minutes. Makes 4 servings.

PINWHEEL TURKEY PIE

4 carrots, cut up
2 potatoes, cut up
½ cup chopped parsley
3 cups cut-up leftover turkey
2 cups turkey gravy or chicken bouillon, thickened
   Salt and pepper to taste
   Parsley Pinwheels

Partially cook carrots and potatoes in boiling salted water. Drain; add remaining ingredients except Parsley Pinwheels and simmer until vegetables are tender, adding more water if necessary. Serve topped with Parsley Pinwheels. Makes 6 servings.

Parsley Pinwheels

Cut ½ cup butter or margarine and ½ pound cream cheese into 2 cups sifted all-purpose flour and ¼ teaspoon salt. Roll out ¼ inch thick on floured board to form a rectangle about 12 x 8 inches. Sprinkle with parsley. Beginning at end, roll up jelly-roll fashion. Cut into ½-inch slices, and bake on cookie sheet in preheated hot oven (400°F.) for about 20 minutes.

LAYERED TURKEY LOAF

3 envelopes unflavored gelatin
3 cups cold turkey or chicken broth
2 cups diced cooked turkey
   Celery salt
   Salt
2 tablespoons chopped parsley
1½ cups bottled cranberry-juice cocktail
1 cup diced celery
½ cup chopped walnuts
   Salad greens
   Mayonnaise

Soften 2 envelopes gelatin in ½ cup of the broth; stir over very low heat until gelatin is dissolved. Add to remaining broth. Chill until slightly thickened. Add turkey, seasonings to taste, and parsley. Put half in a loaf pan (9 x 5 x 3 inches) and chill until firm. Soften 1 envelope gelatin in ¼ cup cranberry cocktail. Dissolve over very low heat; add to remaining cocktail with ¼ teaspoon salt, the celery, and nuts; chill until slightly thickened. Spoon over firm layer; chill until firm. Pour remaining turkey mixture over cranberry layer; chill until firm. Unmold on greens; serve with mayonnaise. Good with mushroom soup, baked potatoes, chocolate meringue pie. Makes 6 to 8 servings.

CALIFORNIA TURKEY BAKE

4 slices of bread
   Prepared garlic spread
4 eggs, separated
2 cups milk
2 teaspoons seasoned salt
⅛ teaspoon pepper
¼ cup sliced ripe olives
2 pimientos, chopped
2 cups diced cooked turkey

Trim crusts, and spread each slice of bread with small amount of garlic spread. Cut into 1-inch squares. Beat egg whites until stiff; set aside. Beat egg yolks and next 3 ingredients until foamy. Add bread, olives, pimientos, and turkey. Fold in egg whites. Pour into shallow baking dish; bake in preheated slow oven (325°F.) for 50 minutes, or until firm. Good with frozen peas, grapefruit and avocado salad, and raisin pie. Makes 6 servings.

TURKEY-SAUSAGE SQUARES

1 pound sausage meat
1 onion, minced
2 cups soft stale-bread crumbs
1 cup diced celery and leaves
2 eggs, beaten
2 cups diced cooked turkey
1 cup milk
1 teaspoon poultry seasoning
   Turkey gravy
   Seasoned salt and pepper to taste

Cook sausage meat until done but not browned, breaking up with fork. Remove meat, and pour off all but 2 tablespoons of the fat. Cook onion in the fat for 5 minutes. Mix meat and onion with all ingredients except gravy and salt and pepper. Stir in 1 cup leftover gravy and salt and pepper. Pour into shallow baking dish, and bake in preheated moderate oven (350°F.) for about 45 minutes. Cut into squares, and serve with additional heated gravy. Good with baked acorn squash, mixed green salad, and Tokay grapes. Makes 6 to 8 servings.

TURKEY SALAD

2 cups diced leftover turkey
1 cup sliced celery
¼ cup French dressing
2 cups halved seeded Malaga or Tokay grapes
   Salt and pepper
   Salad greens
½ cup cooked salad dressing
⅓ cup dairy sour cream
¼ cup toasted slivered almonds

Marinate turkey and celery in French dressing for 1 hour. Add grapes, and season to taste with salt and pepper. Arrange on salad greens. Combine salad

Turkey Hawaiian

Turkey Creole in Rice Ring

dressing and sour cream. Top salad with this mixture, and garnish with slivered almonds. (Mayonnaise or bought salad dressing can be substituted for the cooked dressing and sour cream.)

BROILED TURKEY SALAD

- 1 teaspoon instant minced onion
- 1 tablespoon fresh lemon juice
- 2 cups diced cooked turkey
- ¾ teaspoon salt
- ⅛ teaspoon pepper
- ½ cup mayonnaise
- 1½ cups finely diced celery
- ¼ cup canned buttered chopped almonds
- 2 cups finely crushed potato chips
- 1 cup grated Cheddar cheese

Mix onion and lemon juice. Add remaining ingredients except last 2. Mix well; chill. Divide among 4 individual baking dishes, or put in 9-inch pie pan. Mix chips and cheese and completely cover top of salad. Put under broiler just until top is golden, but salad is still cold. Good with marinated tomatoes, cucumbers, watercress, French bread, and fruit cup. Makes 4 servings.

FRESH TANGERINE AND TURKEY SALAD

- 2 cups diced cooked turkey
- 1 cup diced celery
- 1 teaspoon finely chopped onion
- 1¼ teaspoons salt
- ¼ teaspoon ground white pepper
- 2 cups diced tangerine sections, well drained (about 5 tangerines)
- 3 tablespoons mayonnaise
- 1 tablespoon fresh lemon juice
  Lettuce

Tangerine sections for garnish

Mix together first 6 ingredients. Blend mayonnaise with lemon juice; add and mix lightly. Serve on lettuce. Garnish with tangerine sections. Makes 4 servings.

OPEN TURKEY SANDWICHES WITH CHEESE SAUCE

- 4 slices of toast
- 4 large slices of cooked turkey
- 3 tablespoons butter or margarine
- 3 tablespoons all-purpose flour
- ¼ teaspoon salt
- ⅛ teaspoon pepper
- 1 cup milk
- ¼ pound process American cheese, cut up (1 cup)

Arrange toast in shallow baking dish. Cover with turkey. Melt butter in saucepan; blend in flour, salt, and pepper. Add

Turkey and Broccoli Amandine

Turkey Pie, with Breadstick Topping

milk gradually and cook until thickened, stirring constantly. Add cheese and cook until cheese is melted. Pour sauce over turkey. Then brown under broiler. Makes 4 servings.

BAKED TURKEY-CHEDDAR SANDWICHES
12 slices of firm bread
3 eggs, beaten
¾ cup milk
½ teaspoon seasoned salt
Butter or margarine
1 can (10½ ounces) cream-of-mushroom soup
½ cup each of undiluted evaporated milk and turkey or chicken broth
½ teaspoon bottled thick condiment sauce
¼ teaspoon pepper
2 cups diced cooked turkey
½ cup grated Cheddar cheese

Dip bread into mixture of eggs, milk, and seasoned salt. Brown on both sides in hot butter. Put 6 slices in shallow baking dish. Mix soup, evaporated milk, broth, condiment sauce, pepper, and turkey. Spoon on toast slices. Top with remaining slices, and sprinkle with cheese. Bake in preheated hot oven (400°F.) for 15 to 20 minutes. Good with succotash, sliced-tomato and watercress salad, and baked fresh pears. Makes 6 servings.

TURKEY COMBINATION SANDWICHES
2 packages (3 ounces each) cream cheese, softened
1½ ounces (¼ cup) blue cheese, crumbled
⅓ cup minced pimiento-stuffed olives
1 teaspoon grated onion

6 slices of whole-wheat bread
Mayonnaise
6 slices of cooked turkey
Sliced leftover poultry stuffing
2 cups (one 1-pound can) whole-berry cranberry sauce, chilled and sliced
Lettuce leaves
6 slices of white bread

Mix first 4 ingredients. Spread whole-wheat bread with mayonnaise. Cover with turkey and poultry stuffing. Top with cranberry sauce, then with lettuce. Spread cheese mixture on white bread and invert on lettuce. Secure with picks and cut diagonally into halves. Makes 6 sandwiches.

Note: If not available, stuffing can be omitted. Or prepare stuffing and bake in a small loaf pan. Cool; chill.

TURMERIC—The irregularly shaped root of a tropical plant which is related to ginger. It is one of the essential spices in Indian cooking. When washed, cooked, and then dried, the turmeric root has a mild aroma and a mustardlike bitter taste. One of its characteristics is the brilliant gold color it adds to the dishes in which it is used. Turmeric is the "secret ingredient" of many prepared mustards with a bright yellow color, and it is always present in curry powder.

Turmeric flavors and colors curried meat, poultry, fish, and shellfish; deviled and creamed eggs; sauces for eggs, chicken, fish, or shellfish; egg, potato, or chicken salads; and rice dishes. It may be cooked in butter and the butter added to potatoes, corn, snap beans, and cabbages, or it may be used plain in all sorts of relishes and pickles.

Ground turmeric is widely available and the whole root may be purchased in herb specialty shops.

SAFFRON PILAU

¼ cup butter
1 small onion, minced
1 garlic clove, minced
2 whole cloves
½ teaspoon ground turmeric
⅛ teaspoon ground cuminseed
1½ cups uncooked rice
Salt
Few shreds of saffron

In the butter gently cook onion and garlic until they are transparent but not brown. Add cloves, turmeric, and cuminseed, and cook for 2 or 3 minutes. Then add rice, salt, the saffron which has been softened in a bit of warm water, and boiling water to cover rice by 1 inch. Proceed with favorite method for boiling or steaming rice until done. Makes 4 servings.
Note: If unaccompanied by other eastern dishes, serve with a sprinkling of tiny

onion rings, fried crisp and brown; slivers of almonds, fried or toasted; or seedless raisins, puffed in water, then fried a bit.

PEAR CHUTNEY

2 pounds onions, chopped
10 pounds hard cooking pears, peeled and quartered
2 tablespoons salt, or more to taste
½ cup preserved gingerroot, cut into chunks
2 hot dried peppers or ½ teaspoon cayenne
8 sweet green peppers, chopped
4 cups sugar
3 tablespoons flour
2 tablespoons ground turmeric
¼ cup powdered mustard
2 quarts cider vinegar

Grind onions and pears in grinder, using coarse blade. Mix with salt and let stand overnight. In morning drain off liquid. Cover pulp with cold water and drain again. Mix remaining ingredients and stir until smooth. Boil for 5 minutes. Add to pear mixture and boil for about 40 minutes, or until thick, stirring constantly to prevent sticking. Pour while hot into sterilized jars. Seal and cool. Makes about 8 pints.

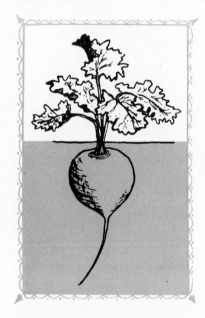

TURNIP—A root vegetable that is a member of the *Brassica* genus; there are several varieties. The flesh varies in texture; the finer-fleshed turnips are eaten as a vegetable and the coarser ones are fed to livestock. Turnips are white-fleshed. Some varieties have purple tops. (The so-called yellow turnip or Swedish turnip is actually the closely related rutabaga.) Turnip tops are eaten as greens and are used for forage.

Turnips originated in the temperate zone of Europe and have been grown for some 4,000 years. They are a cool-weather vegetable and are popular in northern Europe and Great Britain. They

came to the New World via Mexico, arriving in Virginia in 1610 and New England in 1628. Since they are not much trouble to grow and are useful to man and beast, the early and later settlers raised them for both. Turnips and turnip greens are particularly appreciated in our Southern states.

Availability—Fresh turnips are available year round with peak season from October to March.

Turnip greens are also available canned and frozen.

Purchasing Guide—Turnips are sold either bunched, with the tops left on or with tops removed. The tops should be fresh and green and the roots smooth, firm, and a good weight for their size.

Storage—Turnips keep best in a very cool, well-ventilated storage place at about 55° F., the old root cellar, in fact. If such storage is unavailable, refrigerate.

☐ Fresh, refrigerator shelf, raw: 1 month
☐ Fresh, refrigerator shelf, cooked: 2 to 3 days
☐ Fresh, prepared for freezing; or frozen, refrigerator frozen-food compartment: 2 to 3 months
☐ Fresh, prepared for freezing; or frozen, freezer: 1 year

Nutritive Food Values—A fair source of vitamin C. The greens are an excellent source of vitamins A and C, and a good source of calcium, iron, and riboflavin.

☐ Turnip, 3½ ounces, cooked = 23 calories
☐ Fresh turnip greens, 3½ ounces, solids and liquid = 20 calories
☐ Canned turnip greens, 3½ ounces, solids and liquid = 18 calories
☐ Frozen turnip greens, 3½ ounces, cooked and drained = 23 calories

Basic Preparation—Wash, pare, and slice or dice. Small turnips may be left whole.
☐ **To Cook**—Cook, covered, in 1 inch of boiling salted water until tender, for 12 to 15 minutes. Drain; season, and serve with melted butter or margarine. Sliced turnips may be seasoned and baked in a covered casserole in preheated moderate oven (375°F.) for about 45 minutes.
☐ **To Freeze**—Wash, peel, and cut into 1-inch cubes. Blanch in boiling water for 2 to 2½ minutes. Chill in cold water for 3 to 4 minutes. Drain. Pack into freezer container, leaving ½-inch headspace. Seal.

TURNIPS IN SOUR CREAM

2 pounds fresh turnips
1¼ teaspoons salt
½ teaspoon celery salt
1 cup dairy sour cream
¼ teaspoon ground ginger
⅛ teaspoon white pepper

Peel turnips and dice into medium cubes. Cook in boiling salted water until soft.

Drain. Mash, and season with remaining ingredients. Serve hot. Makes 6 servings.

FLUFFY TURNIPS

2 pounds fresh turnips
1 can (10½ ounces) beef consommé
½ teaspoon sugar
2 teaspoons finely chopped onion
2 tablespoons chopped parsley

Pare and cube turnips. Cook with consommé over medium heat for 12 to 15 minutes, or until tender. Mash in same liquid until fluffy. Add remaining ingredients. Reheat and serve with meat dish. Makes 6 servings.

FINNISH STUFFED TURNIPS

12 small to medium-size turnips
   Boiling water
1 tablespoon salt
¼ cup butter or margarine
⅔ cup soft bread crumbs
¼ cup chopped almonds

Scrub turnips, rinse, drain, and peel. Cook, covered with salted boiling water, for 12 to 15 minutes, or until soft. Drain, and cool. Spoon out a little of the center. Chop removed centers and mix with 2 tablespoons butter and all but 2 tablespoons of the bread crumbs. Stuff hollowed turnips with crumb mixture and sprinkle with about half of almonds. Brown remaining butter. Put stuffed turnips in a casserole, pour browned butter over, and sprinkle well with remaining crumbs and almonds. Bake in preheated moderate oven (350°F.) for 20 minutes, or until lightly browned. Baste frequently with any butter in casserole or extra melted butter. Makes 6 servings.

TURNIP SALAD

Mix together 4 cups finely grated young raw turnips, 1 cup thick dairy sour cream, 1 tablespoon sugar, 1 tablespoon vinegar, and 1 teaspoon salt. Serve on crisp shredded lettuce. Makes 6 to 8 servings.

TURNOVER

TURNOVER—A filled pastry in a triangular or semicircular shape. The pastry used may be a standard pastry, puff paste, or egg pastry, rolled out into a circle or a square. The filling, which may be savory or sweet, is placed on half the pastry, which is then folded over to enclose the filling and either baked or deep fried. Turnovers can be served hot or cold.

Commercially made apple, blueberry, and cherry turnovers are sold frozen; other turnovers are sold in the bakery department of food stores; refrigerated bake-and-serve turnovers are sold in the dairy department.

CHICKEN-LIVER TURNOVERS

Cook 2 slices of bacon until crisp, and crumble. In the bacon fat cook ½ pound chicken livers. Chop livers fine; mix with bacon and a little mayonnaise; season. Roll Flaky French Crust about ⅛ inch thick. Cut into 2-inch rounds. Put a dab of filling on one side of each round, and fold over, pinching together. Prick with fork and crimp around edge. Brush with egg yolk beaten with 1 tablespoon milk. Bake in preheated very hot oven (450° F.) for 10 minutes. Makes about 3 dozen.

Flaky French Crust

2 cups plus 2 tablespoons sifted all-purpose flour
¾ teaspoon salt
1 cup soft butter
2 egg yolks
¼ cup light cream
2 tablespoons dry white wine

Sift flour and salt into bowl. Cut in butter. Add combined egg yolks, cream, and wine; mix with fork until blended and smooth. Knead lightly in bowl until bubbles begin to appear on the surface of dough. Cover and chill for 1 hour. Roll to ⅛-inch thickness on floured board. Fold twice lengthwise and then twice crosswise. Chill for 15 minutes. Roll and fold twice more. Store, wrapped in moisture-proof paper, in refrigerator until needed.

CORNED-BEEF TURNOVERS, MUSHROOM SAUCE

Mince half of 12-ounce can corned beef; add ¼ cup undiluted cream-of-mushroom soup from 10½-ounce can, 1 grated small onion, and 2 chopped parsley sprigs. Add seasoning to taste. Roll pastry (made with 1½ cups all-purpose flour) into a rectangle (16 x 8 inches) on floured board. Cut into eight 4-inch squares. Spoon meat mixture on one corner of each square; moisten edges with water; fold over in triangles; crimp edges with fork; brush with undiluted evaporated milk. Put on cookie sheet; bake in preheated hot oven (425°F.) for about 20 minutes. Dilute remaining soup with ⅓ cup milk; heat; add ½ teaspoon Worcestershire. Serve as sauce for turnovers.

SAMOSAS
(Curried Meat Turnovers)

2 tablespoons instant minced onion
2 tablespoons water
2 tablespoons butter or margarine
¼ teaspoon each of garlic powder, ground cinnamon, ground ginger, and cayenne
2 teaspoons ground coriander
¼ cup chopped fresh tomato
1½ cups finely ground lamb or beef
1¼ teaspoons salt
¼ cup water
2 teaspoons fresh lemon juice
   Pastry for Samosas
   Egg white, beaten slightly

Soften onion in 2 tablespoons water. Sauté in butter. Add spices and stir and cook for 1 minute. Add tomato, lamb, and salt. Stir and cook for 2 to 3 minutes.

Add water and lemon juice, and cook until all the liquid is absorbed. Turn out onto a plate to cool. Roll Pastry very thin on a lightly floured board. Cut into circles with a 2½-inch cookie cutter. Brush edges lightly with beaten egg white. Place rounded ½ teaspoon of mixture in center of each. Fold over dough and crimp edges with a fork, being sure they are well sealed. Fry in hot deep fat (360°F. to 375°F. on a frying thermometer) until golden-brown. Drain on absorbent paper. If desired, use your own pastry recipe and bake the puffs in preheated hot oven (400°F.) for 12 to 15 minutes. Serve as an accompaniment to cocktails or tomato juice. Makes about 60 turnovers.

Pastry for Samosas

2 cups sifted all-purpose flour
1 teaspoon salt
¼ cup butter or margarine
7 tablespoons yogurt

Sift flour with salt. Melt butter and add to flour. Mix well. Stir in yogurt gradually, working it with hands for about 5 minutes. Knead until satiny and smooth. Makes pastry for 60 turnovers.

BLUEBERRY TURNOVERS

In saucepan mix ¼ cup sugar, ⅛ teaspoon salt, and ⅓ cup all-purpose flour. Add 2 tablespoons fresh orange juice and about 1⅔ cups (one 14-ounce can) blueberries with syrup. Cook, stirring constantly until very thick; cool. Roll 1 recipe of pastry (2¼ cups all-purpose flour) and cut into twelve 4½-inch rounds. Put 2 tablespoons blueberry mixture on half of each round, moisten edges, and fold over. Seal edges with a fork. Fry in small amount of fat until golden-brown on both sides.

RAISIN-ORANGE TURNOVERS

1¾ cups seedless raisins
1¾ cups water
¼ cup orange juice
⅓ cup brown sugar, firmly packed
1 tablespoon quick-cooking tapioca
½ teaspoon ground cinnamon
¼ teaspoon salt
1 tablespoon vinegar
1 tablespoon butter or margarine
2 teaspoons grated orange rind
   Standard pastry made with 2 cups flour
   Light cream (optional)

Combine raisins, water, and orange juice in saucepan. Bring to a boil and boil for 5 minutes. Then add sugar, tapioca, cinnamon, and salt. Cook, stirring constantly, until mixture comes to a boil. Remove from heat; add vinegar, butter, and orange rind. Cool. Roll pastry very thin (less than ⅛ inch) and cut into 6-inch circles or 5-inch squares. Put about 3 tablespoonfuls of filling on one side of each circle or square, moisten edges, fold over, and seal edges with floured fork.

Brush lightly with cream, if desired. Bake in preheated hot oven (425°F.) for about 20 minutes. Makes 8 to 10.

MARMALADE TURNOVERS

Roll standard pastry ⅛ inch thick and cut into 4-inch circles. Put 1 tablespoon marmalade on one side of circle. Dot with butter and sprinkle lightly with cinnamon. Moisten edges, fold over, and press edges together. Seal with floured fork. Bake in preheated hot oven (425° F.) for about 15 minutes.

TURTLE and TORTOISE—These are
members of the reptilian order Chelonia. They live in salt and fresh waters as well as on land, and are distinguished by their shells. Most of them have hard shells or carapaces, but there are soft-shell varieties. They come in many sizes and colors. In general usage the word turtle is used to describe aquatic types, while the word tortoise is reserved for the forms living on land.

Some turtles are enormous, growing to more than seven feet and weighing as much as 1,000 pounds. For eating purposes, the most famous one is the green turtle, which lives in warm ocean waters and sports a smooth greenish or olive shell. This turtle is made into a thick gelatinous soup which is considered an extraordinary treat by many people. Turtle soup is always served with the addition of sherry or Madeira, with a thin slice of lemon floating on it.

The people of Philadelphia prize the snapping turtle, a large fresh-water turtle of North America. It is traditionally made into snapper stew, and the meat is dished up in a rich cream sauce.

Turtle steak, another delicacy, is highly regarded in the South, especially on the Florida Keys, where commercial turtle fishing is concentrated. At its best it tastes like fine veal, but it can also be very tough. It is seldom available except locally.

There are many varieties of tortoise, known by such local names as the gophers of Florida. These are eaten in stews and soups.

Turtles and tortoises lay eggs which in many cases are also eaten as a delicacy. The eggs most widely eaten are those of the green sea turtle. Usually, turtles' eggs are boiled in heavily salted water. The white does not get hard, as with hens' eggs, but the yolk does and it is rich.

Generally speaking, turtles and tortoises are far more popular in America, with its tradition of living off the land, than in Europe. The exception is turtle soup, which was and is greatly fancied by English gourmets.

Availability—The fresh-water common snapping turtle or snapper is occasionally sold live in food stores, generally in the eastern half of the United States. Market sizes range from 4 to 25 pounds. The alligator snapping turtle is found in southern areas and is usually marketed in New Orleans and St. Louis. It often attains a weight of 200 pounds. Several species of soft-shell turtles are available in the southern areas of the United States where they are caught. Other fresh-water turtles are the Mississippi turtle, the Pacific pond turtle, the Mobile and Suwanee turtle, and the chicken turtle. These are available in local areas only. Green turtles, the most famous of the sea turtles, are available only in local areas. Fishing for them is centered around Key West, Florida.

Frozen turtle meat from the snapping turtle is available in some markets.

Canned turtle meat, green-turtle meat, turtle soup, green-turtle soup, and snapper soup are available.

Storage—Live turtle must be cooked immediately.

☐ Fresh, cooked; and canned, opened, refrigerator shelf: 1 to 2 days

☐ Canned, kitchen shelf: 1 year

☐ Frozen, refrigerator frozen-food compartment: 2 months

☐ Frozen, freezer: 1 year

Nutritive Food Values—High in protein.

☐ Green turtle, 3½ ounces, raw = 89 calories

☐ Canned green turtle, 3½ ounces = 106 calories

Basic Preparation

☐ **To Dress a Live Turtle**—The head must be removed first. Cause snapping turtle to grasp a stick. The head can then easily be pulled forward and cut off. Heads of other species can be forced to protrude by pressing the upper shell. Run a sharp knife along the edges of the skin where it joins the shell; then pull the skin back over the legs to the feet and disjoint the feet. Remove the lower part of the shell by cutting through the bridges which join the upper and lower shell. In both the snappers and soft-shells the bridges are soft. When the bridges are cut, the lower shell is readily removed by inserting a sharp knife under it and lifting the shell up and off. Remove entrails; then remove four quarters from the upper shell.

TURTLE SOUP
    3 pounds turtle meat
      Water
  ¼ cup butter or margarine
    2 medium onions, minced
  ¼ cup all-purpose flour
    1 cup canned tomatoes
  ½ garlic clove, minced
    2 bay leaves
      Few parsley sprigs
    6 whole cloves
  ¼ teaspoon ground mace
    1 teaspoon sugar
      Juice of 1 lemon
  ½ cup sherry
    2 hard-cooked eggs, minced

Have turtle meat cut into 1-inch cubes. Put meat with 3 quarts water in kettle and bring to boil; simmer for 10 minutes. Strain, reserving broth. Melt 3 tablespoons of the butter in kettle. Add turtle meat and brown on all sides. Remove meat and add remaining butter to kettle. Add onions and brown lightly. Add flour and stir until browned. Add turtle meat and next 8 ingredients. Add enough water to broth to make 4 quarts and add to mixture in kettle. Bring to boil, cover, and simmer for 3 hours. Strain, add sherry, and reheat, if necessary. Serve with a garnish of minced egg. Makes about 3 quarts.

TURTLE STEAK WITH SOUR-CREAM SAUCE
1½ pounds of turtle steaks, cut paper-thin
    All-purpose flour
  6 tablespoons butter or margarine
    Salt and pepper
    Paprika
½ cup dry white wine
  1 cup dairy sour cream
    Chopped parsley

Pound turtle steak with the edge of a plate. Dip steaks in flour. Melt butter in skillet with cover, add turtle steaks, and brown quickly on both sides. Season with salt and pepper to taste and add 1 tablespoon paprika. Add wine, cover, and simmer for 1 hour. Remove turtle to a hot platter. Stir sour cream into drippings in skillet and heat, stirring constantly. Pour over turtle and sprinkle with paprika and parsley. Makes 4 to 6 servings.

UPSIDE-DOWN CAKE

UPSIDE-DOWN CAKE—A cake baked in a different manner from other cakes, and one that does not necessarily require an oven. Brown or white sugar and butter are spread in the bottom of a pan and covered with a design of fruit and occasionally nuts which are then topped with a cake batter of some kind. After baking, the cake is turned out of the pan upside down. The sugar and butter mixture forms a glaze with the fruit juices and the cake remains moist. The cake batter may be a spongecake, a muffin batter, a yellow cake made from scratch or from a mix, a spice cake, or perhaps, for an old-fashioned version, gingerbread. Smaller versions may be made in custard cups or muffin pans. Upside-down cakes are also called skillet cakes because they can be baked on top of the stove, using a covered skillet over either gas or electric thermostatically controlled surface units. They can also be baked in covered electric skillets.

Usually an upside-down cake is served warm, either plain or with whipped cream or a dessert sauce. On some occasions main-dish upside-down cakes may be made, using ground meat and perhaps corn bread as a topping.

Upside-down cakes are typically American and are not found in European cooking. They date back to the days of the early settlers who did not always have a bake oven in their homes. Thanks to the ingenuity of these early homemakers, their families did not have to forego the pleasure of eating cake.

APRICOT-PRUNE UPSIDE-DOWN CAKE

¼ cup water
½ cup brown sugar, firmly packed
½ cup butter or margarine
1 cup sweetened cooked dried-apricot halves
1 cup cooked pitted prunes
2 cups sifted cake flour
2 teaspoons baking powder
¼ teaspoon salt
1 cup granulated sugar
1 egg
¾ cup milk
1 teaspoon vanilla extract
  Whipped cream (optional)

Mix water, brown sugar, and ¼ cup of the butter, melted. Pour into wax-paper lined pan (9 x 9 x 2 inches). Arrange fruits in mixture, alternating apricots and prunes. Sift flour, baking powder, and salt together. Cream the remaining butter; gradually add granulated sugar and beat well. Add egg and beat until light.

Add sifted dry ingredients alternately with milk, beating until smooth after each addition. Stir in vanilla. Pour into pan over fruit. Bake in preheated moderate oven (350°F.) for 45 to 50 minutes. Then invert pan on serving plate and peel off paper. Serve warm, with whipped cream, if desired. Makes 6 large or 9 small servings.

Pineapple Upside-Down Cake

Combine ¼ cup melted butter and ⅔ cup firmly packed brown sugar. Mix well and spread in pan (9 x 9 x 2 inches). Drain 1 can (8½ ounces) sliced pineapple and sprinkle 2 tablespoons of the syrup over sugar mixture in pan. Cut pineapple slices into quarters and arrange on sugar mixture. Sprinkle with ½ cup chopped nuts. Prepare cake batter as directed in recipe above. Pour into pan over pineapple and proceed as directed. Makes 6 large servings.

Blueberry Upside-Down Cake

Combine ¼ cup melted butter and ½ cup firmly packed brown sugar. Mix well and spread in pan (9 x 9 x 2 inches). Mix 2 cups washed fresh blueberries and

Ambrosia Upside-Down Cake

2 teaspoons grated lemon rind. Put in pan, distributing evenly. Prepare cake batter as directed in recipe for Apricot-Prune Upside-Down Cake. Pour into pan over berries and proceed as directed. Makes 6 large servings.

Cherry Upside-Down Cake

Combine ¼ cup melted butter and ½ cup firmly packed brown sugar. Mix well and spread in pan (9 x 9 x 2 inches). Mix 2 cups (one 1-pound can) water-packed pitted red sour cherries, drained (reserve liquid), and 2 teaspoons grated lemon rind. Put in pan, distributing evenly. Prepare cake batter as directed in recipe for Apricot-Prune Upside-Down

Cake. Pour into pan over cherries and proceed as directed. Serve baked cake with Cherry Sauce. Makes 6 large servings.

Cherry Sauce

Blend 2 tablespoons sugar and 2 teaspoons cornstarch. Add reserved cherry juice and cook until thickened.

AMBROSIA UPSIDE-DOWN CAKE

- ⅓ cup butter or margarine
- ¾ cup firmly packed light brown sugar
- 6 slices of canned pineapple
- 1 package cake mix: yellow, orange, or orange-coconut
- 1 can (11 ounces) mandarin oranges Coconut
- 6 maraschino cherries

Melt butter in pan (13 x 9 x 2 inches). Sprinkle with brown sugar. Arrange slices of pineapple on sugar. Prepare cake mix as directed on label. Pour over pineapple slices and bake as directed for pan size. Turn out on rack, and cut into 6 serving pieces. Drain mandarin oranges. Arrange sections around each cake serving; sprinkle with coconut; put a maraschino cherry in each pineapple ring. Makes 6 large servings.

GINGER-MINCE UPSIDE-DOWN CAKE

- 1 package dry mincemeat
- ½ cup boiling water
- 3 tablespoons butter
- 2 tablespoons brown sugar

1½ cups canned sliced apples
1 package gingerbread mix

Break mincemeat into saucepan. Add boiling water, and cook for 3 minutes, stirring occasionally. Cool. Melt the butter in a baking pan (8 x 8 x 2 inches). Sprinkle brown sugar on butter. Arrange apple slices in pan, and pour mincemeat over apples. Prepare gingerbread mix as directed on the package. Pour over the mincemeat. Bake in preheated moderate oven (350°F.) for about 35 minutes. When done, turn upside down on serving plate. Makes 8 servings.

UTENSIL—An instrument, vessel, tool, or implement. When the word is applied to kitchen equipment, it refers to the utensils used in the preparation, cooking, serving, or storing of food. Following is a check list of utensils needed in a well-equipped kitchen. Those preceded by an asterisk are probably most essential to the largest number of families.

Baking pans: corn-stick pan; custard cups; loaf pan (9 x 5 x 3 inches) for bread, loaf cakes, meat loaf; muffin pans

*Beaters and mixers, 2 or more of following: whisk for beating and mixing; rotary beater with heavy-duty gear construction; portable electric mixer; stationary electric mixer

Blender, electric, for puréeing, chopping, mixing batters, sauces, beverages

*Boards for cutting and rolling: small one for cheese, vegetables; medium for carving meats; largest for piecrust and breadmaking

*Bowls, graduated (from 1 pint to 4 quarts), for mixing and storing

*Broiling pan, if there isn't one in the range

Cake pans: *8- or 9-inch round or square layer pans (2 or 3); 8- or 9-inch square loaf pan; *13 x 9-inch loaf pan; angel-food pan; springform pan

*Can, bottle, jar openers; alone or in combination:
  Bottle opener
  Corkscrew
  Electric can opener, a real convenience item
  Hand can opener, either mounted on wall or to keep in a drawer (an emergency one needed for odd cans and odd times even if an electric opener is available)
  Jar opener
  Punch-type can opener

*Casseroles with covers: graduated sizes, starting with 2-quart

*Coffeemaker, electric or non-electric percolator, drip, vacuum, or espresso

*Cookie sheets, cutter, press; decorating tubes and tips; cake racks

*Colander, sieve, strainers—need at least 1 large and 1 tea-strainer size

*Covered pan, at least 6 to 10-quart with trivet. May be a Dutch oven, kettle, or saucepan to be used for meats, soups, quantity cooking, canning, and blanching.

*Cutlery (paring knives, chef or butcher knife, carving knife, slicer, utility) and other small tools (rubber and metal spatulas, spoons—including slotted and wooden, forks, apple corer, baster, pastry fork or blender, vegetable peeler, nutcracker, skewers, ladle, shears, potato masher, tongs, pastry brush).

Deep fryer, electric or non-electric

*Double boiler, 2- or 3-quart. Use bottom as an extra saucepan; some upper pans can be used as casseroles.

Egg poacher, electric or non-electric

*Flour sifter, 1-cup and 5-cup sizes most frequently used

*Graters, grinder, shredders, juicer, ice crusher, electric or non-electric. Frequently available in combination or as attachments to mixer. Singly they are more frequently non-electric.

*Griddle, grill, waffle iron; electric or non-electric. One appliance often serves two purposes, and some of the grills serve as heated serving trays.

Ice-cream freezer, electric or non-electric

*Knife sharpener, electric, available alone or in combination with another appliance. Non-electric usually serves this one purpose only.

*Measuring cups graduated from ¼ cup to 1 cup for dry measure; 1 cup, 2 cups, and 4 cups for liquid measure.

*Measuring spoons

Molds for salads, desserts, breads, cakes, puddings

*Pantryware: canisters, salt and pepper shakers, scoops

*Pie pans, one or two each 8-inch and 9-inch

Pressure cooker, electric or non-electric. Useful for certain stews, soups, pot roasts, canning

*Protective mats, tiles, trivets

*Roasting pan, with a rack. Useful size is 10 x 12 inches; 12 x 15 inches, or in between.

Rolling pin, cover, pastry cloth

*Saucepans, for a small family, start with a 1-quart and a 2-quart.

Scales, especially for families on special diets

*Skillets: 7-inch and 10-inch are good starting sizes. Other sizes and omelet pan can come later.

Steamer for steaming rice, puddings, vegetables; for blanching

*Storage accessories: vegetable bins, dinnerware racks, utensil trays, and drawer dividers for use in drawers

*Storage containers with covers for pantry shelves, refrigerator, and freezer storage

*Teakettle, 2- or 3-quart size

Teapot, 1 or 2 depending on tea service

*Thermometers: candy, frying, freezer, meat, and oven

*Toaster, electric or non-electric

Warmers: electric hot trays, casseroles, etc., and their non-electric cousins, the chafing dishes, casseroles, etc., which use canned heat or candles to keep foods warm

VACHERIN—A delicious creamy white dessert cheese made in France and Switzerland from whole milk mixed with cream. It has a firm leathery crust over a very soft paste, similar to ripe Brie.

Vacherin is also the name of a French or Swiss meringue cake made usually in the shape of rings which are stacked on each other and filled with fruit, ice cream, whipped cream, mousse, etc. It is a very festive dessert.

VACHERIN À LA SUISSE
(Meringue Shell)

Beat 5 egg whites, a pinch of salt, and ¼ teaspoon cream of tartar until the whites are stiff and form soft peaks. Gradually add 1¼ cups sugar, 1 tablespoon at a time, beating after each addition. When the meringue becomes very stiff, after about ⅔ of the sugar has been added, fold in remaining sugar at one time and add 1 teaspoon vanilla extract. Grease and flour 2 cookie sheets or cover them with baking paper. Trace 5 circles, 7 inches in diameter, on the sheets. Spread one of the circles with a layer of meringue ¼ inch thick. Put rest of meringue in a large pastry bag with a plain tube and pipe rings of the mixture around the rims of the other 4 circles. Make about 12 small rosettes of meringue in addition, but reserve some of the mixture. Bake the meringue in preheated very slow oven (250°F.) for about 45 minutes. Meringue should be crisp and dry with no tears adhering to it. Remove from oven and loosen meringues carefully. Around the edge of the flat circle spread a thin ridge of unbaked meringue. Put one of the baked rings on this. Brush the top of the ring lightly with more unbaked meringue and top with another ring. Repeat this process until all the rings' are piled up and you have a large meringue shell. Coat the outside with the remaining unbaked meringue and return to the oven until the shell is thoroughly dried out.

Turn off the heat and let the *vacherin* remain in the oven for several hours to cool and dry slowly. To serve, fill the shell with fresh fruit, sweetened whipped cream, sherbet, frozen mousse, or scoops of variflavored ice creams. Decorate with the meringue rosettes and chopped pistachio nuts. Cut into wedges at the table. Makes 6 to 8 servings.

VANILLA *by Lucy Kavaler*—One of the loveliest of orchids with lemon-yellow waxy outthrust petals; it has no odor, yet it is the source of the most aromatic of flavors. The tropical plant *Vanilla planifolia* bears its fruit in the form of a bean pod, which also has virtually no scent or flavor. When dried and cured, however, the bean develops the taste and smell that is generally associated with vanilla, a delicate sweetness ideal for flavoring baked goods, ice cream, and candies.

Vanilla is a part of our earliest memories; its haunting fragrance carries us back to childhood, to cakes baking in the oven, to little bottles of dark-brown extract sniffed and surreptitiously applied as perfume. Even as grown-ups, we find that the scent, like that of cinnamon, cloves, and other spices, brings an aura of far-off places into our everyday kitchens.

It is indeed only fitting that vanilla's history takes in the romantic Spanish conquistadors. More than four centuries have passed since the day when bold dashing Hernán Cortés drank his first cup of *xocoatl* at the court of Montezuma, ruler of the Aztecs. To make this beverage, he learned, the Indians powdered the beans of the cacao tree together with bean pods, renamed *vainilla,* meaning "little scabbard," by the Spaniards.

The combination of vanilla and chocolate has been a particularly happy one from Aztec times to the present. A rich creamy flavor results, and so the best chocolate candy, cakes, and frostings are enhanced with vanilla. Hot chocolate can leave the nursery and become a drink for grown-ups when a few drops of vanilla extract are added.

With the invention of ice cream in the 17th century, vanilla began to outrank other flavors. "Make mine vanilla," cry the vast majority of ice-cream eaters today. It is three times as popular as any other flavor and accounts for half of the staggering three-quarters of a billion gallons of ice cream consumed here in a year. The ice-cream industry thus seizes the lion's share of vanilla bean imports, but enough is left to add mellow sweetness to cakes, cookies, candies, and other desserts. Leaf through any cook book and observe how many such recipes call for vanilla.

This widespread use is particularly surprising, because few natural products have been as difficult to obtain in cultivation as vanilla. It remained a luxury flavor for three centuries, as no one, outside of the Mexican Indians, could manage to obtain a crop of beans.. The problem was that the transplanted orchid would bear no fruit. Superstitious plantation owners were convinced that the curse of Montezuma lay upon them. At last in 1836 a French botanist discovered that the curse lay in the sexual structure of the plant; it could be pollinated by a single species of bee, native only to Mexico. A freed slave then worked out a way of pollinating the plants by hand. This slow and painstaking method, used to this day, made it possible to raise vanilla in many areas of the world. Madagascar, in particular, became a center for the French "Bourbon" beans, so called because the crop was also produced on the island of Bourbon, now Réunion, in the Indian Ocean. But artificial pollination and the appearance of the fruit are merely the preamble to a long and tedious curing and drying process. Fully six months are devoted to transforming the thick green pods into the long thin dark-brown green-bean-shape sticks we know. Even then the job is not done, as most cooks and food processors find it easier to use extracts, made by dissolving the chopped beans in alcohol and water, filtering the resulting liquid, and aging it in glass-lined tanks.

In this form the flavor, as the skilled cook knows, is highly concentrated, and the tiniest quantity carries its sweetness through an entire cake or batch of cookies. A number of chefs, especially in Europe, still like to work with the vanilla bean, both for baking and for making ice cream. In one family of French origin a recipe handed down for generations advises splitting the pod, separating the pulp from it, scalding both pulp and pod with heavy cream, then removing the pod and retaining the flavored cream as a base for old-fashioned ice cream. Many ice-cream lovers will buy only those commercial brands that contain black seed specks, proof that natural vanilla was utilized. The absence of these specks, however, does not necessarily imply the presence of artificial flavor. When manufacturers use extracts, the seeds have been filtered out.

The suspicious gourmet, though, has good reason for his doubt. All too often there is no more than a drop of pure vanilla extract in mass-produced vanilla ice cream, cakes, cookies, and candies. Instead the taste comes from such unromantic origins as waste wood-pulp liquor. Unpalatable though this sounds, the flavor created is a brother, albeit not a twin, of the natural product. Where the planters had trouble in making the orchid reproduce, chemists have been baffled in their efforts to determine the chemical composition of the bean. They have succeeded in duplicating only vanillin, the chief but not the sole source of the taste. The synthetic is stronger and cheaper than the natural extract, which accounts for its wide commercial use. One artificial-flavor producer insists doggedly that despite its centuries-long popularity in ice cream, natural vanilla endures cold poorly and should be reinforced by at least a little of the stable synthetic.

However it is made, we all eat and serve vanilla ice cream. As Ralph Waldo Emerson, American essayist, pointed out more than a century ago: "We dare not trust our wit for making our house pleasant to our friend and so we buy ice cream."

Availability—Pure vanilla extract is widely available. Vanilla beans are available in specialty food stores.

VANILLA SUGAR
Cut a 1-inch piece of vanilla bean into small pieces. Place in covered jar with 1 cup sifted confectioners' sugar. Let stand at least overnight before using. Used for sprinkling on cookies and cakes.

VANILLA FRESH-FRUIT CUP
1 large unpeeled pear, diced
2 cups fresh orange sections
½ cup seeded grapes
2 tablespoons sugar
1 tablespoon fresh lemon juice
1 teaspoon vanilla extract
Fresh mint leaves

Combine all ingredients except mint leaves. Chill for 2 to 3 hours. Garnish with mint and serve as appetizer or dessert. Makes 6 servings.
Note: Vanilla brings out the sweetness in fruits so less sugar is necessary.

SUGGESTED USES FOR VANILLA
• Add 6 to 8 drops of vanilla extract to a cup of hot tea. The vanilla flavor won't be discernible but it will bring out the flavor of the tea.
• Add vanilla extract to taste to the egg-and-milk mixture when making French toast.
• For fruit-salad dressing, mix ¼ teaspoon vanilla extract, ¼ cup mayonnaise, and ¼ cup heavy cream, whipped.
• Add vanilla extract to taste to the cream or milk to be used for morning cereal. Less sugar will be needed.

VARIETY MEAT—The name given to those edible parts of an animal other than the skeletal muscle which is usually known as "meat."

Variety meats include liver, sweetbreads, kidneys, brains, heart, tongue, tripe, and oxtails. Partially prepared meats, such as sausages, are also sometimes looked upon as variety meats. For additional information see entries for individual variety meats.

RAGOUT OF VARIETY MEATS
½ pound each of beef liver, beef kidney, beef heart, fresh tongue, and oxtail
1 cup cider vinegar
1 cup red wine
2 garlic cloves, minced
1 bay leaf
6 whole cloves
1 teaspoon pepper
3 tablespoons bacon fat
1 teaspoon dried hot pepper
3 tablespoons chopped chives
1 tablespoon salt
1 large onion, sliced
2 medium green peppers, seeded and chopped

3 tablespoons chopped parsley
½ pound Italian sweet sausages, sliced
2 tablespoons tomato paste
½ cup pitted green olives
Cornmeal Sauce

Pour boiling water over the variety meats. Drain and chop meat, removing bone from oxtail, into small cubes. Cover with vinegar and wine, 1 garlic clove, the bay leaf, cloves, and pepper. Marinate for several hours. Melt bacon fat and add remaining garlic, hot pepper, and chives. Add meat and cook until brown. Add water to cover, and salt. Allow mixture to come to a boil and add onion, green peppers, parsley, sausages, and tomato paste. Cover and cook until meats are tender. Add olives. Serve with Cornmeal Sauce. Makes 6 to 8 servings.

Cornmeal Sauce

1 tablespoon bacon fat
1 small onion, chopped
3 cups water
1 teaspoon salt
Yellow cornmeal

Melt bacon fat and sauté onion until golden. Add water and salt and bring to a boil. Stir in enough cornmeal to give mixture the consistency of a very thick cream sauce.

VEAL—Young beef four to fourteen weeks of age is known as veal. It is most abundant in late winter and spring. During the rest of the year most of the meat sold as veal is actually calf, from animals fourteen weeks to one year of age.

Availability—All year round. Most plentiful in late winter and spring. For information on the cuts of veal available, see Retail Cuts of Veal—Where They Come From, page 1887.

The veal variety meats available are liver, kidney, heart, brains, sweetbread, and tongue.

Boneless veal rolls weighing from 4 to 8 pounds, boneless veal leg roasts weighing from 4 to 6 pounds, and small veal steaks are all available frozen.

Strained and chopped veal and veal with vegetables and cereal are available in baby and junior foods.

Purchasing Guide—The color of lean veal meat varies with the age of the animal, becoming redder with increasing age. Young, milk-fed veal will have grayish-pink lean. The texture should be fine and velvety. Veal has very little exterior fat and what it has should be firm and creamy white. It has no marbling.

Storage—Remove from market paper or loosen wrapper; store unwrapped or loosely wrapped in coldest part of refrigerator.

☐ Ground veal, stew meat, and variety meats, refrigerator shelf, raw: 1 to 2 days

☐ Chops, steaks, roasts, and cutlets, refrigerator shelf, raw: 2 to 3 days

☐ Veal and gravy, refrigerator shelf, cooked and covered: 4 to 5 days

☐ All types, refrigerator frozen-food compartment, raw, prepared for freezing: 1 to 2 weeks

☐ All types except ground, freezer, raw, prepared for freezing: 6 to 7 months

☐ Ground veal, freezer, raw, prepared for freezing: 2 to 3 months

☐ Veal and gravy, freezer, cooked, prepared for freezing: 2 to 3 months

Veal, once thawed, should not be refrozen.

Nutritive Food Values—An excellent source of protein, iron, and niacin; a fair source of riboflavin.

☐ Arm steak, 3½ ounces, cooked = 298 calories

☐ Blade steak, 3½ ounces, cooked = 276 calories

☐ Breast, 3½ ounces, stewed with gravy = 346 calories

☐ Cutlet, 3½ ounces, cooked = 277 calories

☐ Loin chop, 3½ ounces, cooked = 421 calories

☐ Rib chop, 3½ ounces, cooked = 318 calories

☐ Rump chop, 3½ ounces, cooked = 232 calories

☐ Rump, 3½ ounces, roasted = 174 calories

☐ Sirloin, 3½ ounces, roasted = 175 calories

Basic Preparation—The cuts of veal generally used for roasting come from the

shoulder, rib, loin, or leg sections. The cuts used for stuffing and braising are the breast, birds, and chops. The neck, flank, and shanks are used for cooking in liquid. See Retail Cuts of Veal—Where They Come From, page 1887. Since veal is a very lean meat, broiling, except for kidneys and sweetbreads, is not recommended.

☐ **To Roast**—Wipe meat with a damp cloth and put on a rack in shallow roasting pan. Sprinkle with salt and pepper. If desired, rub with a cut garlic clove. Or sprinkle with herbs such as marjoram, thyme, or crumbled bay leaf. If roast has little fat covering, lay several strips of fat bacon or salt pork on top. Do not cover or add water. Insert a meat thermometer into center of thickest part of meat. Roast in preheated slow oven (300°F. to 325°F.) until meat thermometer registers 170°F. See Timetable for Roasting, below, for length of time required. Plan to have roast done 15 to 20 minutes before serving to allow for making gravy.

☐ **To Make Gravy**—For each cup of gravy desired, use 2 tablespoons drippings, 2 tablespoons all-purpose flour, and 1 cup liquid. Lift roast from pan and pour off all fat except the amount needed. Leave any brown bits in the pan. Blend in flour completely. Put pan over moderately low heat and cook and stir until mixture bubbles and begins to brown. Remove from heat and gradually stir in water or other liquid; combine thoroughly. Return pan to heat. Continue cooking and stirring over low heat until gravy thickens and is cooked, for 3 to 5 minutes. Season, and strain, if desired. **Note:** If pan drippings are not brown, a liquid gravy coloring may be added to attain proper color.

☐ **To Panfry Chops, Patties, and Steak**—Brown meat on both sides in a small amount of fat in heavy skillet. Enough fat should be used to cover the surface of the skillet. After meat is browned on both sides, season to taste with salt and pepper. Continue cooking over medium

TIMETABLE FOR ROASTING VEAL

CUT	APPROX. WEIGHT (POUNDS)	OVEN TEMPERATURE	INTERIOR TEMPERATURE WHEN REMOVED FROM OVEN	APPROX. COOKING TIME (MINUTES PER POUND)
Leg	5 to 8	300 to 325°F.	170°F.	20 to 35
Loin	4 to 6	300 to 325°F.	170°F.	30 to 35
Rib (rack)	3 to 5	300 to 325°F.	170°F.	35 to 40
Rolled Boned Shoulder	4 to 6	300 to 325°F.	170°F.	40 to 45

heat, turning occasionally, until meat is done. Do not cover during cooking.

☐ **To Braise**—Meat is browned slowly, seasoned, and a little liquid such as water, broth, or vegetable juice is added; the heat is lowered to the point where the meat barely simmers, the pan is covered tightly, and cooking continues until meat is completely tender. The meat cooks by steam. For cooking time, see Timetable for Braising Veal, below.

☐ **To Cook in Liquid**—The procedure is almost exactly as above, but a larger quantity of liquid is added, usually enough to cover the meat. Recipes, however, are generally required because of the differences in flavors, other foods to be added, the size, shape, and thickness of the meat, and a few changes in procedure, such as flouring the meat. The cut of meat is also usually specified, although this may be interchangeable within a group according to size and taste.

☐ **To Prepare Brains**—Veal brains weigh about ½ pound. Soak in cold salted water for 15 minutes. Wash in cold running water. Drain, cool, and remove outer membrane. Simmer for 10 minutes in boiling salted water. Drain, cut into slices, and dredge with seasoned flour. Or dip in fine dry bread crumbs seasoned with salt and pepper. Sauté in butter or margarine until lightly browned, sprinkle with parsley, and serve with lemon wedges.

☐ **To Prepare Hearts**—Veal hearts weigh about ¾ pound. They are tender and delicate in flavor and are usually cooked by moist heat, as in braising. To braise hearts, wash well under cold running water. Remove veins and arteries. Put in a bowl and cover with cold water, add 2 tablespoons vinegar, and let stand overnight in the refrigerator. Then drain and wipe dry. Brown on all sides in hot butter or margarine. Sprinkle with all-purpose flour and brown slightly. Add 2 cups beef bouillon. Bring to boil, cover, and simmer for 2½ to 3 hours, or until tender. Serve sliced, with the pan liquid.

☐ **To Prepare Kidneys**—Veal kidneys weigh 8 to 12 ounces each and are so tender that they need very little cooking. They are usually broiled or panfried. To broil kidneys, remove the capsule and white core, rinse well, and cut crosswise into ½-inch slices. Saturate with melted butter and season with salt and pepper. Broil 3 inches from heat for about 5 minutes on each side. To panfry kidneys, prepare and slice as above. Season with salt and pepper and brown in hot butter for about 2 or 3 minutes on each side.

☐ **To Prepare Liver**—Veal liver weighs 2 to 3 pounds and comes from milk-fed animals. It is mild in flavor, light in color, and tender. Calf's liver is also mild in flavor and tender but is slightly darker in color. Liver is often panfried. To panfry, try to get slices that are of the same thickness, about ¼ inch. Remove capsule and thin outer membrane to prevent curling. Dredge with all-purpose flour, if desired, and panfry in hot butter for 1 to 3 minutes on each side.

☐ **To Prepare Tongue**—Veal tongue weighs ½ to 2 pounds. It is cooked in liquid. To cook tongue, put in kettle. Add ½ teaspoon salt per pound of tongue and water to cover. Add a few peppercorns, 1 large onion stuck with 2 or 3 whole cloves, 1 bay leaf, 1 sliced carrot, 1 celery stalk, and a few parsley sprigs. Bring to boil, cover, and simmer for 2 to 3 hours, or until tender. Cool in the liquid, pull off skin, and cut off roots. Serve sliced with mustard or horseradish.

☐ **To Prepare Sweetbreads**—Veal sweetbreads are white and tender. A pair weighs about 1 pound. They should be precooked before using them in recipes. Put in saucepan and cover with boiling water. Season with salt. Simmer, covered, for 25 minutes. Drain. Hold under cold running water and slip off membrane with fingers. With knife, cut out dark veins and thick connective tissue. Split very thick sweetbreads into halves lengthwise. Use at once or refrigerate.

RETAIL CUTS OF VEAL— WHERE THEY COME FROM

TENDER
1. Shoulder Section
    Arm roast
    Blade roast
    Arm steak
    Blade steak
    Rolled shoulder
2. Rib Section
    Rib roast
    Crown roast
    Rib chops
    Frenched rib chops
3. Loin Section
    Loin roast
    Rolled stuffed loin
    Loin chops
    Kidney chops
    Sirloin roast
    Sirloin steak
    Rolled double sirloin
    Cube steak
4. Leg Section
    Standing rump
    Shank half of leg
    Rolled leg
    Center leg
    Boneless cutlets
    Round steak
    Escallops
    Rolled cutlets (birds)
    Heel of the round
5. Breast Section
    Breast
    Stuffed breast
    Stuffed chops

LESS TENDER
    Neck slices
    Riblets
    Fore shanks
    Brisket pieces (front of breast section)
    Brisket rolls

GROUND VEAL (may come from any section, but generally from neck, breast, shanks, and flank)
    Ground veal
    Patties
    Mock chicken legs (ground veal on skewers)

CUBE STEAKS
    Cube steaks
    Rolled cube steaks (birds)

DICED VEAL
    City chicken (diced veal on skewers)
    Veal for stew (generally from forequarter cuts)

TIMETABLE FOR BRAISING VEAL

CUT	AVERAGE WEIGHT OR THICKNESS	APPROX. TOTAL COOKING TIME
Breast, stuffed	3 to 4 pounds	1½ to 2½ hours
Breast, rolled	2 to 3 pounds	1½ to 2½ hours
Veal birds	½ x 2 x 4 inches	45 to 60 minutes
Chops (all except shoulder)	½ to ¾ inch	45 to 60 minutes
Steaks or cutlets	½ to ¾ inch	45 to 60 minutes
Shoulder chops	½ to ¾ inch	45 to 60 minutes
Shoulder cubes	1 to 2 inches	45 to 60 minutes

VEAL COOK BOOK

LEG AND SHOULDER OF VEAL IN LARGE PIECES

ROAST LEG OF VEAL

3 pounds boneless leg of veal
¼ pound lean salt pork
3 to 4 slices of prosciutto or cooked ham
3 garlic cloves, cut into small pieces
1 teaspoon each of salt and pepper
½ teaspoon each of ground ginger and nutmeg
Crumbled dried basil
Olive or corn oil
½ cup each of tomato juice and sherry or Madeira

Buy a leg of veal and have the butcher bone, roll, and tie it. Have the butcher lard the meat with strips of the pork and small rolls of the ham. If you own a larding needle, you can do it yourself. Jab the meat in several places with a sharp knife and insert the pieces of garlic. Combine salt, pepper, ginger, and nutmeg and rub this mixture on the leg. Arrange it in a baking dish and sprinkle with a little dried basil and plenty of olive oil. Mix tomato juice with sherry and add to the pan. Insert a meat thermometer in the flesh and roast in preheated moderate oven (350°F.) for 30 minutes. Baste with the pan juices and continue roasting for another 30 minutes. Baste again, adding more wine and tomato juice if needed. Lower heat to slow (300°F.) and continue cooking for another 30 minutes, or until the thermometer registers an internal temperature of 165°F. Serve with roasted potatoes, a good green salad, and hot French bread. Use the pan juices as a sauce. Makes 6 servings.

BRAISED LEG OF VEAL

½ cup plus 2 tablespoons butter
1 garlic clove, minced
1 teaspoon salt
¼ teaspoon ground rosemary
Pinch of thyme
Pepper to taste
1 small leg of veal, boned and tied
2 cups thinly sliced onions
2 celery stalks, trimmed and cut into 2-inch lengths
1 carrot, scraped and cut into 1-inch lengths
1 bay leaf
Chicken bouillon or water
1 tablespoon cornstarch
¼ cup dry sherry

Cream 2 tablespoons butter with garlic, salt, rosemary, thyme, and pepper. Rub this over the meat. Put remaining butter, onions, celery, carrot, and bay leaf in heavy casserole or Dutch oven. Put meat on the bed of vegetables and cover. Bake in preheated moderate oven (375°F.) for about 2 hours, or until veal is very tender. Turn the meat several times as it cooks and, if necessary, add a little bouillon to keep it from becoming dry.

Remove meat and strain broth. Measure it and add enough bouillon to make 2 cups. Boil the liquid rapidly. Blend cornstarch with wine and stir it into the gravy. Cook, stirring constantly, until smooth. Serve the meat with the sauce. Makes about 8 servings.

VITELLO TONNATO (Veal with Tuna)

3½ pounds veal cut from the leg
Celery (about 8 stalks)
Olive oil (1⅓ cups)
3 carrots
10 anchovy fillets
½ sour pickle
2 cans (7 ounces each) tuna fish
1 cup dry white wine
2 garlic cloves
Salt, pepper, and ground thyme to taste
2 egg yolks
1½ cups uncooked rice
6 green onions, sliced
1 red onion, chopped
½ green pepper, chopped
12 each ripe and green olives, chopped
¼ cup minced parsley
Tarragon vinegar

Simmer veal, 4 celery stalks, ½ cup olive oil, 1 carrot, next 5 ingredients, and seasonings for about 3 hours. When tender, cool in pot. Purée ingredients except meat in an electric blender or force through a food mill. Beat egg yolks and stir in ½ cup oil, a few drops at a time. When thickened, beat in puréed mixture. Cook, and cool rice. Add 2 chopped carrots, 1 cup diced celery, green and red onion, green pepper, olives, parsley, remaining oil, and vinegar, salt, and pepper to taste. Add a little purée. Serve veal sliced very thin with the purée as a sauce and with the rice salad. Garnish with artichokes and pimientos, if desired. Makes 8 servings.

JELLIED VEAL SLICES

4 to 5 pounds veal shoulder
2 garlic cloves
3 to 4 tablespoons butter
1 teaspoon each of salt and pepper
1 cup white wine
1½ cups bouillon or water
Bones from the meat
1 pound veal neck
1 teaspoon chopped fresh tarragon
1 onion, stuck with 2 cloves
½ bay leaf

Have the shoulder boned, rolled, and tied. Make small incisions in the meat with a sharp knife and insert slivers of garlic. Melt the butter in a deep Dutch oven or a heavy kettle and brown meat on all sides. Sprinkle with salt and pepper. Add white wine and bouillon. Add bones, veal neck, tarragon, onion, and bay leaf; cover with a tight lid. Bring to boil, remove to preheated slow oven (325°F.), and bake for 2½ hours, or until the meat is fork-tender. Cool the meat. Remove strings, cut into serving slices, and arrange on a deep platter.

Strain the broth through a linen towel or several thicknesses of cheesecloth and cool very quickly over ice. Remove every trace of fat. Cook down by one third and spoon over veal slices. Chill. Serve with a garniture of chopped parsley, sliced stuffed olives, and hard-cooked eggs, and pass a tarragon-flavored mayonnaise or anchovy vinaigrette sauce. Makes 8 servings.

ARROSTO DI VITELLO (Veal Roast)

3- pound boneless veal roast
Salt and pepper
½ cup butter or margarine
½ cup minced onion
½ cup white wine
1 tablespoon all-purpose flour
1 cup sliced fresh mushrooms
1 tablespoon crumbled rosemary leaves

Season meat with salt and pepper to taste. In a skillet, sear meat on both sides in butter until golden-brown. Remove from skillet. Brown onion; add wine and flour and stir well; add mushrooms and rosemary. Put meat on a rack in a roasting pan. Pour contents of skillet over meat. Roast in preheated moderate oven (350°F.) for 1¾ hours. Serve sauce with mashed potatoes or polenta. Makes 6 to 8 servings.

VEAU SAUMONÉ (Veal with Salmon)

3 to 4 pounds leg of veal
1 cup white wine
3 parsley sprigs
2 fresh dill sprigs or 1 teaspoon dillweed
2 cans (7 ounces each) salmon
1 teaspoon salt
1 teaspoon pepper
2 egg yolks
½ cup cooking oil (about)

Have the butcher bone, roll, and tie veal. Place meat in a deep casserole or baking dish with a tight cover and add white wine, parsley, dill, salmon, salt, and pepper. Cover tightly and bake in preheated moderate oven (350°F.) for 2½ to 3 hours, or until the meat is tender. Let it cool in the juices and then remove it to the refrigerator to chill. Put the salmon and juices through a food mill or fine sieve, or purée them in an electric blender. Beat egg yolks until light and lemon-colored and gradually add oil. Slowly beat in the puréed salmon mixture. Taste for seasoning and add more chopped parsley or dill if necessary. You can do this whole process in an electric blender if you have one. When ready to serve, cut the veal into thin slices and arrange them on a platter. Pour the sauce over and serve with a rice salad. Makes 6 to 8 servings.

Veau Saumoné with Tarragon

Substitute fresh or crumbled dried tarragon for the dill in recipe for *Veau Saumoné.*

VEAL SHOULDER WITH CHEESE SAUCE

- 3 to 4 pounds boneless shoulder of veal, rolled and tied
  Melted butter and white wine
  Slices of baked ham
- ¼ cup butter or margarine
- ¼ cup all-purpose flour
- 1½ cups scalded milk
- 2 egg yolks
- ¼ cup lukewarm cream
  Salt
  Grated Swiss cheese
  Grated Parmesan cheese
  Chopped parsley

Place veal in a roasting pan and insert a meat thermometer. Roast in preheated slow oven (325°F.), basting often with a mixture of melted butter and white wine. When the veal has reached an internal temperature of 160°F. (in about 2 hours), remove it and cut into even slices. Arrange these slices, alternating them with slices of baked ham, in a baking dish. Pour the pan juices over the meat. In a skillet melt butter and blend in flour. Cook for a few minutes and slowly add scalded milk. Cook and stir until smooth and thickened. Continue cooking for a few minutes, stirring constantly. Beat egg yolks lightly and beat in cream. Slowly add this mixture to the sauce, blend it in thoroughly, and heat well but do not let it boil or the sauce will curdle. Season to taste with salt. Sprinkle the meat liberally with grated Swiss cheese, pour the sauce over it, and sprinkle the top with grated Parmesan cheese. Run under the broiler, sprinkle with chopped parsley, and serve from the baking dish. Makes 6 to 8 servings.

SHOULDER OF VEAL WITH RAVIOLI STUFFING

- 1 veal shoulder (4 to 5 pounds) with pocket for stuffing
  Salt and pepper
- 3 cups finely ground or minced cooked chicken meat
- 4 cooked chicken livers, finely ground or minced
- ½ cup each of sliced green onions with tops and chopped fresh parsley
- ¼ cup grated Parmesan cheese
- ¼ cup heavy cream
- 1 teaspoon salt
- ½ teaspoon each of ground black pepper and crumbled dried tarragon
- ⅛ teaspoon ground nutmeg
  Olive oil
  About ¾ cup chicken broth or bouillon
- ½ cup dry white wine

Sprinkle veal, inside and outside pocket, generously with salt and pepper. To make stuffing, thoroughly mix together the remaining ingredients except olive oil, chicken broth, and ¼ cup of the white wine. Taste stuffing and correct seasoning with salt and pepper. Spoon stuffing lightly into veal pocket; close with small skewers or sew. Tuck under and skewer tight any thin edges of meat to make a compact shape. Then with string tie into a roll. Rub roast surface with olive oil.

Shoulder of Veal with Ravioli Stuffing

Place on rack in roasting pan. Bake in preheated slow oven (300°F.) for 3 to 3½ hours. Baste frequently with chicken broth. During last 30 minutes, baste with reserved wine. Allow to stand for 30 minutes before carving. Makes 10 10 servings.

Note: To make a sauce to serve over veal slices, loosen pan drippings. Add dry white wine (about 2 cups). Heat, stirring, until wine is slightly reduced. Garnish with whole cherry tomatoes or, if desired, hollow out tomatoes and fill with whipped cream, seasoned with grated Parmesan cheese and chopped parsley.

VEAL STEAK, CHOPS, CUTLETS, AND ESCALLOPS

MARINATED VEAL STEAK

Have a 1-inch-thick steak cut from the leg; remove the outside skin. In a shallow dish put ½ cup olive oil and 2 crushed garlic cloves and let the steak marinate in this for several hours, turning occasionally. Broil over a low fire for 7 to 9 minutes on each side. No further basting should be necessary, as the meat will have absorbed enough of the oil to moisten it. Serve with fettuccine and a zucchini and tomato casserole.

VEAL CHOPS PAPRIKA

- 6 loin veal chops
- 1 egg, beaten
- 2 tablespoons milk
- ¼ cup cracker meal
- ¼ cup cooking oil
  Salt and pepper
- 1 medium onion, chopped
- ¼ pound mushrooms, sliced
- 1 tablespoon paprika
- 1 bay leaf
- 1 can (10½ ounces) condensed tomato soup
- ⅓ cup water
- ½ cup dairy sour cream

Dip chops into combined egg and milk, then into cracker meal. Brown on both sides in 3 tablespoons oil in skillet. Remove chops to shallow casserole and sprinkle with salt and pepper. Put 1 tablespoon oil in skillet. Add onion and mushrooms; brown lightly and place on chops. Mix remaining ingredients and pour over top. Bake in preheated moderate oven (350°F.) for about 45 minutes. Makes 6 servings.

VEAL CHOPS SOUBISE

- 6 large veal chops
  Milk
- 4 large onions, minced
  Butter or margarine (about ⅔ cup)
  All-purpose flour
- 2 tablespoons cooking oil
- 1 teaspoon salt
- ½ teaspoon pepper
- ½ cup grated Parmesan cheese
  Grated Swiss cheese

Soak veal in enough milk to cover for 1 hour. Sauté onions in ¼ cup butter in a heavy skillet, then steam the onions in the butter over a very low heat. They should be transparent and just tender, not browned. Remove the chops from the milk and dry them on absorbent paper. Dust them lightly with flour and, in a separate pan, brown on both sides in ¼ cup butter heated with the oil. Lower heat and season the chops with salt and pepper. Continue to cook, turning once, until they are tender. Arrange the chops in a flat baking dish. Blend the liquid

Veal Chops Soubise

from the onion with the milk in which the chops were soaked. You will need about 1½ cups liquid. To the pan in which the chops were cooked, add enough butter to make 3 tablespoons fat. Blend in ¼ cup flour and simmer gently for 3 or 4 minutes. Slowly add the milk-onion liquid, stirring constantly. Cook and stir until the sauce is smooth and thickened. Season to taste with salt and pepper and add grated Parmesan cheese. Continue cooking until the cheese is thoroughly blended into the sauce. Spread each chop with some of the drained steamed onion. Pour the sauce over all and sprinkle liberally with grated Swiss cheese. Run under the broiler or heat in preheated hot oven (475°F.) until the cheese melts and browns lightly. Serve with duchesse potatoes, green peas, and seeded breadsticks. Makes 6 servings.

BREADED VEAL CUTLET
(Wiener Schnitzel)
This is the classic veal dish of Vienna. For 4 persons, buy 4 cutlets, or 1½ pounds veal cutlet. Beat 2 eggs lightly;

set out a bowl of all-purpose flour seasoned with salt and pepper and another bowl of fine dry bread crumbs. Heat cooking oil and butter mixed in a large skillet. You will need at least ½ inch of fat in the pan. Dip each cutlet into flour, then into beaten egg, and finally into bread crumbs. Sauté the cutlets in the hot oil and butter until they are well browned on both sides and tender. Arrange the cutlets on a hot platter and on each one place a slice of lemon topped with a rolled anchovy. Surround with mounds of chopped hard-cooked egg and tiny mounds of capers. Sprinkle the whole lightly with chopped parsley.

VEAL CUTLETS, SICILIAN STYLE
3 slices of leg of veal, about ¼ inch thick
½ pound salami, sliced
½ pound mortadella or bologna, sliced
½ pound sliced prosciutto or cooked ham
¼ cup fine dry bread crumbs
5 garlic cloves, minced
2 tablespoons chopped parsley
1 teaspoon crumbled dried basil

5 or 6 hard-cooked eggs
¼ cup olive oil
Salt and pepper to taste
5 or 6 slices of bacon
2 cups tomato sauce

Have the bone removed from the veal slices, but leave each slice in one whole piece. Ask the butcher to pound these large cutlets very thin. On a large sheet of heavy wax paper, arrange the slices side by side the long way, so that they overlap slightly. Pound the overlapping areas thoroughly to press them together. On the veal arrange rows of overlapping slices of salami. Top these with rows of mortadella and finally with prosciutto or cooked ham. Sprinkle the surface with bread crumbs, 3 garlic cloves, the parsley, and basil. Down the center place a row of shelled hard-cooked eggs. Sprinkle with olive oil and salt and pepper. Roll up very carefully in the paper as for a jelly roll, making certain that the eggs stay in place in the center. Remove paper, and tie the rolled meat firmly in several places. Place the roll in a baking dish and stripe the top with bacon slices.

Veal Cutlets, Sicilian Style

Pour tomato sauce over all and add remaining garlic. Bake in preheated moderate oven (350°F.) for 1 hour, basting from time to time with the tomato sauce. Remove to a hot platter, or serve from the baking dish. Serve with green noodles, good green salad, and hot crisp Italian bread. Makes 8 servings.

Note: This is exceptionally good sliced and served cold the next day.

STUFFED VEAL ROLLS

6 pieces of veal cutlet (about 1¼ pounds)
    Salt and white pepper to taste
¾ cup fine dry bread crumbs
    Few parsley sprigs, chopped
    Grated rind of 1 lemon
¼ teaspoon ground thyme
¼ teaspoon crumbled dried basil
5 tablespoons butter or margarine
3 tablespoons milk
1 tablespoon all-purpose flour
1 teaspoon seasoned salt
1 cup chicken bouillon
1 tablespoon fresh lemon juice

Season veal with salt and pepper. Mix next 5 ingredients, 2 tablespoons melted butter, milk, and salt and pepper to taste. Spread on veal pieces and roll up. Secure with toothpicks or string. Brown on all sides in remaining butter. Remove meat rolls to shallow 1½-quart casserole. Blend flour and seasoned salt into butter remaining in pan. Add bouillon, lemon juice, and pepper to taste. Bring to boil, stirring; pour over meat rolls. Cover and bake in preheated moderate oven (350° F.) for about 45 minutes. Makes 6 servings.

VEAL ESCALLOPS
(Scaloppine, Escalopes, Scallops, or Collops)

Veal escallops are small slices of veal cut very thin and then flattened even more with a meat pounder. They can be cut from the tenderloin, the sirloin, or the leg; the best come from the tenderloin. Be sure they are paper-thin. If your butcher doesn't pound them enough, do it yourself. Place each escallop between 2 pieces of wax paper, and pound with a meat pounder; or, if you don't have one, use the flat side of a cleaver or any heavy flat object. You might even use the bottom of a heavy skillet.

VEAL ESCALLOPS, MARSALA

1½ pounds thin veal escallops
    All-purpose flour
3 tablespoons butter or margarine
3 tablespoons cooking oil
    Salt and pepper
    Ground ginger
    Marsala
¼ cup chopped parsley

Dust veal with flour and brown quickly on both sides in butter mixed with oil. Season to taste with salt and pepper and add a dash of ground ginger. Cover with Marsala and continue cooking until the wine is reduced to half. Turn the escal-

lops once during this process. When the wine is reduced and the meat is tender, remove the escallops to a hot platter and add another ¼ cup Marsala to the pan. Bring the juices to a boil, add parsley, and pour over the meat. Serve with rice. Makes 4 servings.

Note: This is the classic *scaloppine* dish of southern Italy.

VEAL ESCALLOPS WITH LEMON

Place 8 (1½ pounds) very thin veal escallops on large shallow plate and cover with fresh lemon juice. Place another plate on top and let meat stand for 30 minutes. Remove from lemon juice, dust lightly with flour, and sauté for 3 or 4 minutes on each side. Season; add ¼ cup finely chopped parsley. Toss escallops in parsley. Makes 4 servings.

VEAL AND BACON TERRINE

12 bacon slices
2 pounds veal escallops
¾ cup chopped green onions
¾ cup chopped parsley
    Pepper
    Crumbled dried thyme
½ bay leaf, crumbled
1½ pounds Canadian bacon, thinly sliced
½ cup dry white wine or dry vermouth

Line a bread pan or mold, both bottom and sides, with slices of bacon. In the bottom put a layer of veal escallops and sprinkle them slightly with green onions and parsley, a little pepper, thyme, and bay leaf. Place a layer of sliced Canadian bacon on this and add another layer of veal scallops. Repeat the seasonings. Continue these layers until all the veal and Canadian bacon are used. Stripe the top with more slices of regular bacon and add wine. Place a lid on the mold or cover with several layers of heavy foil. Bake in preheated slow oven (300°F.) for 2 hours. Remove the mold from the oven and take off the lid. Add several layers of heavy foil and place a plate on top. Put weights on the plate. You can use canned goods, a heavy electric iron, or any weighty object. Let the terrine stand until thoroughly cool. Place in the refrigerator to chill. When ready to serve, turn the meat with the jellied broth that formed around it onto a decorative platter. Serve cut into very thin slices. Makes 8 servings.

Note: Excellent for cocktails or for a picnic or buffet.

ROLLATINE WITH HAM

Rollatine are escallops of veal spread with stuffing and then rolled and tied or fastened with toothpicks.

8 very thin veal escallops
8 thin slices of ham
8 sage leaves
¼ cup butter or margarine
¼ cup cooking oil
    All-purpose flour
    Salt and pepper to taste
⅓ cup white wine

On each escallop place a piece of ham and pound thoroughly to press the two together. Top the ham with a leaf of sage and roll the escallop up firmly. Tie it with string or fasten with toothpicks. In a large skillet heat butter and oil. Dust the rolls with flour and brown them in the hot butter and oil, rolling them around to be sure they are evenly colored. Season with a little salt (the amount depends on the saltiness of the ham) and pepper, and add white wine. Cover the skillet and cook gently for 8 to 10 minutes, turning the rolls once or twice during the cooking. In the center of a hot platter, place a mound of cooked noodles dressed with butter and cheese, and arrange the rolls around the noodles. Makes 4 servings.

BREAST OF VEAL

BREAST OF VEAL WITH SAUSAGE STUFFING

1 breast of veal, about 3 pounds
1½ pounds sausage meat
3 cups soft bread crumbs
½ cup sliced green onions
¼ cup chopped parsley
6 anchovy fillets, chopped
1 egg, slightly beaten
1 teaspoon salt
½ teaspoon pepper
1 teaspoon crumbled dried thyme
4 large onions, sliced
4 carrots, scraped and cut into strips
4 or 5 parsley sprigs, chopped
    Butter (about ⅓ cup)
1 cup chicken bouillon or white wine

Have the butcher cut a pocket in veal breast. Combine the sausage with bread crumbs, green onions, parsley, anchovy fillets, egg, salt, pepper, and thyme. Stuff the pocket of the veal breast with this mixture and sew it up or fasten it with skewers. Mix onions, carrots, and parsley together and spread them on the bottom of a baking pan. Dot the bed of vegetables with butter and place the veal on top. Add bouillon and sprinkle the meat with salt and pepper. If you use a seasoned bouillon for liquid, you may not need additional seasoning. Rub the veal breast with butter and roast in preheated hot oven (450°F.) for 30 minutes, basting from time to time. After 30 minutes, or as soon as the veal begins to brown nicely, cover the pan and lower the heat to slow (325°F.). Continue roasting for 1¾ to 2 hours. About 15 minutes before the meat is done, remove the cover to finish browning the top. Makes 6 servings.

Note: To serve cold, slice, and serve with a well-seasoned mayonnaise and a green salad.

SIMMERED BREAST OF VEAL

3- pound breast of veal

½ pound lean bacon
1 tablespoon salt
 Water
4 onions, peeled
6 carrots, scraped
1 celery stalk
2 or 3 parsley sprigs
1 pound garlic sausage or Kielbasa
3 turnips, peeled and halved
6 medium potatoes, peeled
1 small head green cabbage, quartered
 About 2 cups (one 1-pound can)
 tiny French-style peas, drained

Place veal and bacon in a large kettle and add salt and water to cover. Place a lid on the kettle and bring to a boil. Lower the heat and simmer gently for 1¼ hours. Add onions, carrots, celery, and parsley; continue cooking for 30 minutes. Add sausage, turnips, potatoes, and cabbage. Cook for a final 15 minutes, adding peas during the last few minutes. Remove the veal breast to a hot platter and arrange the sausage, bacon, and vegetables around it. Serve with a good hot mustard and a tomato and cucumber salad. Makes 6 servings.

BELGIAN VEAL BLANQUETTE

2 pounds breast of veal, cut for stew
5 tablespoons butter or margarine
2½ cups beef consommé
⅛ teaspoon crumbled dried thyme
1 bay leaf
12 shallots or 12 scallions,
 bulb end only
⅛ teaspoon ground nutmeg
 Salt and pepper
½ pound ground veal
½ pound ground pork
½ cup fresh bread crumbs
¼ cup milk
1 egg
12 fresh mushroom caps
2 tablespoons all-purpose flour
2 egg yolks
 Juice of ½ lemon

In a flameproof casserole lightly brown pieces of veal in 3 tablespoons butter. Add 1 cup consommé and herbs, shallots, and nutmeg. Season to taste with salt and pepper. Add water to cover. Bring to a boil. Lower heat, cover, and simmer over low heat until meat is just tender, about 1 hour. In a bowl mix ground veal, pork, bread crumbs, milk, and egg. Roll mixture into tiny meatballs the size of a nut. Sauté balls in remaining butter. Add mushroom caps and sauté until lightly browned. Add to stew. Cover and simmer for 10 minutes. To the pan drippings, add flour. Gradually stir in remaining consommé. Cook, stirring constantly, over low heat until smooth and thickened. Gradually stir hot sauce into egg yolks and lemon juice. Simmer sauce for 5 minutes. Add to stew. Blend well and reheat slightly. Serve with rice or mashed potatoes. Makes 6 servings.

BARBECUED VEAL BREAST AND VEGETABLES

2 to 2½ pounds veal breast
2 tablespoons shortening
4 large potatoes, halved
4 carrots, halved lengthwise
1 onion, chopped
1 garlic clove, minced
1 can (8 ounces) tomato sauce
¼ cup vinegar
1 tablespoon sugar
1½ teaspoons salt
⅛ teaspoon pepper
 Dash of cayenne
1 teaspoon Worcestershire
1 teaspoon powdered mustard

Cut meat into serving pieces. In Dutch oven or top-stove casserole, brown meat slowly on all sides in shortening. Remove from heat and add potatoes and carrots. Mix remaining ingredients and pour over meat and vegetables. Bake, covered, in preheated moderate oven (350°F.) for 2 hours, or until meat and vegetables are tender. Makes 4 servings.

VEAL BREAST IN MUSHROOM SAUCE

2 pounds veal breast
2 tablespoons shortening
1 can (10½ ounces) cream-of-mushroom soup
¼ soup-can water

Brown veal in shortening. Add soup and water. Simmer, covered, for about 2 hours, or until tender. Makes 4 servings.

VEAL SHANKS, NECK, AND SHIN

VEAL WITH BULGUR AND DILL

¼ cup all-purpose flour
2 teaspoons salt
 Few grindings of pepper
3 pounds veal-neck slices
2 tablespoons shortening
1 cup chopped onions
2 cups undiluted canned consommé
½ cup white wine
2 garlic cloves, crushed
1 cup bulgur (cracked wheat)
 Salted water
1 package (9 ounces) frozen artichoke hearts
1 cup dairy sour cream
1 tablespoon dillweed
 Salt and pepper

Combine flour, salt, and pepper; rub into veal slices. Brown veal in shortening slowly, using a large flameproof casserole or a skillet. Add onions, consommé, wine, and garlic. Cover and simmer for 1½ hours, or until tender. In the meantime cook bulgur in 2 cups salted water for 15 minutes; also cook artichoke hearts. Strain meat juice and vegetable juices, and purée in blender. Add sour cream, dill, and salt and pepper to taste. Combine half of this sauce with the bulgur and mound in the center of a platter or chop plate. Surround with veal slices and garnish with artichoke hearts. Serve remaining sauce separately. Makes 6 servings.

Note: If you wish, sprinkle with minced parsley or dill, or paprika for more color.

VEAL IN ASPIC

2 pounds carrots
2 pounds onions
2 pounds shank of veal
1 celery stalk
1 teaspoon Worcestershire
¼ teaspoon hot pepper sauce
2 bay leaves
 Salt and pepper to taste
2½ quarts water
2 envelopes unflavored gelatin
 Watercress
 Radish roses

Scrape carrots and peel onions; put in kettle with meat, celery, and seasonings. Add water and bring to a boil over a gentle heat. Cook very slowly until the meat falls from the bones. The broth should then be strained through a dampened linen napkin into a clean pan, placed back over heat, and reduced to half its quantity. Remove all bones from the meat and cut meat into small even dice. When the broth has reduced sufficiently, remove from heat, stir in gelatin softened in ½ cup cold water, and pour over the diced meat. Pour all into a 2-quart mold and chill until set; stir occasionally while still liquid to prevent meat from sinking to the bottom of the mold. Unmold on platter and garnish with watercress and radish roses. Makes 6 to 8 servings.

JELLIED HERB VEAL LOAF

4 pounds neck of veal
2 pounds shin of veal
1 veal knuckle
1 onion stuck with 2 whole cloves
1 bay leaf
1 teaspoon crumbled dried thyme
2 or 3 carrots
 Celery stalks and leaves
 Water
1½ tablespoons salt
 Pepper
 Sliced hard-cooked eggs
 Worcestershire

Place meat and bones in a deep kettle and add onion stuck with cloves, bay leaf, thyme, carrots, and some celery. Cover with cold water and bring to a boil. Boil rapidly for 5 minutes and then skim off any scum that has formed. Add salt and a few grinds of pepper. Lower the heat, cover the kettle, and simmer for 2½ hours, or until the meat is very tender. Remove the meat and set the broth aside to cool. When the meat is cool enough to handle, separate all the lean and discard bone, fat, and gristle. Chop the meat rather coarsely. Oil a mold and place a layer of the chopped veal in the bottom. Add a layer of sliced hard-cooked eggs and more chopped meat. Continue until the meat is used. Skim the fat from the broth. Strain it and return it to the heat to cook down. Season with Worcestershire. Cool the reduced broth and pour over the meat in the mold. The broth should just barely reach the top of the chopped veal. Place in the refrigerator to chill and gel. Serve sliced, with a vegetable salad and thin bread-and-butter sandwiches, or thin slices of bread spread with chive and parsley butter. Makes 12 servings.

INDIVIDUAL JELLIED HERB VEAL LOAVES

Arrange the layers of meat and egg in recipe for Jellied Herb Veal Loaf in individual molds. Top with broth, chill, and gel. Turn out onto individual salad plates garnished with lettuce. Add a dollop of herbed mayonnaise (mayonnaise blended with chopped chives and parsley) and serve as a main course for a summer luncheon. Makes 10 to 12 servings.

SMALL PIECES OF VEAL

VEAL STEW

1 pound dried marrow beans
6 cups water
½ pound salt pork, thinly sliced
2 pounds boneless veal stew meat
1 large onion, sliced
2 garlic cloves, minced
1 tablespoon paprika
¼ teaspoon crumbled dried thyme
½ teaspoon crumbled dried marjoram
¼ teaspoon pepper
4 large carrots, sliced
1 green pepper, cut into eighths
4 outer celery stalks, sliced
  Chopped parsley

Wash beans, add the water, and bring to boil; boil for 2 minutes. Let stand for 1 hour. Fry salt pork for about 5 minutes; add veal, onion, and garlic; brown lightly. Stir in paprika, thyme, marjoram, and pepper. Add to beans and water. Simmer, covered, for 1½ hours, or until beans and meat are almost tender, adding more water if necessary. Add carrots, green pepper, and celery; simmer for 25 minutes longer, or until vegetables are tender. Add salt if desired. Sprinkle chopped parsley over stew. Makes 8 servings.
Note: Stew can be made a day or two before. Cool, refrigerate, and reheat at serving time. (Or serve 4 for 2 meals.) Green pepper can be omitted or pimiento can be substituted for it.

VEAL WITH DANDELION GREENS

1 pound boneless veal, diced
2 tablespoons butter or margarine
2 onions, sliced
3 small carrots, quartered
½ cup diced celery
2 large mushrooms, quartered
½ cup water
1 pound dandelion greens, cooked
  Pinch of basil or ½ bay leaf, crushed
  Salt and pepper

Brown veal in butter in heavy kettle; add vegetables and water. Cover and simmer until tender, about 1 hour. Add greens; season with basil and salt and pepper to taste and heat for 5 minutes. Makes 4 servings.

HAWAIIAN VEAL STEW

1½ pounds stewing veal, cut into 2-inch pieces
3 tablespoons butter or margarine
2½ cups (one 1-pound, 4-ounce can) pineapple cubes, drained
1½ teaspoons seasoned salt
1 tablespoon paprika
1 bay leaf
¼ teaspoon pepper
1 onion, sliced
2 tablespoons all-purpose flour

Brown veal on all sides in butter in kettle. Add next 6 ingredients and 4 cups water. Bring to boil, cover, and simmer for 1½ hours. Thicken with flour blended with ¼ cup water. Serve plain, on toast, or on hot cooked rice. Makes 6 servings.

VEAL AND PEPPERS, ITALIAN STYLE

1½ pounds boneless lean veal
3 tablespoons olive oil
2 green peppers, cut into eighths
1 can (3 ounces) sliced mushrooms
  Pinch of crushed red pepper
2 cans (8 ounces each) tomato sauce
  Salt and pepper

Cut meat into bite-size pieces. Heat oil in skillet and brown meat on all sides. Add green pepper, cover, reduce heat, and cook for 10 minutes, stirring occasionally. Add mushrooms and liquid, red pepper, and sauce. Simmer, covered, for 30 minutes longer, or until tender. Season to taste. Makes 4 servings.

VEAL MEXICAN

2½ pounds shoulder of veal, cubed
  Butter or lard
3 garlic cloves
1 tablespoon chili powder
1 teaspoon crumbled dried oregano
1 teaspoon salt
  Dash of hot pepper sauce
2 cups tomato sauce
1 can (6 ounces) peeled green chilies, chopped

Brown veal cubes on all sides in butter (the Mexicans use lard). When the cubes are all nicely browned, add garlic, chili powder, oregano, salt, hot pepper sauce, and tomato sauce. Cover and simmer very gently for about 2 hours, or until veal cubes are thoroughly tender. Add chilies to veal and heat through. Taste for seasoning; you may want to add more chili powder and hot pepper sauce. Serve on hot rice with refried beans or black beans. Makes 6 servings.

VEAL WITH GARLIC SAUCE

This is a French version of Veal Mexican. Prepare the dish as above, but omit the chili powder and chilies and add 4 garlic cloves. Makes 6 servings.

GROUND VEAL AND LEFTOVER COOKED VEAL

OLD-FASHIONED VEAL LOAF

2 pounds veal, ground
1 pound pork, ground

1 cup fine dry bread crumbs
2 garlic cloves, chopped
¼ cup grated onion
½ cup chopped parsley
2 eggs, slightly beaten
1 teaspoon crumbled dried thyme
1 teaspoon salt
1 teaspoon pepper
  Bacon slices

Place the ground meats in a deep bowl and mix thoroughly with bread crumbs, garlic, onion, parsley, eggs, thyme, salt, and pepper. Form the meat mixture into a firm loaf shape. Place a layer of bacon slices on the bottom of a shallow roasting pan or baking dish and arrange the loaf on top. Stripe the top of the meat with more bacon slices. Roast in preheated moderate oven (350°F.) for 1½ hours, basting occasionally with the pan juices. Serve hot with creamy mashed potatoes and green beans. Makes 8 servings.

VEAL LOAF WITH ITALIAN SAUSAGES

This is an elegant buffet dish to be served hot or cold. Make veal-and-pork mixture in recipe above. Buy 6 to 8 Italian sausages and boil them for 10 minutes. Cool and remove the skins. Arrange half of the veal-pork mixture on bacon slices in the bottom of a baking dish. Put the skinned sausages on the meat and add the rest of the mixture. Press down firmly. Top with more bacon and bake as above. Makes 8 to 10 servings.

WHITE DOME

½ cup sliced mushrooms
  Lemon juice
  Butter or margarine
2 cups ground cooked veal
¾ cup condensed cream-of-chicken soup
2 cups mashed potatoes
  Grated cheese
¼ cup fine dry bread crumbs

Sprinkle mushrooms with lemon juice. Sauté mushrooms in butter. Add meat and soup to mushrooms. Heat until thick. Grease baking dish; fill with heated pudding mixture, piling it up in the shape of a pyramid. Cover with a thick layer of mashed potatoes which have been mixed with 2 tablespoons grated cheese. Pour over a little melted butter; top with ¼ cup bread crumbs mixed with 2 tablespoons grated cheese. Bake in preheated hot oven (425°F.) for 20 minutes. Makes 6 servings.

AVOCADOS STUFFED WITH VEAL

2 large ripe avocados
1 teaspoon onion juice
  Salt and pepper to taste
2 cups cold cooked veal
  Dash of hot pepper sauce
1 tablespoon melted butter or gravy
½ teaspoon poultry seasoning

Cut avocados lengthwise into halves and remove seeds. Mix other ingredients and pile into the halved shells. Bake in preheated hot oven (400°F.) for 20 minutes. Makes 4 servings.

VEAL SALAD

2 cups diced cooked veal
¼ cup chopped onion
¼ cup chopped celery
½ cup toasted blanched almonds
1 cup mayonnaise
1 teaspoon crumbled dried tarragon
1 tablespoon fresh lemon juice
Salad greens

Mix veal with onion, celery, and almonds. Blend mayonnaise with tarragon and lemon juice. Add enough of the mayonnaise to the veal mixture to bind it. Heap on greens; garnish with the rest of the mayonnaise, and with tomatoes, ripe olives, and toasted almonds, if desired. Serve with herbed French bread. Makes 4 servings.

VEAL AND CHEESE STEAKS

Juice of 1 lemon
Salt and pepper
½ cup bouillon or white wine
4 slices of cooked veal
1 egg, beaten
½ cup fine dry bread crumbs
4 slices of Swiss cheese
Slivered blanched almonds
Paprika

Mix lemon juice with salt, pepper, and bouillon. Pour mixture over veal. Let stand for 1 hour. Drain. Dip veal into egg and then into crumbs. Brown in hot fat on one side only. Cover unbrowned side with cheese, almonds, and paprika. Bake in a shallow pan in preheated hot oven (400°F.) until cheese sizzles, about 10 minutes. Makes 4 servings.

VEAL VARIETY MEATS

VEAL BRAINS IN MUSHROOM SAUCE

1 pound veal brains
1 teaspoon salt
1 tablespoon vinegar
1 can (10½ ounces) cream-of-mushroom soup
¾ cup milk
2 tablespoons grated cheese
2 tablespoons dry bread crumbs
1 tablespoon margarine

Wash brains in cold water; remove membrane. Cover with water, add salt and vinegar, and simmer for 15 minutes. Drain; drop into cold water and drain again. Heat mushroom soup with milk. Add coarsely cut brains. Pour into shallow 1-quart casserole or pie plate. Sprinkle with cheese and crumbs; dot with margarine. Brown in preheated hot oven (400°F.) for 10 minutes. Makes 4 servings.

ROAST VEAL KIDNEYS

Have the butcher leave all the fat on veal kidneys. Put the whole kidneys on the spit, and roast them over the charcoal for about 40 minutes, or until a small incision shows that they are done to your liking. Slice through fat and all, and

serve with *Maître d'Hôtel* Butter made by creaming together ½ cup butter, 1 teaspoon minced parsley, 1 tablespoon fresh lemon juice, and a little freshly ground black pepper.

VEAL KIDNEYS IN VERMOUTH

4 veal kidneys
Milk
6 tablespoons butter or margarine
1 medium onion, chopped
¼ cup parsley, chopped
Salt and pepper
Boiled rice
¼ cup dry vermouth
¼ cup beef bouillon

Remove the fat and cut the kidneys into thin slices. Soak in milk for 1 hour. Melt butter in a skillet and sauté onion and parsley gently. Drain sliced kidneys and dry them on absorbent paper. Add them to the pan and cook quickly, turning slices to brown on both sides. Season to taste with salt and pepper and arrange on a bed of rice. To the pan add vermouth and bouillon. Heat and blend with the onion and parsley. Pour over the kidneys and rice. Makes 4 servings.

MOTTRAM KIDNEY IN CREAM

Mince 1 veal kidney into very small pieces. Sauté 2 tablespoons chopped onion in 2 tablespoons butter until transparent. Add another tablespoon butter and the kidney, and cook quickly for 2 to 3 minutes. Sprinkle with 1 teaspoon flour, pour in ¼ cup heavy cream, and season with salt and pepper. Cook for a few seconds so that the cream will heat, and serve on toast. This is enough for 4 persons, 6 if each serving is topped with a poached egg.

VEAL LIVER STEAK, BÉARNAISE

You will need about 8 ounces of veal or calf's liver per serving. Ask the butcher to cut it rather thick, 1 to 1½ inches. Broil over charcoal or in a broiler until crusty brown on the outside and still pink and rare in the center. Brush with a mixture of melted butter and oil several times during the broiling. Season to taste. If you are broiling over charcoal, move the coals close to the meat for the last minute to char the outside a bit. Sprinkle with parsley; serve Quick Béarnaise Sauce separately. Good with onion slices baked in beef broth and sprinkled with grated cheese, and fried or sautéed potatoes.

Quick Béarnaise Sauce

1 teaspoon crumbled dried tarragon
2 teaspoons chopped green onion
2 teaspoons chopped parsley
3 tablespoons wine vinegar
1 tablespoon water
3 egg yolks
2 teaspoons fresh lemon juice
½ teaspoon salt
Few grains of cayenne
½ cup butter

In a small pan cook tarragon, green onion, parsley, wine vinegar, and water. Cook gently until almost a glaze. Put egg yolks in an electric blender with lemon juice, salt, and cayenne. Flick the blender on and off rapidly just long enough to blend the eggs. Melt butter and bring just to boiling. With the blender on high, add the butter until sauce is blended and thickened. Add the tarragon mixture and beat until well mixed.

SWEETBREAD AND CUCUMBER SALAD

Prepare 2 or 3 pairs of veal sweetbreads as directed on page 1887. Chill, and cut into ¼-inch slices. Peel 2 medium or 1 large cucumber. Split, remove seeds, and cut into very thin slices. Arrange sliced cucumbers in a bowl and sprinkle with salt. Let stand for 30 minutes. Wash off salt and drain well. Mix cucumbers with 6 thinly sliced green onions and the sliced sweetbreads. Add enough well-seasoned homemade mayonnaise to bind, and heap in a salad bowl. Garnish with more mayonnaise, tomato wedges, sliced hard-cooked eggs, and ripe olives. Makes 6 servings.

VEGETABLE—Although the word can properly be used as an adjective to describe any kind of plant life, as distinguished from animal life, in common usage vegetables are those plants or parts of plants eaten by man. They include the leafy vegetables such as spinach, lettuce, and cabbage; the stem vegetables, such as celery and asparagus; the roots and tubers of which beets, turnips, carrots, and potatoes are examples; flower vegetables such as broccoli and cauliflower; seeds and seed pods, which include beans and peas; edible fungi, such as mushrooms and truffles; and those fruits classed as vegetables because of the way they are cooked and served: tomatoes and squash, for example.

Modern methods of transportation, refrigeration, and storage have made most vegetables available year round. Canned and frozen vegetables are universally available. Some vegetables are available dried; a few are available pickled. Puréed and chopped vegetables are sold as baby and junior foods.

Nutritive Food Values—Vegetables are a source of vitamins and minerals. They are good sources of vitamin A and C. Vegetables supply varying amounts of thiamine, riboflavin, and niacin. The minerals present are calcium, phosphorus, and iron. Vegetables are necessary in maintaining the neutrality of the blood and the regularity of the digestive system. For specific food values see the individual vegetable entries.

VEGETABLE COOKERY

by James A. Beard

A colorful display of fresh vegetables is a magnificent sight to behold. Deep-purple eggplant, plump green peppers, bright tomatoes, slender young scallions, miniature beans and carrots make as beautiful a centerpiece as any bouquet of flowers. But often it is dismaying to encounter them after they have been cooked—overdone, waterlogged, colorless, and tasteless. It is amazing to me that most people mistreat these crisp delicacies.

Indeed, the art of vegetable cookery has been tragically neglected in most of the world's cuisines. The English are noted for overcooking vegetables until they are mushy; most Europeans do little better; we Americans use scant imagination and less variety; Latins tend to ignore them. The French and Italians do some vegetable dishes well, but it is only the Chinese who approach vegetables with true appreciation and artistry.

I recall some of my vegetable-eating experiences with horror. I was once served beans cooked for hours with hog jowl, and spinach drowned in water and cooked with salt pork. Then I have tried to gulp down Brussels sprouts cooked to a gray mass. This was in England, of course.

On the other hand, I have enjoyed beans cooked just until barely tender and still crisp and then sautéed in good sweet butter, a dish so delicious I could have made a meal of it. I have eaten perfect spinach, barely wilted in the skillet with oil and garlic and soy sauce—one of my favorites; and Brussels sprouts steamed in butter until crisply done, each one a buttery nugget of flavor.

Vegetable cookery, then, need not be dull. With our bountiful supply in this country, there is no excuse for not giving vegetables a chance to shine at the table. Using choice tender young vegetables, good butter or oil, fine seasonings, and some care, anyone can turn out tasty dishes. Vegetables need not always be boiled. They can go into the skillet to be braised; they can be cooked in interesting combinations; they can go into delicate soufflés; they can be dressed with a variety of sauces. If you do boil them, and some are most delicious this way, do not drown them in a large pot full of water. Spread them out in skillet and use just enough water to cover them barely. Cook until they are crisply done, not mushy, and drain them well. A watery vegetable is most unappetizing. This method retains the garden-fresh flavor and texture that is the vegetable's most appealing quality.

For example, here is asparagus:

ASPARAGUS

True asparagus lovers can eat a pound per serving; for others, perhaps ½ to ¾ pound will do. Break or cut off the tough stalk ends and peel them up a ways if you wish. Remove scales and wash off sand which may collect under them. Arrange the stalks in a skillet and add just enough salted water to cover. Bring to a boil and cook for 4 to 6 minutes, testing frequently with a fork. The asparagus stalks should be just pierceable and still crisp. Drain thoroughly. Good fresh asparagus really needs nothing but freshly ground pepper and salt. But here are a variety of ways to dress it: melted butter and freshly ground pepper, hollandaise sauce or maltaise sauce, freshly grated Parmesan cheese.

• As a main luncheon dish: for each portion top several stalks of asparagus with a fried egg and spoon 2 tablespoons of melted butter and some freshly grated Parmesan cheese over all. Top with freshly grated black pepper.

• Another luncheon dish: for each portion, top several stalks of buttered asparagus with a thin piece of frizzled ham. Or place the asparagus on top of a slice of ham. Add melted butter and grated cheese.

• Combine 3 tablespoons of Dijon mustard with 1 tablespoon of fresh lemon juice and about 6 tablespoons of softened butter. Beat with a fork until it is a creamy paste. Serve with hot asparagus.

• Serve cold asparagus with a good vinaigrette sauce: 6 tablespoons of olive oil to 2½ tablespoons of wine vinegar, and salt and pepper to taste. Or you may add a tablespoon of Dijon mustard to the vinaigrette and beat it in well.

• Serve cold asparagus with a well-flavored homemade mayonnaise.

• Serve either cold or hot asparagus as follows: for each portion, add a hard-cooked egg to the plate. Pass lemon quarters, olive oil, and mustard. Each person crushes the egg with a fork and blends in olive oil, mustard, and lemon juice to taste, making a rather thick sauce. This is seasoned to taste with salt and pepper and eaten with the asparagus.

CORN

Good fresh corn is another vegetable that is at its best when cooked quickly and served simply. The sooner corn is cooked after picking the sweeter it is.

Put the ears in a skillet with cold water to cover. Omit salt; it tends to toughen the corn. Bring just to a boil and then let the ears stand in the boiling water for 1 minute. Eat at once with coarse salt,

freshly ground pepper, and plenty of sweet butter.

• Corn steamed in butter: Just before cooking, cut the kernels from 6 ears of corn. Melt ½ cup butter in a skillet, and when it is just bubbling, add the corn. Cook until the kernels are just heated through, 3 or 4 minutes. Shake the pan well and add salt and freshly ground pepper to taste. Spoon onto hot plates or onto rounds of toast fried crisp in butter or oil.

• Variations: Add 3 tablespoons of finely chopped green pepper and a hint of finely chopped garlic to the pan 3 minutes before you put in the corn. Blend well.

• Add ½ cup of crisp bacon cracklings.

• Add 2 tablespoons of finely chopped pimiento and 2 dashes of hot pepper sauce.

• Cook the corn in ¼ cup butter, season to taste, and just before serving stir in 4 to 6 tablespoons of heavy cream.

• Cook corn in ¼ cup butter and stir in 3 tablespoons of *Duxelles* (see below).

DUXELLES

This is a delicious addition to many vegetable dishes as well as a fine seasoning for sauces and eggs. It will keep in the refrigerator for a fortnight and is also good when frozen.

½ cup butter, approximately
2 pounds mushrooms, chopped very fine (stems and all)
1 garlic clove, finely chopped
2 shallots or 1 small onion, finely chopped
Additional butter, if needed
Salt

Melt the butter in a heavy skillet and add the mushrooms, garlic, and shallots. Cook very slowly, stirring occasionally, until the liquid is cooked out and the mushrooms are fairly black in color. Add more butter if needed and season with salt to taste when the mixture begins to cook down. Store in a jar or crock.

MADAME FRAIZE'S TOMATOES PROVENÇAL

This is another simple but perfect vegetable dish that takes advantage of the fresh ripe flavor. Madame Fraize has a small restaurant in Maillane, France, near Avignon. She treats vegetables with real respect. She not only cooks them beautifully, but even serves a "vegetable course."

Use ripe but firm tomatoes. Split them into halves and sauté, cut side down, in olive oil until the cut side is delicately caramelized in the oil. Season to taste.

VEGETABLES À LA GRECQUE

Any number of vegetables may be cooked in this sauce and served cold. They are thoroughly delicious as a first course, or

Vegetables à la Grecque ■ **Gratin of Greens**

with cold meats or fish as a main luncheon dish. Or you may serve several vegetables *à la grecque* on a combination hors-d'oeuvre luncheon tray with any or all of the following: stuffed eggs, sliced salami, sliced tomatoes, sardines, anchovies, thinly sliced ham. Such a tray, plus good French bread, makes a fine buffet luncheon for summer.

Most vegetables cooked in this manner may be kept in the refrigerator for several days.

Sauce à la Grecque

1½ cups water
¼ cup olive or peanut oil
   Juice of 2 lemons
1 teaspoon salt
2 or 3 garlic cloves
1 bay leaf
1 parsley sprig
1 celery top
1 teaspoon crumbled dried thyme
   Fennel sprig or fennel seeds (optional)
½ teaspoon white pepper
   Dash of hot pepper sauce

Combine all ingredients and bring to a boil. Boil for 5 minutes. Add the vegetables and simmer until just tender. Do not overcook. Let them cool in the sauce and serve chilled with some sauce spooned over. Or drain and serve with vinaigrette sauce.

Or the vegetables can be removed when they are done, the sauce cooked down until somewhat reduced, then cooled and poured over the vegetables. Top with chopped parsley, chives, and fresh tarragon. Variations on the Sauce: Substitute white wine for half of the water. Use wine vinegar instead of lemon juice. Add 1 to 2 tablespoons tomato paste.

Vegetables to be cooked à la grecque:

12 small artichokes (about 2 inches) or 12 hearts
2 pounds large-stalked asparagus
   About 20 scallions
12 to 14 leeks (about 2 inches) (trim and soak in acidulated water)
12 tiny whole eggplants (about 2 inches) or 1 large eggplant, sliced
12 to 16 small whole zucchini (about 2 inches) or 8 larger zucchini, halved
12 to 16 young whole carrots (about 2 inches)
   About 1 pound mushrooms, small ones preferred
4 to 6 celery hearts, halved
3 fennel heads, quartered
28 to 30 small white onions

■ **Variation** for Onions *à la Grecque*— Use 1 cup oil and 1 cup water. When the onions are just beginning to be tender, add 1 tablespoon tomato paste, a pinch of ground saffron, and ½ cup raisins. Cook for several minutes, or until the raisins are puffed and the sauce is thick and rich.

Makes approximately 8 servings for a first course.

BRAISED VEGETABLES

There are several ways to braise vegetables. The old French method was to cook them in boiling water for an hour or more and then bake them for another hour. The result is absolutely tasteless.

I prefer to poach vegetables in broth, or water plus bouillon cubes or beef extract, until they are just barely tender, and then finish them off in butter or oil. You may save the broth for sauces and gravies. Or sometimes I use half broth and half white wine for the poaching. This gives added flavor.

Poached vegetables may be drained and then tossed in hot butter or oil and seasonings; or they may be arranged in a flat baking dish, dotted with butter, and covered loosely with a piece of foil or parchment paper to be finished off in a preheated moderate oven (350°F.). This takes 12 to 15 minutes.

When serving braised vegetables, remember most of them are properly knife and fork foods.

Braised Celery

Choose 1 good heart of celery for each person. Trim them neatly and cut off the tops. Tops can be saved for seasoning other dishes. Split the hearts into halves and wash well. Place them in a skillet large enough for all to lie flat. You may need 2 skillets. Barely cover the celery with broth, water, and bouillon cubes, or broth and white wine. Season with salt to taste and add a dash of hot pepper sauce. Bring to a boil and reduce the heat at once to a simmer. Cook the celery, turning once or twice, until it is just tender. The time will vary according to the thickness of the hearts and your taste for tenderness. Drain the broth from the skillet and turn the celery cut side down. For 6 celery hearts, add 4 to 5 tablespoons butter and 2 or 3 twists of the pepper grinder. Heat for 5 minutes over a medium heat. Turn the celery over and heat for another 3 or 4 minutes.

If you wish, you may add a few spoonfuls of the broth during the last minute or two.

To braise in the oven, remove the cooked celery hearts from the broth and place them cut side up in a baking dish. Add a few spoonfuls of broth. Dot heavily with butter and place a piece of foil or parchment very loosely over the top. Heat in a preheated moderate oven (350° F.) for 12 to 15 minutes. Variations: 1. Sprinkle with freshly grated Parmesan cheese just before serving.

2. To serve cold, let the poached celery cool in the broth and serve with a vinaigrette sauce or French dressing. When topped with anchovy fillets and a bit of pimiento, this dish is called Celery Victor.

Braised Fennel

Prepare in the same way given for celery hearts (see above). I find that sometimes, if the fennel heads are very large, it is better to quarter them or cut them into slices. This is an excellent accompaniment for fish or game.

Braised Endive

Choose uniform-size heads of Belgian endive. Follow the recipe for braised celery, but add 1 or 2 thin slices of lemon to the broth.

Braised Lettuces

Tiny heads of limestone (Bibb) lettuce or Boston (butter) lettuce are best for braising. Romaine braises well. Iceberg lettuce is not good. Proceed as for braised celery, but watch the poaching closely for there is a great difference in cooking time, since some lettuces are more tender than others. If you are poaching rather loose-leafed heads, it is wise to tie them together lightly so they will hold their shape. Remove the strings before serving, of course.

Braised Chinese Cabbage

Cut this vegetable into quarters trimmed to fit your skillet and leave the root on. Proceed as for celery.

Braised Leeks

Clean the leeks well and poach as for celery. Reheat in butter and serve.

■ **Variations**—1. Poach leeks until just tender, remove from the broth, and wrap with strips of partially cooked bacon. Place on a rack and bake in preheated slow oven (250°F.) until the bacon is crisp.

2. Chill the cooked leeks in the broth. Drain and arrange in a serving dish. Add a good vinaigrette sauce or French dressing, and top with strips of anchovy if you wish.

BRAISED LEEKS, NIÇOISE

Another method of braising calls for steaming or simmering the vegetables in butter or oil plus seasonings. This gives a richer dish.

12 uniform-size leeks
⅓ cup olive or peanut oil
2 garlic cloves, finely chopped
2 tomatoes, peeled and cut into sixths
   Finely grated rind of 1 lemon, or thinly sliced and chopped rind
1 tablespoon fresh lemon juice
   Salt and pepper to taste
½ cup soft black olives, pitted
   Chopped parsley

Wash the leeks well and cut into 1- to 1½-inch rounds. Heat the oil in a heavy skillet and add the leeks. Cover and cook for exactly 9 minutes over a medium heat. Add the remaining ingredients except the parsley and cook, uncovered, for another 6 to 8 minutes. Do not let the mixture become mushy. Top with chopped parsley. This is excellent with veal or lamb. Makes about 8 servings.

BRAISED ONION SLICES
- 2 tablespoons butter or margarine
- 2 tablespoons olive oil
- 4 large onions, peeled and cut into 1-inch slices
- 1 teaspoon salt
- ¼ cup broth
- ½ teaspoon pepper
- ¼ cup whiskey (optional)

Melt the butter in a heavy saucepan. Add olive oil. Add the onions and sear over high heat for 2 minutes. Add salt, broth, and pepper and reduce the heat. Cover and simmer for 10 minutes. Add the whiskey, if desired, and let the sauce cook down slightly. Makes 4 to 6 servings.

■ **Variation**—Add 2 tablespoons of raisins that have been soaked in the whiskey.

CLASSIC RATATOUILLE
Interesting combinations of vegetables and seasonings can make rich, flavorful dishes. These are often cooked in butter or oil in the skillet. This is a classic example.

- ⅓ cup olive oil
- 2 large onions, sliced
- 3 garlic cloves (or more, to taste), chopped
- 2 small eggplants, cubed
- 4 small zucchini, sliced
- 2 green peppers, cut into strips
- 1 head of fennel, sliced
- 2⅓ cups (one 1-pound, 3-ounce can) Italian plum tomatoes
- 1 teaspoon crumbled dried basil
- 1½ teaspoons salt
  Pepper to taste
- ½ teaspoon chopped parsley

Heat the olive oil in a heavy skillet and add the onions and garlic. Heat and toss until wilted. Add the eggplants, zucchini, peppers, and fennel, and mix well over a brisk heat. Add the tomatoes, seasonings, and parsley; cover, and simmer for about 1 hour, stirring occasionally. Remove the cover and cook down until most of the liquid has evaporated and the mixture is thick. Serve hot or serve cold with additional oil and a little vinegar. Makes 6 servings.

■ **Variations**—1. Add 2 celery hearts cut into thin slices.

2. Thirty minutes before the ratatouille is done, add 1 pound of small whole mushrooms or 1 pound of large mushrooms, sliced.

3. Substitute 1 or 2 sliced cucumbers for the zucchini.

CAPONATA
This is the Italian *ratatouille* and it is almost always served cold. There are many versions but this is the one I have enjoyed most.

- 1 large or 2 small onions, thinly sliced
- 1 celery stalk, thinly sliced
- ½ cup olive or peanut oil
- 2 medium or 3 small eggplants,

unpeeled and cut into strips
- 1½ cups Italian plum tomatoes
  Salt and pepper
- 1 teaspoon crumbled dried basil
- 2 garlic cloves, chopped
- 2 tablespoons tomato paste
- ⅓ cup capers
- ½ cup soft black Italian or Greek olives, pitted
- 1 lemon, thinly sliced
  Tomato quarters
  Chopped parsley

Sauté the onions and celery in oil until just golden. Add the eggplant strips and sauté lightly, tossing them well with the onions and celery. Add the tomatoes and cook down, uncovered. Do not let the vegetables overcook. Season with salt and pepper to taste and add the basil and garlic. Cook for 10 minutes. Stir in the tomato paste, capers, olives, and lemon slices and cook for another 10 minutes.

Chill the *caponata* for a day or so before serving. Serve garnished with tomato quarters and chopped parsley. Add oil and vinegar if you wish. Makes 4 servings.

CAULIFLOWER SAUTÉ WITH LEMON
- 1 medium-size cauliflower
  Olive oil
  Salt and pepper
  Fresh lemon juice

Wash the cauliflower and soak it in salted cold water for 1 hour. Drain, and cut into flowerets. Cover with fresh cold salted water and cook slightly. The flowerets should be quite firm.

Heat olive oil in a large skillet and add the drained flowerets. Sauté them quickly, turning to brown on all sides. Remove to a hot serving dish and season to taste with salt and pepper; add lemon juice. Makes 4 servings.

■ **Variation**—serve cold, dressed with lemon juice, sesame-seed oil, salt and pepper.

OKRA AND TOMATOES WITH LEMON
- 1 pound small fresh okra
- ½ cup olive oil
- 3 or 4 onions, peeled and coarsely chopped
- 2 garlic cloves, peeled and chopped
  About 3½ cups (one 1-pound, 13-ounce can) tomatoes
  Salt and pepper
- 1 teaspoon coriander, tied in a cheesecloth bag
  Lemon wedges

Trim the cone-shape tops from the okra, wash them, and dry them thoroughly with paper towels.

Heat the oil in a large skillet and add the onions and garlic. Cook gently until tender. Add the okra and cook, tossing lightly, until they are slightly browned. Add the tomatoes, salt and pepper to taste, and the bag of coriander. Cover the skillet and simmer gently until the okra is tender; this depends on its size and age. Remove the cheesecloth bag.

Serve with lemon wedges. Steamed rice is a good accompaniment. Makes 4 servings.
Note: This dish is equally good served cold with lemon wedges. If fresh okra is not available, substitute the frozen.

ZUCCHINI IN TOMATO SAUCE
- 3 tablespoons olive oil
- 1 garlic clove, finely chopped
- 7 cups (two 1-pound, 13-ounce cans) Italian plum tomatoes
- 1 teaspoon salt
- 1 teaspoon sugar
- ½ teaspoon pepper
- 3 tablespoons tomato paste
- 12 small zucchini, peeled
- 2 tablespoons chopped fresh basil

Heat the olive oil, add the garlic, and cook for 3 minutes. Add the tomatoes and bring to a boil. Lower the heat and simmer slowly for 20 to 25 minutes, stirring occasionally. Add next 3 seasonings and tomato paste, and simmer for 10 more minutes. Add the zucchini and cook until just pierceable with a fork, about 15 minutes. Stir in the basil, and cool. Serve cold. Makes 8 to 10 servings.

MADAME FRAIZE'S CABBAGE AND ZUCCHINI SKILLET
- 5 tablespoons olive oil, goose fat, or bacon fat
- 1 head cabbage (about 1½ pounds), coarsely chopped
- 1 large onion, thinly sliced
- 3 or 4 zucchini, peeled and cut into ½-inch slices
- 1 garlic clove, finely minced
  Salt and pepper

Heat the oil in a skillet and add the cabbage. Toss it about well, and cover. Cook quickly for 5 minutes, stirring twice. Add the onion and re-cover. Reduce the heat and cook slowly for 45 minutes. Add the zucchini and garlic, re-cover, and cook slowly for another 30 to 45 minutes. Add more oil if needed. Season to taste and cook for another 15 minutes. Serve very hot with braised meats or boiled beef. It is good with sausage also. Makes 6 servings.

■ **Variations**—1. Add another garlic clove and ¼ cup tomato paste with the zucchini. 2. Add pitted black olives and crisp bits of bacon for the last 10 minutes.

HARICOTS VERTS MAILLANOISE
(Green Beans, Maillane Style)
Vegetables simply boiled until tender but still crisp often gain added interest when tossed with imaginative seasonings.

- 2 pounds tiny green beans
  Salted water
- 3 tablespoons olive oil
- 1 garlic clove, finely chopped
  Chopped parsley
  Salt (optional)

Cook the beans in salted water until just crisply tender. Drain well. In a skillet heat the olive oil and garlic. Add the beans and toss as you would a salad. Add parsley, and additional salt if needed. Makes 6 to 8 servings.

CARROTS WITH DILL

Boil 12 whole carrots until just crisply tender. Drain. Melt ½ cup of butter in a skillet and roll the carrots around in the butter until they are well saturated. Add salt, chopped fresh dill to taste, and freshly ground pepper.

Serve in a divided dish with fresh or frozen peas in butter.

Makes 4 servings.

BROCCOLI ALLA PIEMONTESE

Cook 1 or 2 bunches of broccoli according to your favorite recipe until it is just barely tender, not mushy. Drain. Sauté 2 finely chopped garlic cloves in enough olive oil to cover the bottom of a large skillet. When the garlic is lightly browned, add the broccoli and spoon the hot oil over it. Season with salt and pepper to taste, toss in ½ cup dry white wine, and let it cook down very quickly. Serve the broccoli with the pan juices poured over it. Makes 4 to 8 servings.

GRATIN OF GREENS

Sometimes vegetable combinations are finished off in the oven with a topping of cheese or crumbs. This makes a hearty dish.

  2 pounds spinach, washed and chopped rather fine
    Olive oil
    Salt and pepper
  2 pounds Swiss chard, washed and chopped fine
  2 pounds zucchini, diced
  1 cup cooked rice
  3 garlic cloves, chopped
  6 eggs
    Crumbs

Cook spinach in skillet with olive oil until just wilted. Season with salt and pepper. Drain. Prepare the chard in the same manner. Cook the zucchini in oil until just tender. Combine the vegetables with the rice and garlic and mix thoroughly. Put in a well-oiled baking dish, add 3 to 4 tablespoons olive oil, and heat in preheated slow oven (300°F.) for 20 minutes.

Beat the eggs well and pour them over the vegetables. Sprinkle with crumbs and return to the oven to cook until the eggs are just set. Serve warm or cold. Makes 6 to 8 servings.

■ **Variations**—1. Add a bit of flaked codfish as well as the rice and omit the eggs.

2. Use some finely chopped celery tops as well as the spinach and chard, and blend ½ cup grated Parmesan cheese with the eggs.

3. Substitute mustard greens for the chard.

4. Substitute finely chopped beet greens or turnip greens for one of the other greens.

5. Add pitted black olives to the dish.

GRATIN OF EGGPLANT

  1 large onion, coarsely chopped
  ½ cup olive oil
  4 tomatoes, peeled, seeded, and chopped, or about 2 cups plum tomatoes
  1 large eggplant, sliced
    Salt and pepper to taste
  ½ teaspoon crumbled dried thyme
  ½ tablespoon all-purpose flour
    Grated Swiss cheese

Sauté the onion in the oil and add the tomatoes. Let them cook for 5 to 8 minutes. Add the eggplant and seasonings and cook very slowly, covering the pan for part of the cooking time. When the eggplant is tender but not mushy, sprinkle with the flour and blend it into the juices. Add the grated cheese and run under the broiler to melt. Makes 4 servings.

STUFFED BAKED EGGPLANT

Many people think of stuffed vegetables as a way of using up leftovers, but the stuffed vegetable dish can be an important taste combination and elegant party fare.

  2 small eggplants
    Olive oil
  2 garlic cloves
  2 cups croutons
  16 to 20 anchovy fillets
    Salt and pepper
    Grated rind of 1 lemon
  2 tablespoons fresh lemon juice

Halve the eggplants and scoop out the flesh. Chop rather coarsely and sauté in ⅓ cup of olive oil with finely chopped garlic. Sauté the croutons separately in garlic-flavored oil. Chop the anchovies rather fine and combine with the eggplant and croutons. Toss well. Season to taste and add the lemon rind and lemon juice.

Stuff the eggplant halves with this mixture and dribble with olive oil. Place in a baking dish with a little warm water. Bake in preheated moderate oven (375° F.) for 35 minutes, or until done and well browned. Makes 4 servings.

STUFFED ZUCCHINI

  12 to 14 small zucchini, halved
    Olive oil
  ⅔ cup bread crumbs or croutons
  3 garlic cloves, finely chopped
  12 black olives, chopped
  2 tablespoons capers
  12 to 14 anchovy fillets, coarsely chopped
  2 tablespoons chopped parsley

Scoop out the zucchini and discard the seeds and a small amount of the flesh. Sauté the halves quickly in olive oil. Then parboil them for 5 to 10 minutes. Cool. Heat 6 tablespoons of olive oil and sauté the crumbs and garlic for 2 minutes. Add the chopped black olives, the

capers, and part of the chopped anchovies. Stuff the zucchini with this mixture; sprinkle with additional crumbs and brush with oil. Arrange in a baking dish and bake in preheated moderate oven (375° F.) for 20 minutes, brushing once with more oil. Serve cold, garnished with chopped parsley and the rest of the anchovies. Makes 6 or 7 servings.

ZUCCHINI WITH WALNUTS

  ¼ pound walnuts
  6 medium zucchini
  2 tablespoons butter or margarine
    Salt and pepper

Reserve a few walnut halves for garnish and chop the remainder. Slice unpeeled zucchini about ⅛ inch thick. Sauté in butter, stirring constantly. When zucchini is almost tender, add the chopped walnuts and salt and pepper to taste. Continue cooking until tender. Garnish with walnut halves. Makes 6 servings.

VEGETABLE SOUFFLÉS
Onion or Shallot Soufflé

This is a spring favorite at the Four Seasons Restaurant in New York.

For the vegetables:

  6 shallots, peeled and chopped, or 1 medium onion, chopped
  3 tablespoons butter

For the basic soufflé mixture:

  3 tablespoons all-purpose flour
  3 tablespoons butter or margarine
  ¼ cup milk
  ½ teaspoon salt
    Dash of hot pepper sauce
  ¾ cup sharp Cheddar or Gruyère cheese, grated
  4 egg yolks
  6 egg whites

Sauté the shallots in butter until nicely colored and cooked through.

Prepare the soufflé mixture: combine the flour and butter in a skillet and cook for a few minutes. Gradually stir in the milk, salt, and hot pepper sauce, and continue stirring until thickened. Add the shallots, the cheese, and the egg yolks, lightly beaten. Cook, stirring constantly, over very low heat for 5 minutes, or until the cheese is melted and the mixture blended. Cool. Beat the egg whites until stiff but not dry. They should still have a fine gloss. Fold half of the whites in quite thoroughly. Add the rest of the whites and fold in lightly. Pour into a buttered 1½-quart soufflé dish and bake in preheated moderate oven (375°F.) for 25 to 30 minutes, or at 400°F. for a little less time. The soufflé is done when it is high and brown. Makes 6 servings.

Broccoli Soufflé

Prepare the basic soufflé mixture as above. Add 1 cup of puréed cooked broccoli and ½ garlic clove, finely minced. Frozen broccoli may be used.

Caponata ■ Celery Victor

Spinach Soufflé

1 garlic clove, chopped
2 tablespoons olive oil
¾ cup chopped fresh or frozen spinach
2 teaspoons fresh lemon juice
Pinch of ground nutmeg

Sauté the garlic in oil for a minute. Add the spinach, lemon juice, and nutmeg and heat through for 4 or 5 minutes. Add to the basic soufflé mixture (page 1904). Cool slightly and fold in the egg whites. Pour into a buttered 1½-quart soufflé dish and bake in preheated moderate oven (375°F.) for 30 to 35 minutes. Makes 6 servings.

Green-Bean Soufflé

To the basic soufflé mixture (page 1904) add:

1 cup finely chopped or puréed cooked green beans
¼ cup crisp bacon pieces

Add the beaten egg whites, pour into a buttered 1½-quart soufflé dish, and bake in preheated moderate oven (375°F.) for 30 to 35 minutes.

TANGERINE SWEETS

6 cooked sweet potatoes
48 tangerine sections
1 jar (8 ounces) honey
Parsley

Peel and slice each potato lengthwise into 4 slices. Put in shallow ovenproof serving dish. Arrange 2 tangerine sections on each potato slice. Cover with honey and bake in preheated moderate oven (350° F.) for 30 minutes, or until heated through. Garnish with parsley. Makes 6 servings.

ONIONS IN ONIONS

3 Spanish onions, 3 inches in diameter
Salt
18 pearl onions (use canned, if preferred)
¼ cup butter or margarine
¼ cup all-purpose flour
2 cups milk
Pepper

Cook Spanish onions in boiling salted water to cover until barely tender. Cook pearl onions in the same manner until done (if using canned ones, heat through). Melt butter, and blend in flour. Gradually add milk, and cook, stirring constantly, until thickened. Season to taste with salt and pepper. Drain the pearl onions, and combine with the sauce. Remove outer skins from Spanish onions, and cut each into halves crosswise. Remove center rings to leave a hole about 1 inch in diameter. Put 3 pearl onions in each hole and pour the cream sauce over all. Put under broiler until golden brown. Makes 6 servings.

Onions in Onions

Tangerine Sweets

Zucchini with Walnuts

VENISON—The edible flesh of a wild animal taken by hunting. The word is most often used in reference to deer meat. It comes from the Latin term for hunt and quarry.

For practically all cooking purposes, recipes for deer, moose, and elk are interchangeable. What should be remembered is that the flavor of venison depends on the animal's food and the tenderness of the meat depends on the animal's age. Venison is apt to be tough; it should, therefore, be treated like any such meat, and be either marinated or pot-roasted.

PIT-COOKED VENISON

This is a favorite way of cooking freshly killed meat in camp. Dig a pit about 18 inches square and line with rocks. Build a fire in the pit and let it burn down until you have about 6 inches of red coals. Place a 5- or 6-pound boned roast on 2 thicknesses of heavy-duty foil large enough to cover roast. Season with salt and pepper and any other seasonings you desire. Fold foil over the roast, sealing edges well. Place in the pit and bank coals around it. Fill the pit with dirt and cover with a dampened piece of canvas weighted down with rocks. Leave for 5 to 6 hours. Carefully remove roast from pit and open foil. Use the juices to serve over the sliced roast. Makes 8 servings.

VENISON STEAKS OR CHOPS

8 venison steaks or chops, 1½ inches thick
Burgundy
Freshly ground pepper
Seasoned all-purpose flour
Butter (about ⅓ cup)
½ pound fresh mushrooms, sliced
6 slices of bacon, cut into julienne strips
¼ cup minced onion
½ cup diced celery

Place steaks in a shallow pan and pour wine over just barely to cover; sprinkle liberally with pepper. Marinate overnight. Remove meat from marinade; dry on paper towels. Turn in seasoned flour and sauté in butter until nicely browned and tender. In another skillet simmer in 2 tablespoons butter the mushrooms, bacon, onion, and celery. When lightly browned, add wine marinade and bring to the boiling point. Serve steaks on a heated platter; pour sauce with vegetables over the meat. Makes 8 servings.

SPICY BARBECUED ROAST VENISON

4- pound venison roast (leg, rump, or shoulder)
2 tablespoons olive oil
1 cup chili sauce
1 cup water
2 tablespoons vinegar
1 tablespoon Worcestershire
1 teaspoon salt
¼ teaspoon pepper
⅛ teaspoon each of celery salt, ground cinnamon, and ground cloves
1 small onion, finely chopped
½ lemon, thinly sliced
½ cup currant jelly

Brown roast on all sides in olive oil, then place in a roasting pan. Add all the remaining ingredients except jelly to the pan juices and heat to boiling, scraping bottom of pan to loosen all particles. Pour sauce over meat and roast in preheated moderate oven (350°F.) until meat reaches the desired degree of doneness, about 1½ hours for rare, 2 to 2½ hours for medium or well done, basting occasionally with sauce. Add more water if necessary. Remove meat to serving platter and strain basting sauce. Measure and add water if needed to make ½ cup of sauce. Add jelly and cook over moderate heat, stirring constantly, until jelly is melted and sauce is smooth. Serve hot in a sauceboat to spoon over sliced meat. Makes 8 to 10 servings.

VENISON POT ROAST

1 cup dry red wine
1 cup water
1½ teaspoons salt
2 bay leaves
10 whole cloves
5 whole allspice
2 chili peppers
1 large onion, sliced
One 5- to 6-pound venison roast (any cut) or chuck or rump beef
2 tablespoons bacon fat

Combine all ingredients except meat and bacon fat to make a marinade. Put meat in deep container; do not use aluminum. Pour marinade over meat. Cover and marinate in refrigerator for 2 days. Drain and reserve marinade. Dry meat. Strain marinade. In Dutch oven brown meat on all sides in hot bacon fat. Add ½ cup reserved marinade. Simmer, covered, over low heat for 2 to 3 hours, or until meat is tender. (Cooking time depends on cut and age of the venison.) Check occasionally, add more marinade to prevent sticking. Remove pot roast to hot serving dish and slice thickly. Keep hot. Make gravy in the usual manner. Pour gravy over meat. Serve with wild rice or buttered noodles. Makes 6 to 8 servings.

MEAT-ON-A-STICK

2 pounds venison round steak
¼ cup olive oil
¼ cup dry red wine
2 tablespoons Worcestershire
1 teaspoon garlic salt
½ teaspoon crumbled dried oregano
½ teaspoon salt
¼ teaspoon pepper

Remove fat and bone from meat and cut meat into 1-inch cubes. Mix remaining ingredients and pour over meat in a mixing bowl. Marinate for 2 hours, stirring occasionally. Thread meat on individual skewers or sticks and broil, either over charcoal or in the oven, until meat reaches the desired degree of doneness, turning to brown each side. About 3 minutes on each side will result in a crusty outside and pink juicy inside if sticks of meat are placed about 5 inches from heat.

When hunters cook meat-on-a-stick in camp, they cut green willow branches and peel them to use for sticks.

Makes enough for ten 8-inch sticks.

VENISON RAGOUT

2 tablespoons butter or margarine
2 tablespoons all-purpose flour
1 cup chicken bouillon or 1 chicken bouillon cube dissolved in 1 cup water
1 tablespoon Worcestershire
1 tablespoon currant jelly
2 cups 1-inch cubes of cooked venison
Salt and pepper to taste

Brown butter in skillet. Add flour and continue to cook until flour browns. Add bouillon, stirring constantly until thickened. Add Worcestershire and jelly and cook over low heat, stirring constantly, until jelly is melted. Add meat and seasonings and heat until meat is heated through. Makes 4 servings.

VENISON STROGANOFF

2 pounds venison round steak, cut ¾ inch thick
2 tablespoons shortening
1 large onion, peeled and chopped
½ teaspoon salt
⅛ teaspoon pepper
1 can (10½ ounces) beef bouillon
¼ pound fresh mushrooms
2 tablespoons butter or margarine
2 tablespoons all-purpose flour
1 teaspoon prepared mustard
1 cup dairy sour cream

Remove bone and fat from meat and cut into strips about ¼ inch wide and 1½ inches long. Brown meat in shortening in a heavy skillet. Transfer meat to a 2-quart casserole and add onion, salt, and pepper. Heat bouillon in skillet, scraping bottom of pan to loosen all particles. Pour over meat and bake, covered, in preheated moderate oven (350°F.) for 1½ hours, stirring occasionally if meat on top becomes dry.

Wash and slice mushrooms and sauté

in butter until golden. Stir in flour. Drain the liquid from the meat and add gradually while stirring. Cook over low heat, stirring constantly, until smooth and thickened. Add mustard and sour cream and blend well. Pour over meat. Serve over cooked rice. Makes 4 to 6 servings.

BRINE-CURED VENISON ROLL

8 to 10 pounds venison flank and scraps
1 medium onion, peeled and chopped
2 quarts water
1½ cups rock salt
¾ teaspoon saltpeter

Spread out flank, sewing together if you have several small ones. Sprinkle with onion and any scraps or meat trimmings. Roll tightly and tie securely. Boil water with salt until salt is dissolved. Add saltpeter (this is to preserve the color of the meat). Cool the brine, add the meat roll, and store in a stone crock or glass or pottery bowl. Put a plate on top with a weight to keep the meat immersed in the brine. The meat may be left in the brine from 2 weeks to 2 months. When ready to use, remove the meat, rinse with fresh water, and boil in water to cover for 2 hours. Then remove from the liquid and place in a loaf pan. Put a weight on top to press it into a firm roll. Cut into thin slices for sandwiches or dice it and serve it cold with a pickle relish or in a salad. Makes 12 to 14 servings.

VENISON SAUSAGE

4 pounds venison scrap meat
½ pound beef suet
¼ cup smoked salt
2 teaspoons salt
1½ teaspoons ground sage
½ teaspoon ground allspice
¼ teaspoon cayenne

Grind the venison and the suet through the coarse blade of a meat grinder. The suet will be easier to grind if it is cold. Mix in the seasonings thoroughly and grind again through the medium blade. Mix again thoroughly, using your hands. Stuff into casings and tie into convenient lengths. Drop into boiling water and cook until the sausage floats, 20 to 30 minutes. After cooking, the sausage may be wrapped in foil and frozen. Makes 8 to 10 servings.

VENISON CHOPS PARMESAN

8 venison chops
1 tablespoon butter
2 medium onions, peeled, quartered, and sliced
1 tablespoon shortening
Salt and pepper
1 cup beef bouillon or 1 bouillon cube dissolved in 1 cup hot water
8 slices of French bread, toasted
1 cup dairy sour cream
1 tablespoon Worcestershire
3 tablespoons grated Parmesan cheese

Trim fat from chops. Melt butter and sauté onions until they are limp and straw-colored. Remove onions and add shortening. Brown chops on both sides and sprinkle with salt and pepper. Top with onions and bouillon. Simmer, covered, until meat has reached the desired degree of doneness, 15 to 30 minutes. Arrange toast on serving dish or individual plates, top each slice with a chop, and keep warm. Add sour cream and Worcestershire to pan drippings and stir until mixed and heated. Pour over chops and sprinkle with Parmesan cheese. Makes 8 servings.

HUNTER'S CHILI

1 pound small red chili or kidney beans
½ teaspoon baking soda
1 tablespoon salt
1 pound each of venison and moose scraps, trimmed from neck, shoulder, shanks, or ribs, (or all venison or all moose may be used)
¼ cup shortening
1 large onion, peeled and chopped
4 to 6 tablespoons chili powder
2 tablespoons all-purpose flour
3 garlic cloves, peeled and minced, or put through garlic press
4 teaspoons crumbled dried oregano
2 teaspoons ground cuminseed
1½ teaspoons crumbled dried sage or ¾ teaspoon ground sage

Soak beans overnight in water. In the morning add baking soda and bring to a boil. Boil for 10 minutes. Drain and rinse. Cover beans with water, add salt, and bring to a boil. Meanwhile, trim all fat and tendons from meat and cut into small cubes. Brown in shortening, then add to the beans. Cook onion in remaining shortening until golden brown, stirring occasionally. Add chili powder and flour, and mix. Then add to beans and meat. Rinse the pan with a little water, stirring to remove all particles, and add to chili. Add remaining ingredients and cover. Simmer for 4 hours, stirring occasionally, adding more water if necessary. Makes 6 to 8 servings.

VENISON SHANKS WITH ROSEMARY

6 slices of venison from upper shank, cut 1 inch thick
Olive oil
6 medium potatoes, peeled and halved
Salt and pepper
Basting Sauce

Rub meat with olive oil and place in a large flat roasting pan. Brown in preheated extremely hot oven (500°F.), turning once to brown both sides. Place potatoes around meat and sprinkle both with salt and pepper to taste. Reduce heat to slow (325°F.) and roast for 1 hour more, basting frequently with Basting Sauce. Makes 6 servings.

Basting Sauce for Venison

1 cup chicken bouillon
½ cup dry red wine
½ cup tomato sauce
2 tablespoons olive oil
2 tablespoons grated onion
1 garlic clove, peeled and minced, or put through garlic press
1 teaspoon salt
½ teaspoon crumbled dried rosemary or 1 teaspoon chopped fresh rosemary
⅛ teaspoon pepper
Pinch of cayenne

Combine all ingredients in a small saucepan and heat to boiling. Keep warm over very low heat while using to baste venison shanks.

VENISON MEATBALLS

2 pounds venison, ground
1 medium onion, peeled and chopped
1 garlic clove, peeled and minced, or put through a garlic press
1 cup tomato juice
1 cup dry bread crumbs
1 teaspoon Worcestershire
1½ teaspoons salt
½ teaspoon pepper
Water
All-purpose flour

Mix together thoroughly all ingredients except water and flour, and form into balls the size of a golf ball. Brown them in shortening and transfer to a 2-quart kettle. Pour a small amount of water into the skillet and heat, scraping the bottom to remove all particles. Pour over meatballs and add enough water to cover them. Simmer, covered, for about 45 minutes. Pour off the liquid and measure. Mix a smooth paste of flour and water, measuring 2 tablespoons water and 1½ tablespoons flour for each cup of liquid. Gradually add the hot liquid, stirring constantly, and cook until thickened. Correct seasoning. Serve with Herbed Wild Rice (page 1940). Makes 6 to 8 servings.

VERBENA, LEMON (Lippia citriodora)

—This perennial shrub, originally from Argentina and Chile, is now found in many mild climates. Its size varies greatly according to the conditions under which it is grown: outdoors in warm climates it reaches over ten feet; inside in pots it grows to a height of less than ten inches. The long, narrow, pointed leaves are yellow-green. Dried or fresh, these leaves have a delicate lemony flavor and smell. They may be used to garnish fruit cups or fruit salads, or put into jellies. A crushed leaf in the bottom of a cup or glass gives a delicious flavor to a sweet drink. Lemon verbena tea is one of the most popular of the herb teas. Its lemony fragrance makes it a natural for cologne and sachets, too.

VERMICELLI—A variety of pasta consisting of long thin strands, thinner than spaghetti. The name is Italian and means "little worms."

Vermicelli is cooked like any other pasta in plenty of boiling salted water, and served either with a sauce or with butter and grated Parmesan cheese. It may be served also as a soup, in bouillon.

VERMOUTH—A fortified wine, heavily aromatized with a formula of herbs, spices, and other flavoring agents. One of its more definite ingredients is taken from the shrub *Artemesia absinthium* or wormwood, which is used in the making of absinthe.

In the United States vermouth is used extensively in preparing cocktails and aperitifs. To a small extent here and to a far greater extent in Europe vermouth is drunk straight, either served frappéed with crushed ice, at room temperature, or slightly chilled. Both the dry and the sweet are made in France and Italy. They are made in the United States, too, where some of the drys especially rank high in the field. Other vermouths come from Latin America and a few from various countries in Europe.

Vermouth is used extensively in cookery. Usually the dry is preferred although there are a few recipes calling for the sweet. As a matter of fact, one may substitute a dry vermouth whenever a recipe calls for a dry white wine.

VICHYSSOISE—A very elegant cold leek and potato cream soup invented by Louis Diat, the great chef of the Ritz-Carlton Hotel in New York.

Chef Diat often told of the origin of Cream Vichyssoise Glacée, as the soup is properly called. When he lived as a child on the family farm in a small village in central France, not far from Vichy, one of Europe's most famous watering places, his mother used to make the hot leek and potato soup that is standard French fare. In the summer, the children cooled their hot soup with milk.

When Chef Diat took over the kitchens of the Ritz-Carlton, he was interested in cool dishes to serve during the hot summer season. The time was shortly before World War I when cold jellied dishes were just beginning to be introduced. As Chef Diat remembered the cooled soup of his childhood, he began to add refinements to it and made it into the perfect summer soup.

As for naming the soup, he first thought of his little native village, but he realized that no one would know the place, and decided that since Vichy was a nearby town, and one that his rich customers would know very well from having taken the cure there, the name "Vichyssoise," "From Vichy," would be the right one.

THE ORIGINAL CREAM VICHYSSOISE GLACÉE
From *Cooking à la Ritz* by Louis Diat (Lippincott, 1941)

    4 leeks, white part only
    1 medium onion
    2 tablespoons sweet butter
    5 medium potatoes
    4 cups water or chicken broth
    1 tablespoon salt
    2 cups milk
    2 cups medium cream
    1 cup heavy cream

Finely slice the white part of the leeks and the onion, and brown very lightly in the sweet butter; then add the potatoes, also sliced finely. Add water and salt. Boil gently for 35 to 40 minutes. Crush and rub through a fine strainer, or whirl in a blender. Return to heat and add milk and the medium cream. Season to taste and bring to a boil. Cool, and then rub through a very fine strainer. When soup is cold, add the heavy cream. Chill thoroughly before serving. Finely chopped chives may be added when serving. Makes 8 servings.

VINAIGRETTE—A sauce which is a mixture of oil, vinegar, salt, and pepper, sometimes with the addition of herbs. The sauce is one of the simplest and best of salad dressings, and there are countless variations of it. It takes its name from *vinaigre*, the French word for vinegar.

VINEGAR *by Lucy Kavaler*—Vinegar, a mixture of acetic acid and water, is a kitchen workhorse, needed for pickling, preserving, tenderizing tough meat and fowl, and adding sour pungency to dishes ranging from vinegar pie to tomato ketchup and salad dressing.

No one can say when vinegar first came into use. It was old when Ruth in the Bible dipped her morsel of bread into vinegar, when Caesar's legions mixed it with drinking water. Vinegar was probably discovered by ancient peoples accidentally, along with wine. Yeasts and bacteria are ever present in the air, too small to be seen by the naked eye. In the days before recorded history, yeasts must have fallen by chance into uncovered earthenware jugs of fruit juice and caused the juice to ferment and become wine. And in time the bacteria *Acetobacter* dropped into the wine and soured and transformed it into acetic acid and water. The name, derived from the French words *vin aigre*, "sour wine," is an apt description of the way vinegar is made. Despite the winy origin, no alcohol remains; the action of the *Acetobacter* sees to that.

Although it started with wine, vinegar making did not stop there, and imaginative cooks throughout the world have invented such variants as banana vinegar, or date, pear, orange, pineapple, peach, raspberry, honey, molasses, rice, or brandy. In America the cider vinegar made out of fermented apple juice is the most popular, and a white distilled vinegar based on dilute alcohol is also widely used. The English years ago began to employ malt in an economical effort to dispose of sour ale and beer, and still like malt vinegar best. Subtleties of flavor àre achieved with herbs and leaves. The chef of a luxury restaurant makes an incomparable marinade for beef by using a vinegar he has flavored himself. He first crushes basil and a garlic clove, then pours boiling vinegar over them, places the mixture in a jar, shakes it once a day for ten days, and at last strains it through a thin cloth.

The strangest of all formulations was devised by a gang of thieves looting Marseille during the Black Plague of the Middle Ages. They choked down a mixture of cloves, sage, rosemary, rue, pimiento, calamus (a root), caraway, nutmeg, and vinegar, in the belief that this hair-raising brew would protect them from the disease. But even they seem unimaginative when compared to Cleopatra who made vinegar history on the night when she dissolved a perfect pearl and drank it down with a flourish to show Mark Antony that she could consume a fortune in one meal. Nobody has ever found out what she thought of the flavor.

Anyone aware that the difference between good and superlative cuisine lies in just such basic ingredients as vinegar, must consider strength as well as flavor. Vinegar's bite and sourness is in direct proportion to the amount of acetic acid in it, and a four per cent vinegar will be far less pungent than one with five per cent or higher. The term "forty- or fifty-grain strength" is used by some manufacturers instead, "grain" standing for ten times the acetic-acid content. The strength

The Original Cream Vichyssoise Glacée

VITAMIN

4

has no effect on the calorie count, which is nil, making vinegar the dieter's delight the world over.

One of the most universal of all foods, vinegar is an essential of characteristic dishes of nations separated by thousands of miles and totally different customs and cooking practices. Consider the German *sauerbraten* and potato salad, the Japanese rice *sushi*, the American barbecued chicken, the Chinese sweet-and-sour pork, the kosher herring. Eating an old artichoke, say the French with a smile, will make you old quickly, but a young one with *sauce vinaigrette* will add years to your life. Although the pickle is definitely not a part of gourmet cookery, few gourmets anywhere in the world would pass up the pleasure of biting into a sharp sour salty one, be it dill, tomato, watermelon, beet, pumpkin, or cauliflower. The natural affinity of vinegar for salads has also won international recognition.

King Richard II of England was so fond of "salat," as it was then known, that his cook wrote down the directions: "Take parsel, sawge (sage), garlec, chibollas (small onions), leeks, myntes, fenel, ton tressis (watercress) . . . waishe hem clene . . . myng (mix) hem wel with rawe oile. Lay one vinegar and salt and serve it forth." In 14th-century England or 20th-century America, the classic salad dressing called "French" is regularly served forth.

Salad dressings, pickles, and seasoning do not exhaust the uses for vinegar; some are completely independent of the palate. Louis XIII of France, for example, ordered his generals to cool their cannons with vinegar. Less royal personages find that it removes the smell of onions from their fingers, helps to hard-cook cracked eggs without mess, controls the pervasive odor of cooking cabbage, and best of all, leaves shampooed hair soft and silky.

Availability and Purchasing Guide—The most common types of vinegar, such as red-wine, cider, and distilled vinegar, come in pint or quart bottles. Many others are available and they vary in size with the manufacturer and the kind of vinegar. Some of the special vinegars are imported: rosé wine vinegar, tarragon, chianti vinegar. Others are made in the United States and include basil white-wine vinegar, eschalot red wine, garlic red wine, red wine, rosé wine, tarragon red wine, white wine, white wine and vinegar with tarragon sprigs.

Table vinegars should be bought in small quantities. Vinegars for canning or preserving can be bought in larger bottles.

Storage—Store in a dark, cool place and keep airtight. Avoid using sediment that may form in bottom of bottle if stored a long time. Mold indicates spoilage; do not use. Cider or distilled vinegar will keep for about 6 months on the pantry shelf once opened, or almost indefinitely if not opened. Other vinegars will keep for 2 to 3 months.

Vinegar which has developed "mother," a jellylike membrane, can still be used. The vinegar should be strained through a fine strainer.

HERB VINEGAR
(from fresh herbs)

Put 2 cups minced fresh herb leaves in 1 quart cider vinegar and let jar stand in a warm place for 2 weeks, shaking mixture every day. Then strain, bottle, and seal. Makes 1 quart.

HERB VINEGAR
(from dried herbs)

Scald 1 quart of cider vinegar. Add 1½ tablespoons dried herbs. Let stand in jar in a warm place for 2 weeks, shaking mixture every day. Strain, bottle, and seal. Makes 1 quart.

SPICED RAISIN RELISH

1½ cups seeded raisins
⅓ cup sugar
⅓ cup cider vinegar
¼ teaspoon ground cinnamon
Dash of ground cloves

Simmer all ingredients, covered, for 15 to 20 minutes. Cool, and serve as a relish with ham or other meat. Makes about 1½ cups.

VITAMIN—A powerful organic compound indispensable to nutrition which is found in small quantities in foods. Absence of vitamins can cause serious health disorders, or even death. The fat-soluble vitamins (vitamins A, D, E, K) found in natural foods are more easily absorbed than vitamins in pill form, but with other vitamins, there is no significant difference. Each vitamin has its own function in the closely interwoven body processes. Vitamin values of commercial preparations, based on feeding tests on animals and on the latest chemical or microbiological methods of assay, are expressed in weights of pure vitamins in milligrams (mg.) or micrograms (mcg.). Vitamins A and D are also expressed in International Units. Research in vitamins has made this subject more complex as additional vitamins are found and their specific functions in the body are determined.

The fat-soluble vitamins are not lost easily in cooking, because they do not dissolve in water. However, water-soluble vitamins (vitamins B complex and C) may be partially lost in cooking water, but in normal practice enough is retained to afford complete protection. The risk is usually greatest in vitamin C loss, but in acid foods this loss is relatively slow. Losses in vitamins occur when fresh produce is stored too long or cooked too long in too much water. Cooking water should be used to prevent the loss of valuable vitamins. Dietary allowances specifying the amounts of vitamins needed are only approximations. These figures vary with age, sex, and activity. A well-varied diet will provide the necessary vitamins. Long-range good eating is important since vitamin deficiencies at their beginning are hard to detect. Once discovered, they may have progressed to a severe and chronic stage which will take months or even years to remedy.

FAT-SOLUBLE VITAMINS

Vitamin A is necessary for good eyesight and eyes that adapt readily to changes from light to dark. It is especially important for skeletal growth and normal tooth structure. Vitamin A is also necessary for the health of the mucous membranes lining the nose, throat, and other air passages, the alimentary canal, and the genitourinary tracts. It also regulates the permeability of membranes inside nearly *all* body cells, and functions in the entire body. Vitamin A can be stored in the body in the liver. The recommended daily allowance is 5,000 International Units per day. The food sources are fish-liver oils, animal livers, yellow-colored vegetables and fruits, green-colored vegetables and fruits, all milk products that include milk fat.

Vitamin D is necessary to prevent rickets and promote normal bone growth. Huge overdoses have been known to have specific toxicity. Daily requirement for children is 400 International Units. Vitamin D can be stored in the body in the liver. Vitamin D is formed from fatty material in the skin by ultraviolet light as in sunlight and is found in limited amounts in food. Fish-liver oils and other vitamin-D-fortified foods, chiefly milk products, are the usual sources of vitamin D. Vitamin D is stable to heating, aging, and storage.

Vitamin E is essential in muscle functions and serves as an anti-oxidant in body cells. The daily requirement is not stated. Food sources include wheat and corn germ and most seed oils, and it is found in moderate amounts in cereals, egg yolk, legumes, nuts, leafy vegetables, and vegetable oils.

Vitamin K is necessary in the formation of prothrombin which is vital to the proper clotting of blood. Large doses have been given to surgical patients and premature babies to prevent hemorrhaging. The adult daily requirement is unknown. Food sources are cabbage, cauliflower, spinach, and other leafy vegetables; pork liver, soybean oil, and other vegetable oils. It is moderately stable to heat, light, and exposure to air.

WOMAN'S DAY

WATER-SOLUBLE VITAMINS

Vitamin C or ascorbic acid is necessary in the prevention of scurvy leading to sore mouth, swollen gums, hemorrhages, bone fragility, weakened capillary walls, and muscle weakness. It is unstable when heated and exposed to air, and may be destroyed by drying and storage. It is found naturally in citrus fruits, strawberries, cantaloupes, tomatoes, sweet peppers, cabbage, potatoes, kale, broccoli, and turnip greens. The adult human daily requirement is 70 mg. for women and 75 mg. for men.

Thiamine (B-1) is necessary to maintain the appetite; in preventing beriberi (a disease affecting the nerves and digestive system), fatigue, and constipation; and in preserving the health of the nerves. It is unstable to heat and air in alkaline foods. In acid foods, such as cereals, meats, breads, peanuts, and walnuts, it is somewhat more stable to heat and air. The adult human daily requirement is 0.8 to 1.2 mg. for women and 0.9 to 1.2 mg. for men. It is found naturally in wheat and nearly all seed germ, pork, liver, organ meats, whole grains, enriched products, nuts, legumes, yeast, and potatoes.

Riboflavin (B-2) is necessary for the proper use in the body of carbohydrates and amino acids, preventing eye sensitivity and cataract. It is stable to heat in cooking, to acids and exposure to air, but unstable in the presence of light. It is found in liver, milk, meat, eggs, legumes, enriched products, yeast, and green leafy vegetables. The adult human daily requirement is 1.2 to 1.8 mg. for women and 1.3 to 1.7 mg. for men.

Niacin or niacinamide (a related compound) is necessary in the prevention of pellagra (a disease involving the nerves and skin), and is an essential part of carbohydrate and amino-acid metabolism. It is stable to heat, light, and exposure to air, acid, and alkali. The adult human daily requirement is 13 to 20 mg. for women and 15 to 19 mg. for men. It is found in liver, poultry, meat, fish, whole grains, enriched products, legumes, yeast, and mushrooms.

Pantothenic acid is necessary to growth and health and serves as a catalyst in the utilization of fats, sugars, and amino acids. It is moderately unstable to acid, alkali, heat, and certain salts, but it is extremely widely distributed. The adult human requirement has not been established. It is found in liver, organ meats, eggs, peanuts, legumes, mushrooms, salmon, yeast, wheat germ, and whole grains.

Vitamin B-6 (pyridoxine, pyridoxal, pyridoxamine) is necessary in nerve functions and to the proper metabolism of fats and amino acids. It is only moderately stable to heat, light, and air. The adult human daily requirement is about 1.5 to 2.0 mg. It is found in liver, pork, organ meats, legumes, seeds, grains, leafy foods, and potatoes.

Biotin is necessary for cell respiration. A deficiency in biotin causes fatigue, loss of appetite, nausea, and anemia. It is found in organ meats, egg yolks, milk, fruits, and leafy vegetables. Deficiencies are extremely rare.

Folacin and B-12 are necessary for blood cell formation and prevention of anemia. B-12 is closely related to nerve function. They are found in organ meats, milk, eggs, fish, and most leafy vegetables.

VODKA—A potent colorless spirit, distilled from a grain or potato mash. Vodka does not have a definite aroma or taste.

Russians, Poles, and other Slavic people toss their vodka down in thimble-size glasses, accompanied by *zakuski* or appetizers. In recent years vodka has become a popular drink in the United States.

VOL-AU-VENT—A delicate light pastry made from puff paste in the shape of a wide tower which looks like an enormous patty shell. Its cavity is filled with a sauced or creamed food. Like a patty shell, a *vol-au-vent* has a lid or top, which is removed before filling and put back afterward, like a hat.

The term is French, and it means "flying in the wind." Supposedly the great French chef Carême was experimenting with puff paste shapes one day. When he baked the first *vol-au-vent,* he noticed that the puff-paste dough had baked into its airy towerlike shape. Joyfully, he cried that it was "flying in the wind," and the name stuck.

CHICKEN-MUSHROOM VOL-AU-VENT

1 pound sweet butter
4 cups all-purpose flour
1 teaspoon salt
1 tablespoon fresh lemon juice
1¼ cups cold water (about)
1 egg, slightly beaten
Chicken-Mushroom Filling

Shape the butter into a brick about 3 x 5 x ¾ inches. Roll butter in 3 tablespoons of the flour, coating all sides. Wrap in wax paper, and chill. Put remaining flour in a large bowl. Make a well in the center. Add salt and lemon juice. Gradually begin to add water, only enough to make a rather firm, slightly sticky dough. Knead dough thoroughly on floured board for 20 minutes. Pound it on the table at intervals to achieve the right consistency. It should be very elastic and smooth. Form it into a ball; place on well-floured cloth. With a rolling pin, make the ball of dough into the shape of a four-leaf clover. Roll ends out, leaving the center thick. Well rolled, the dough will have a thick cushion in the center and four thinner "petals." Put brick of butter in the center of the four-leaf clover. Fold "petals" over dough by stretching them over butter and sealing all the edges so that the butter is completely enclosed. Wrap in wax paper, and chill for 20 minutes. On a well-floured cloth, gently roll out the block of dough as evenly as possible into a rectangle slightly less than ⅓ inch thick, and about 3 times as long as it is wide. Do not roll over the ends but flatten them gently to same thickness as the rest of the dough. Fold dough into thirds, making three layers, and chill for 20 minutes. Turn folded sides toward you, and roll out dough, and fold again into thirds. (Rolling, folding, and turning is called a "turn.") It is necessary to make a total of 6 turns, after which the dough is ready for use. The dough should be chilled between each turn. Roll chilled dough to ½-inch thickness. Cut out two 7-inch circles. Brush one with water and put the other on top. Roll remaining dough ¼ inch thick and cut out 2 more 7-inch circles. Cut out centers to leave two rings 1½ inches wide. Reserve one of the centers. Brush outer edge of double circle with water and lay 1 ring on top. Moisten this ring and top with remaining ring. Prick the bottom inside with a fork and let stand for 10 minutes. Scallop bottom edges with fingers and dull edge of a knife. Cut crisscross lines on reserved center and put on top. Brush whole shell except the edges with egg. (Egg on edges might prevent rising.) Bake in preheated extremely hot oven (500°F.) for 5 minutes. Reduce heat to moderate (350°F.) and bake for 30 minutes longer. Remove the center cover and scoop out soft center. Fill shell with Chicken-Mushroom Filling. Replace cover in center. Makes 6 servings.

Chicken-Mushroom Filling

½ pound mushrooms, sliced
¼ cup butter or margarine
¼ cup all-purpose flour
1 teaspoon salt
¼ teaspoon pepper
2½ cups light cream
3 cups diced cooked chicken
2 egg yolks
2 tablespoons sherry

Cook mushrooms in the butter until lightly browned. Blend in flour and seasonings. Gradually add cream and cook, stirring constantly, until thickened. Add chicken, and heat. Beat egg yolks with the sherry and add to mixture. Cook, stirring, for 2 or 3 minutes longer.

WAFFLE—A crisp, light quick bread made from a pour batter which always contains eggs. Waffles are made in a waffle iron, a utensil with two metal parts hinged together. Each section of the iron has an embossed surface, the crisscross design of which is imprinted on the waffle as it bakes.

Waffles are a very old form of cake or bread, and in Europe there are century-old, elaborately patterned waffle irons, often in the shape of hearts. The word itself is ancient, and traces its origins back to old German words meaning weave and honeycomb. Looking at the pattern of a waffle, we can see both images in it.

Waffles should be uniformly brown, crisp, and tender. Crispness results from baking the waffle for a sufficient length of time.

Serve waffles with butter and syrup, creamed mixtures, sauces, or ice cream.

Commercially prepared waffle mixes are available, as are frozen precooked waffles which can be heated in a toaster.

BASIC WAFFLES

1½ cups all-purpose flour
 2 teaspoons baking powder
 ½ teaspoon baking soda
 ¼ teaspoon salt
 1 tablespoon sugar
 3 eggs, separated
 ¾ cup dairy sour cream
 ¾ cup sweet milk or buttermilk
 ¼ cup lard or vegetable shortening, melted
 ¼ cup butter, melted

Sift dry ingredients together. Beat egg yolks, sour cream, and milk. Add to dry ingredients, alternating with fats cooled to room temperature. Stir until batter is smooth and free from lumps. Fold in egg whites, beaten stiff. Cook waffles according to directions for your particular waffle iron. Serve with syrup, honey, preserves, etc. Makes 4 waffles.

Note: These are fluffy crisp waffles with enough body to hold up when topped with creamed chicken or meat. They freeze well, too.

■ **To Freeze**—Cool; wrap each leftover waffle in foil and freeze. Or freeze flat and wrap. To reheat, it is not necessary to thaw. Place each unwrapped section in toaster set at light and toast until section is heated through. These waffle sections become crisp when cool. If you prefer, place unwrapped sections side by side on a flat cookie sheet and put under grill until heated and sufficiently browned. Do not keep over 2 weeks in the freezer.

■ **To Use Leftover Batter**—Store leftover waffle batter in refrigerator in covered jar. Before cooking add 1 teaspoon baking powder dissolved in 1 tablespoon milk for each cup batter. If batter is still too stiff, add an extra tablespoon or 2 of milk. Cook as directed.

Bacon Waffles

Cut thin strips of breakfast bacon into halves. Place one of these pieces over the top of each waffle section before closing iron. Cook according to directions for your iron, and serve. The bacon should be crisp and brown.

Ham Waffles

Add ½ cup ground baked ham to Basic Waffle batter before cooking.

Blueberry, Currant, Raisin, Nut, or Date Waffles

Add ½ cup blueberries, currants, raisins, chopped nuts, or pitted dates (cut into thirds) to Basic Waffle batter before cooking.

Cheese Waffles

Add ½ cup grated Parmesan or shredded Cheddar cheese to Basic Waffle batter before cooking.

Spice Waffles

Add to Basic Waffle batter before cooking: ½ teaspoon ground cinnamon plus ½ teaspoon coriander seeds (pounded or ground) and ¼ teaspoon ground nutmeg. Or use 1 teaspoon cinnamon alone, or vary it by adding a little nutmeg, clove, or ginger; ½ teaspoon caraway seed is a distinctive addition if you like the flavor.

Rice Waffles

Add ⅔ cup fluffy cooked rice to Basic Waffle batter.

CORN WAFFLES

    2 eggs, separated
 1½ cups milk
  ⅓ cup melted shortening
    1 cup cream-style corn
    2 cups sifted all-purpose flour
    2 teaspoons baking powder
  ½ teaspoon salt

Beat egg yolks with rotary beater until thick. Add milk, shortening, and corn. Add to sifted dry ingredients; mix until smooth. Then fold in stiffly beaten egg whites. Bake in hot waffle iron. Serve hot with butter and syrup. Or serve with creamed chicken or ham, as a main dish. Makes 6 waffles.

BROWNIE WAFFLES

  ½ cup butter, melted (or ¼ cup each
       butter and margarine)
    2 ounces (2 squares) unsweetened
       chocolate, or 2 envelopes no-melt
       chocolate
    1 cup sugar
  ½ teaspoon vanilla extract
    2 eggs
 1½ cups all-purpose flour
    1 teaspoon baking powder
  ⅛ teaspoon ground cinnamon (optional)
  ½ cup milk
    1 cup finely chopped pecans, almonds,
       or walnuts

Melt butter and chocolate in heavy saucepan; add sugar and beat well. Add vanilla, and cool. Add eggs one at a time, beating well. Sift flour, baking powder, and cinnamon. Add alternately with milk to first mixture. Add nuts. Bake according to directions for your particular waffle iron. When first taken from the iron, the waffle will be soft, but it gets crisp as it cools.

If any batter is left over, refrigerate. Before cooking add ½ teaspoon baking powder mixed with 1 teaspoon of water, for each cup of batter. This batter keeps several days, covered, in the refrigerator. Freezing is not advised. Makes 4 waffles.

■ **Variation**—You can use half dairy sour cream, half milk, plus ½ teaspoon baking soda and 1 teaspoon cream of tartar, instead of milk and baking powder.

Note: Serve a waffle section to each person and top each with a scoop of vanilla ice cream and hot fudge sauce. It makes a marvelous dessert and is fun to cook at the table. Cut recipe in half for a small group.

CHERRY WAFFLES

       Waffles for 4 servings
       Grated orange rind
    1 can (1 pound) water-packed pitted
       red sour cherries
  ¼ cup sugar
    1 tablespoon cornstarch
  ⅛ teaspoon salt
    1 tablespoon fresh lemon juice
       Red food coloring
       Buttered chopped blanched almonds

Prepare waffles using mix or your favorite recipe, adding a little grated orange rind to batter. Drain cherries and measure juice. Mix sugar with cornstarch and salt. Add enough water to the juice to make 1 cup. Add mixture gradually to cornstarch mixture. Cook over low heat, stirring constantly, until smooth and thickened. Stir in cherries, lemon juice, and food coloring. Serve hot on waffles with a sprinkling of buttered chopped almonds.

OLD COLONY GINGERBREAD WAFFLES

    1 cup plus 2 tablespoons all-purpose
       flour
 1¼ teaspoons baking powder
  ¼ teaspoon baking soda
    1 teaspoon ground ginger
  ¼ teaspoon ground clove
  ¼ teaspoon ground nutmeg
  ¾ teaspoon ground cinnamon
  ⅓ cup butter and lard, mixed (or use
       vegetable shortening in place of
       lard)
  ½ cup boiling water or coffee
  ⅓ cup firmly packed dark-brown sugar
  ½ cup dark molasses
    1 egg, well beaten

Sift dry ingredients. Add shortenings to boiling water and stir until dissolved. Then add sugar and molasses. Cool to room temperature. Add to dry ingredients; add egg and beat until batter is smooth. Pour into waffle iron. Use about ¾ cup batter for each waffle. Serve one section to a person. These waffles become crisp as they cool. Extra batter can be refrigerated for several days in a covered container. Cooked sections can be frozen. See Basic Waffles, page 1914, for freezing. Makes 2 large waffles.

Note: These waffles are delicious for dessert topped with cinnamon-flavored whipped cream; Mock Devonshire Cream, soft custard or vanilla pudding; with caramel, chocolate, or butterscotch sauces. Other favorite toppings, especially during the Christmas holidays, are: hard sauce, Orange Hard Sauce, brandy sauce, or heated mincemeat, well laced with spirits.

SAUCES FOR OLD COLONY GINGERBREAD WAFFLES
Mock Devonshire Cream

Those who have tasted rich, golden Devonshire Cream know there is no substitute, but here's a recipe which approaches it somewhat and is delicious in its own right. Blend a 3-ounce package of cream cheese, at room temperature, with 2 to 3 tablespoons heavy cream or dairy sour cream. When smooth, fold in 2 tablespoons confectioners' sugar and ½ teaspoon vanilla extract. Makes ½ cup.

Orange Hard Sauce

Blend ¼ cup butter, at room temperature, with 1 cup confectioners' sugar, 1 teaspoon grated orange rind, and 2 to 4 tablespoons fresh orange juice. The mixture should not be stiff or runny. Taste, adding more orange juice if the sauce will take it without separating. If desired, substitute 1 or 2 tablespoons Grand Marnier, Curacao, or Triple Sec for some of the orange juice. Cover and chill until firm. Pass with the waffles. If any sauce is left over, use on puddings, as a filling for cakes, or a frosting for sweet muffins. Makes about ⅞ cup.

HONEY BUTTER

    1 cup honey
  ½ cup butter

Be sure both ingredients are at room temperature. Add honey slowly to softened butter and beat with a fork. When well blended, heat gently. Serve hot. Makes 1½ cups.

WALNUT—The edible nut of the fruit of the walnut tree. The most commonly

Waffles

known walnut is the English, or Persian, walnut, *Juglans regia.* This hard-shelled nut has a wrinkled white kernel with two very irregularly shaped halves covered with a light brown skin. The shell is thin and light tan; it is made up of two distinct halves. In the United States this species of walnut is generally called a California walnut. The black walnut, *J. nigra,* a native American nut, has a dark brown, deeply ridged shell covering a strongly flavored kernel. Butternuts, or white walnuts, *J. cinerea,* are also native to America.

The English walnut was known in Old English as *wealhhnutu,* which meant "Welsh" or "foreign nut." It had been cultivated for centuries in the Mediterranean region, from which it spread to temperate zones everywhere. Pliny the Elder reported in the 1st century A.D. that the tree had been introduced from Persia; it was known in Italy in the 1st century B.C. according to an earlier writer. Many varieties now exist. One in France is called the Titmouse walnut because the shell is so thin that birds, and especially the titmouse, can crack it open and eat the kernel. Walnut oil, expressed from the kernel, is used in France like olive oil.

The Indians of North America relied heavily on butternuts and black walnuts for their food. Butternut oil was used as a seasoning; the kernel thickened and flavored their meat and vegetable dishes. Both black walnuts and butternuts, as the Indians knew, are better when used in combination with other foods than when eaten plain. The black walnut meat is extremely oily, which adds to its food value but does not make it too tasty if eaten fresh. After being stored for a while it dries out and the flavor improves. These nuts are widely used in cakes, cookies, confections, and ice cream.

English walnuts are one of the most popular of all nuts for eating out-of-hand. Walnut meats also make a delicious addition to all sorts of cakes and cookies.

Today, the United States leads the world in walnut production; other countries which grow them include France, Italy, Turkey, Iran, Yugoslavia, Rumania, China, and India.

Availability and Purchasing Guide—Nuts and nutmeats are available year round in bulk, in film bags, and in vacuum cans. They are graded according to variety, size, and grade. Variety is determined by shape, hardness of shell, and flavor. Sizes in the shell and shelled are indicated by the number in an ounce or by the diameter of smallest and largest nuts or nutmeats. There are three sizes of walnuts:

large, medium, and babies. Grade is based on color and condition of nuts and nutmeats. When choosing walnuts in the shell, look for those which are clean and free from scars, cracks, or holes, and well filled, so the kernel does not rattle.

For full flavor and freshness, when choosing shelled walnuts, look for those which are plump and meaty, and crisp and brittle; limp shriveled nutmeats indicate staleness.

☐ 2 pounds in-shell walnuts = 1 pound shelled = 4 cups

Storage—Store in-shell walnuts in a cool dry place; store shelled walnuts, tightly covered, in the refrigerator or freezer. Walnuts remain fresh longer in the shell, in larger pieces, and uncooked.

☐ In shell, kitchen shelf: 2 to 3 months
☐ Shelled; or vacuum-packed, opened, refrigerator shelf: 6 months
☐ Shelled, refrigerator frozen-food compartment or freezer: 1 year
☐ Vacuum-packed, kitchen shelf: 1 year

Nutritive Food Values—Some protein, iron, and B vitamins. Walnuts are high in fat.

☐ English, 3½ ounces, shelled = 651 calories
☐ Black, 3½ ounces, shelled = 628 calories

Basic Preparation

☐ **To Shell**—Use nutcracker; the shell of California walnuts is thin and nutmeat removes easily. Black walnuts must be cracked with a hammer, and the meats picked out with a nut pick.
☐ **To Chop**—Use a long straight knife and wooden board, or a chopping bowl and chopper.
☐ **To Grind**—Use a special nut grinder, except for butters and paste, for which you should use a meat grinder or blender.
☐ **To Roast**—Spread walnuts in shallow baking pan; dot with butter (1 tablespoon for 2 cups walnuts). Bake in preheated moderate oven (350°F.) for about 20 minutes, or until golden, stirring occasionally. Spread on paper towels to cool.

HO T'AO CHI JING
(Walnut Chicken)
2 pounds chicken breasts
2 tablespoons cornstarch
2 egg whites, unbeaten
1 cup California walnut meats
¼ cup cooking oil
1 cup diced celery
1 can (5 ounces) water chestnuts, quartered
⅓ cup chicken bouillon
3 tablespoons soy sauce
1 tablespoon sherry
1 teaspoon sugar
3 slices of fresh gingerroot, minced

Remove chicken meat from bones and cut into ½-inch cubes. Mix 1 tablespoon cornstarch with 1 tablespoon water and

beat into egg whites with a fork. Add chicken and mix until each piece is coated. Boil walnuts in water to cover for 3 minutes. Drain and dry between paper towels. Deep fry in hot oil (375°F. on a frying thermometer) until golden-brown. Remove and keep warm. In another pan, heat oil. Add chicken, celery, and water chestnuts. Fry for 3 to 4 minutes. Mix bouillon, soy sauce, sherry, sugar, gingerroot, and 1 tablespoon cornstarch. Add to chicken mixture; cook, stirring, until thickened. Serve garnished with walnuts. Makes 4 to 6 servings.

WALNUT SHORTBREAD
1 cup soft butter
1 cup confectioners' sugar
1 teaspoon vanilla extract
2⅓ cups sifted all-purpose flour
Walnut halves

Cream butter. Gradually beat in sugar. Add vanilla extract. With hands work in flour and knead until bowl is clean. Chill thoroughly. Roll out on lightly floured board to ½-inch thickness. Cut with 2-inch scalloped or other fancy cutter. Decorate with nuts. Bake on ungreased cookie sheets in preheated moderate oven (350°F.) for 20 to 25 minutes. Store airtight. Makes 24.

BLACK-WALNUT BRITTLE
In saucepan mix ½ cup light corn syrup, 2 cups sugar, ⅓ cup water, ¼ teaspoon salt, and 3 tablespoons butter. Bring to boil, stirring until sugar is dissolved. Add 1 cup coarsely broken black walnuts and cook, stirring almost constantly, until a small amount of mixture separates into hard brittle threads when dropped into very cold water (300°F. on a candy thermometer). Add 1 teaspoon vanilla extract and pour onto buttered cookie sheet to cool. When cold, break into pieces. Makes about 1¼ pounds.

WALNUT BONBONS
⅓ cup soft butter
⅓ cup light corn syrup
½ teaspoon salt
1 teaspoon vanilla extract
4½ cups (1 pound) sifted confectioners' sugar
Red and green food coloring
California walnut halves

Blend first 4 ingredients; mix in sugar and knead until blended. Divide mixture into halves and color one half red and the other green. Shape mixtures into 1-inch balls and press a walnut half on each side of each ball. Store airtight. Makes 4 dozen.

BLACK-WALNUT WAFERS
2 eggs
1 cup firmly packed light brown sugar
⅔ cup sifted all-purpose flour
¼ teaspoon each of salt and baking powder
1 cup finely chopped black walnuts

Beat eggs until light. Add sugar and beat

until thick. Add sifted dry ingredients and nuts; mix well. Drop by scant teaspoonfuls onto greased cookie sheets. Bake in preheated hot oven (400°F.) for 5 minutes. Let stand for ½ minute before removing. Makes about 5 dozen.

CHOCOLATE BUTTERSCOTCH BARS

⅔ cup shortening, melted
2¼ cups firmly packed light brown sugar
3 eggs
2¾ cups sifted all-purpose flour
½ teaspoon salt
2½ teaspoons baking powder
1 cup chopped California walnuts
1 cup (6 ounces) semisweet chocolate pieces
1 teaspoon vanilla extract

Add shortening to sugar and mix well. Add eggs, one at a time, beating well after each addition. Add sifted dry ingredients, nuts, chocolate, and vanilla. Spread in greased pan (15 x 10 x 1 inch). Bake in preheated moderate oven (350°F.) for about 25 minutes. While warm, cut into 50 bars.

HUNGARIAN WALNUT BARS

2¼ cups sifted all-purpose flour
¼ teaspoon salt
1 cup granulated sugar
1 cup soft butter
2 egg yolks
1 tablespoon brandy
4 cups finely chopped California walnuts
½ cup firmly packed light brown sugar
1½ teaspoons ground cinnamon
4 unbeaten egg whites
Confectioners' sugar (optional)

Sift flour, salt, and ½ cup of the granulated sugar. Blend in butter; add egg yolks and brandy. Pat evenly into greased and floured pan (15 x 10 x 1 inch). Bake 15 minutes. In heavy saucepan put remaining granulated sugar, the walnuts, brown sugar, cinnamon, and egg whites. Cook, stirring, over low heat until sugars dissolve. Increase heat and cook until mixture no longer clings to sides of pan. Spread on baked mixture. Return to oven for 15 minutes longer. Cool slightly. Cut into bars 1 x 3 inches. Dust cookies with confectioners' sugar, if desired. Store in airtight container. Makes 50.

SERBIAN WALNUT STRIPS

4½ cups (1 pound) walnuts, ground
1 cup granulated sugar
1 teaspoon fresh lemon juice
4 egg whites, unbeaten
¾ cup confectioners' sugar

Mix walnuts and granulated sugar. Add lemon juice and 3 egg whites. Knead until mixture sticks together. Pat out on sugared board to rectangle 3 inches wide and ½ inch thick. Beat remaining egg white stiff and gradually beat in confectioners' sugar. Spread over walnut mixture. Cut into strips 1½ x ¾ inch. Arrange cookies in rows on well-greased cookie sheets. Bake in preheated very slow oven (200°F.) for 20 minutes. Makes 6 dozen.

WALNUT CRESCENTS

1 cup soft butter or margarine
Confectioners' sugar
1½ teaspoons water
2 teaspoons vanilla extract
2 cups unsifted all-purpose flour
1 cup chopped California walnuts

Cream butter and ¼ cup confectioners' sugar. Add remaining ingredients and mix well. Shape into rolls about ½ inch in diameter and cut into 1-inch pieces. Put on ungreased cookie sheets and pull ends down slightly to form crescent shapes. Bake in preheated moderate oven (375°F.) for about 15 minutes. While warm, roll in confectioners' sugar; roll again when cool. Makes about 6 dozen walnut crescents.

BAKED BONBONS

2½ cups (1 pound) pitted dates
2 cups (½ pound) shelled California walnuts
3 egg whites
¾ cup sugar
1 teaspoon vanilla extract
Food coloring

Grind dates and nuts together twice and shape into 72 small balls. Beat egg whites until they begin to hold their shape. Gradually add sugar and continue beating until mixture is stiff but not dry. Add vanilla and divide into halves. Tint half pink and half green. With a teaspoon roll date balls in meringue and put on greased cookie sheets. Swirl top of each. Bake in preheated very slow oven (250°F.) for 30 minutes. Makes 6 dozen.

WASSAIL—A drink once popular in England for special occasions such as Christmas and Twelfth Night. It consisted of ale or wine flavored with spices. Other ingredients such as toast, sugar, and especially roasted apples were added.

A wassail was originally a toast made to someone's health or good luck as you gave him a cup of wine. The word came from the Old Norse *ves heill,* or "Be in good health." Wassail bowls and wassailing were Old English festive customs. The wassail bowl was surrounded with merriment. Often at Christmas, groups of Christmas carolers would go a-wassailing, traveling from house to house caroling their hosts in return for a cup of the delicious wassail. In those days the custom of singing was so connected with the drink itself that a wassail meant a carol. It is hard to tell whether more drinking or singing went on.

OLD-TIME WASSAIL BOWL

6 baking apples
½ cup sugar
Whole cloves
½ teaspoon each of ground cinnamon and nutmeg
1 tablespoon grated lemon rind
2 quarts muscatel
4 eggs, separated

Core apples and peel down to about 1 inch from the stem end. Fill cavities with the sugar and bake in preheated moderate oven (350°F.) for 30 minutes to 1 hour, or until tender but still firm. Time will depend on kind of apples. When done, stud apples with whole cloves. Add ground spices and lemon rind to the wine and heat in top part of a double boiler over hot water. Beat egg whites until stiff. Then beat egg yolks until thick and lemon-colored. Fold egg yolks into whites. Put apples in bottom of wassail (punch) bowl. Add egg mixture to wine and pour over apples. Serve in warm mugs. Makes 2 quarts, plus the apples.

WASSAIL BOWL

4 quarts apple cider
1 cup firmly packed brown sugar
1 can (6 ounces) frozen lemon-juice concentrate
1 can (6 ounces) frozen orange-juice concentrate
6 each of whole cloves and allspice
1 tablespoon ground nutmeg
24 cinnamon sticks

Put cider, sugar, and fruit juices (undiluted) in kettle. Tie cloves and allspice in a small cheesecloth bag. Add to cider with nutmeg. Cover and simmer for 20 minutes. Remove spice bag. Serve beverage hot in mugs with a cinnamon stick in each mug. Makes twenty-four 6-ounce mugs.

WATER—Water is one of the most essential substances on the face of the earth, if not the most important. Technically it is a chemical compound, H_2O, which consists of two atoms of hydrogen united with one atom of oxygen in every water molecule. Water is present in a solid state as ice or snow; as a liquid it is the water we know; in a gaseous state it is steam or water vapor. All vegetables and animals, certainly not excluding man, contain water. Man can live longer without food than he can without water.

Chemically pure water of two parts hydrogen and one part oxygen is obtainable only by filtration and distillation. It does not exist naturally. The purest water obtainable in natural form is rain water in places remote from human habitation, taken after the rain has been falling long enough to have cleared the atmosphere, or water obtained from melting snow that has fallen in the polar regions. Water in some mountain lakes resulting from melting snow and resting on impermeable rocks is also relatively pure.

Such water is known as "soft," in contrast to "hard" water which implies a mineral content of eight or more grains to the gallon. Minerals vary greatly.

Those most often found in hard water are lime and magnesia salts. These minerals are not harmful in any way and a small amount actually improves the flavor of the water. Soft water is often flat by contrast.

So called "pure water" provided by communities for drinking water is not pure in the chemical sense, but is uncontaminated by sewage. In large cities, chlorine is sometimes added to insure further protection.

Spring water is frequently regarded as the highest type of pure water because of its bright and sparkling appearance. This is due primarily, however, to the presence of minerals. When minerals are present in sufficient amount to be of alleged medicinal value, the water is classed as mineral water.

Distilled water is ordinary water filtered, boiled in vacuum boilers to remove volatile organic matter, converted into steam in stills, and finally condensed and aerated. Aeration removes the flat taste of the distilled product. This water is free of salts and organic matter. It should be stored in siphons or corked bottles to insure its continued purity.

Water can be sterilized at home by boiling, thus killing all organic matter. It, too, should be carefully stored.

Spring water and mineral water are widely available; bottled and distilled water can be bought in small quantities in drugstores. Electric water distillers are available for homes. They remove taste and odor-producing minerals and salts, and eliminate fluorides and detergents. Water-tap filters which remove objectionable taste, odor, discoloration, and cloudiness are also available. Activated charcoal within the filter removes chlorine, sulphur, rust, scale, and algae.

Electric water coolers of half-gallon size are available for home use, as well as water containers with spigots for refrigerators. These are helpful in conserving water since they eliminate the prolonged running of tap water to obtain a cool drink.

WATER CHESTNUT—The fruit of a water plant of the genus *Trapa* with floating leaves and small white flowers. The nutlike fruit kernel resembles a true chest-

nut in shape and color, but is crunchy in texture. Native to Asia, it is widely used in Oriental cookery. Water chestnuts can be used in poultry, meat, seafood, and egg dishes, and add a pleasant crispness when combined with soft foods.

Canned water chestnuts are widely available in the United States and can be bought in most food stores. Pickled water chestnuts are also available.

Caloric Value

☐ 3½ ounces, raw = 79 calories

DUCK HASH

¼ cup butter or margarine
1 small onion, chopped
2 cups diced cooked potatoes
2 cups chopped cooked duckling
½ cup chopped water chestnuts
½ cup diced green pepper
½ cup consommé
1 teaspoon salt
¼ teaspoon pepper
½ teaspoon grated lemon rind
¼ cup heavy cream
Buttered soft bread crumbs

Melt butter, add onion, and cook until golden. Add potatoes and brown lightly. Add next 8 ingredients and cook for several minutes. Put in shallow baking dish and sprinkle with crumbs. Bake in preheated moderate oven (350°F.) for about 30 minutes. Makes 4 servings.

ROAST PORK WITH CHINESE VEGETABLES

¼ teaspoon salt
½ cup diced mushrooms
½ pound Chinese cabbage, diced
¾ cup diced water chestnuts
¼ cup diced bamboo shoots
12 snow-pea pods (frozen can be used)
¼ cup diced celery
¼ cup water
2 cups diced roast pork
1 teaspoon cornstarch
Dash of pepper
¼ teaspoon sugar
½ teaspoon monosodium glutamate
¼ cup blanched almonds, toasted

Put salt in hot, well-greased skillet. Add mushrooms, cabbage, water chestnuts, bamboo shoots, snow-pea pods, and celery. Stir-fry for 30 seconds. Add the water, cover, and cook for 2 minutes. Add the roast pork and stir. Blend cornstarch with a little water and add to first mixture with pepper, sugar, and monosodium glutamate. Cook, stirring, for 30 seconds. Put in serving dish and garnish with almonds. Makes 4 servings.

WATER-CHESTNUT AND RICE STUFFING

1 medium onion, minced
1½ cups diced celery
⅓ cup butter or margarine
1⅓ cups cooked rice
1 cup chopped water chestnuts
2 teaspoons grated fresh gingerroot or other spice or herb to taste
Salt and pepper to taste

Cook onion and celery in the butter for

5 minutes. Add remaining ingredients and mix lightly. Use as stuffing for duck. Makes about 4 cups.

WATERCRESS—This is the most popular and widely eaten of the cresses, plants of the mustard family which includes peppergrass or garden cress, winter cress or rocket, and spring or Belle Isle cress. All have crisp green leaves and a pungent, rather bitter taste, each variety with its own characteristics. Peppergrass is sometimes sprinkled over such dishes as beet soup; the more bitter winter and spring cresses should be cooked with another herb like spinach to cut their strong flavor. All the cresses may be boiled as potherbs; and all of them are delicious in salads, usually with other greens. Minced cresses are sprinkled on cream soups, or used minced to garnish vegetables. Watercress, the most widely available of the cresses, is used as garnish for canapés and seafood appetizers; as garnish for meats, poultry, and fish; minced and blended into cottage- or cream-cheese spreads or omelets and egg dishes; minced and added to biscuit dough or piecrust; used like sorrel; sprinkled over carrots, cauliflower, potatoes, green beans, and sweet vegetables.

Watercress gets its name because it grows in cold running water. It is a native of temperate Europe, and is naturalized in the brooks and ponds of North America. The word "cress" alone has a long history; it is perhaps related to the Latin word for grass, and even further back to the Sanskrit verb meaning "to eat," especially gnawing or nibbling. It would then be a distantly removed linguistic cousin to the word "grass." Humans, having only one stomach, cannot digest grass, but cress has long been eaten by man.

The Greeks and Romans both esteemed watercress. The old Greek proverb, "Eat cress and learn more wit," was taken seriously by the Romans who ate it with vinegar as a remedy for deranged minds. Later, cress's reputation for curing madness diminished, but it was thought to have other miraculous qualities. One Renaissance Englishman wrote: "The eating of water cress doth restore the wanted bloom to the cheeks of old-young ladies." John Evelyn, the 17th-century Englishman of letters who wrote a book about salads, decided that watercress was "best for raw and cold Stomachs, but nourish little." Evelyn was right about many things but wrong about watercress. Modern nutritionists recommend its use for its high vitamin content, as well as its goodly amounts of iron.

Availability—Watercress is available all year round with peak supplies in May,

June, and July.

Purchasing Guide—It is sold in small bunches. Look for fresh deep greens and crisp stems with no yellowing or wilting.

Storage—Store away from light and heat. To keep, wash well, shake water from the leaves, and refrigerate in a tightly covered jar.

☐ Refrigerator shelf: 7 days

Nutritive Food Values—A good source of vitamins A and C and supplies a variety of minerals including iron if eaten in large amounts.

☐ 3½ ounces = 19 calories.

Basic Preparation—Wash thoroughly in several changes of water to remove all traces of sand. Remove all tough stems and wilted portions. When cooked, it should be cooked for a very short time.

CREAM-OF-CORN-AND-CRESS SOUP

    1 small onion, chopped
    ¼ cup butter or margarine
    1½ cups cut fresh corn
    1½ teaspoons suet
    ½ teaspoon sugar
    1 cup water
    1½ cups milk
    ⅛ teaspoon white pepper
    1 cup chopped watercress
    2 egg yolks, beaten
    ½ cup light cream
      Paprika

Sauté onion in butter in saucepan for 2 or 3 minutes. Add corn, suet, sugar, and water. Bring to boil and simmer, covered, for about 10 minutes. Add milk, pepper, and cress; cook for 2 or 3 minutes longer. Force mixture through a food mill or purée in a blender. Add egg yolks and cream; heat gently. Serve with a sprinkling of paprika. Makes about 1 quart or 4 servings.

CHICKEN AND WATERCRESS SOUP

Heat together 1 can (10½ ounces) chicken soup, 1 can water, and 1 vegetable bouillon cube. Stir until cube dissolves. Add ½ cup chopped watercress. Serve immediately. Makes 2 or 3 servings.

WATERCRESS SALAD

To a bowlful of freshly washed and crisped watercress in bite-size pieces, add 2 or 3 hard-cooked eggs, peeled and sliced. Add 2 or 3 chopped fresh green onions and salt and pepper to taste. Top with 1 or 2 tablespoons olive oil to taste. Toss with a dash or so of wine vinegar. Makes 4 servings.

WATERCRESS SANDWICH

Mix potted meat with chopped watercress and celery. Moisten with mayonnaise or salad dressing.

SOUR-CREAM WATERCRESS SAUCE

    ½ cup salad dressing
    ½ cup dairy sour cream
    ½ teaspoon salt
    ¼ teaspoon pepper

      Few drops of hot pepper sauce
    ½ cup chopped watercress

Mix together all ingredients. Makes about 1½ cups sauce.

WATERMELON—A member of the gourd family, native to Africa, and most commonly a spherical fruit with pink or red flesh and many seeds. There are many varieties among which are yellow and white watermelons as well as the red. Seeds may be white, red, brown, black, green, or speckled. The rind is usually dark green. Watermelons average twenty-four to forty pounds, although there are some small two- to ten-pound varieties, and even some monstrously large ones. The flesh is sweet with a high water content.

In the United States watermelons are a universally popular summer dessert, but in the dry countries of Africa and in Near Eastern countries such as Iraq, watermelons are not confined to the dessert course. There they are an important staple food and an animal feed. They are especially valuable in countries where water is scarce, because they are such a thirst-quenching delight. In some parts of Asia the seeds are roasted and eaten as snacks. Americans prize their watermelon-rind pickles; the Orientals preserve entire halves of watermelon in salt or brine.

Watermelons were cultivated by the ancient Egyptians. The warmer parts of Russia and the Near East have long been able to grow these melons. Eventually, with many other foods, their culture spread to Europe. The botanists of the 16th and 17th centuries described all the varieties of watermelon we know today.

Watermelons were grown in this country quite early in its history. They were found in Massachusetts gardens as early as 1629, and in Florida not too long afterward. Watermelons are most successfully raised in a warm climate, and they flourish throughout the South of this country.

Availability—Watermelons are sold whole, halved, quartered, or by the slice. They are available in May, June, July, and August.

Pickled watermelon rind and dried watermelon seeds are also available.

Frozen melon-ball mixtures which include watermelon are available.

Purchasing Guide—Watermelons should be symmetrical in shape and firm to the touch. The shape varies from long oval to small cannonball. The skin is smooth with a deep green to gray color with a yellowish underside. The flesh is red with black seeds dispersed throughout.

Storage—Wrap cut surfaces in wax paper.

Use within 1 or 2 days.

☐ Refrigerator shelf: 1 to 2 days

Nutritive Food Values—A good source of vitamin A and a fair source of vitamin C.

☐ 3½ ounces = 26 calories

Basic Preparation—Chill before serving. Cut into wedges or cubes, removing seeds. Serve with fresh lime or lemon juice, if desired.

FROSTY WATERMELON SOUP

    1 envelope unflavored gelatin
    ¼ cup cold water
    6 cups diced fresh watermelon
    ¼ cup sugar
    ⅓ cup fresh lime juice
    ¼ teaspoon salt
      Fresh mint sprigs

Soften gelatin in cold water. Place over hot water to melt until ready to use. Press watermelon through a sieve. Add sugar, lime juice, and salt. Stir in melted gelatin. Chill until mixture has thickened slightly, 3 to 4 hours. Serve in chilled bouillon cups. Garnish with sprigs of fresh mint. Makes 1 quart, or 5 servings.

MOLDED WATERMELON SALAD

    1 box (3 ounces) watermelon-flavored gelatin
    1 cup hot water
    3 tablespoons fresh lemon juice
    ¼ cup fresh orange juice
    ½ cup muscatel
    2 cups diced watermelon
      Salad greens
      Dairy sour cream

Dissolve gelatin in hot water. Add next 3 ingredients. Chill until slightly thickened. Fold in melon and pour into 1½-quart mold. Chill until firm. Unmold on greens: serve with sour cream. Makes 6 servings.

RIPE WATERMELON PICKLE

    4 quarts diced red watermelon, seeded
    5 cups sugar
    ¼ teaspoon salt
    ½ cup cider vinegar
    2 slices of lemon
    1 tablespoon cracked whole cinnamon
    1 teaspoon whole cloves

Put diced melon in colander and with the hands squeeze out as much juice as possible. Let drain for 1 hour. Put melon, sugar, salt, vinegar, and lemon in large heavy kettle. Add spices tied in cheesecloth bag. Cook slowly for 50 to 60 minutes. Stir occasionally to prevent sticking. Pack at once into hot sterilized jars and seal. Makes about 2 pints.

WATERMELON-LIME COOLER

Take one-fourth of a good-size watermelon, and remove all seeds. Pound flesh or press through a food mill to remove juice. There should be about 3 cups. Add the juice of 1 large lime, and sugar to taste. Put a cube of watermelon and a slice of lime in each of 4 tall glasses. Add ice cubes, and pour watermelon-juice mixture over ice. Makes 4 servings.

Watermelon-Lime Cooler

SPICED WATERMELON HONEY
3 pounds watermelon rind
1 cup water
6 cups sugar
3 lemon slices
3 pieces of whole dried gingerroot
½ teaspoon whole cloves
2 cinnamon sticks
¼ teaspoon salt

Remove all green outer rind and red meat from watermelon rind; discard. Force remaining rind through food chopper, using coarse blade. Measure; there should be 6 cups. Put in kettle with water. Cook slowly, uncovered, for 25 minutes, or until melon is translucent. Add sugar and lemon. Tie spices in a cheesecloth bag and add with salt to first mixture. Cook slowly, stirring frequently, for 1 hour, or until thickened. Remove spice bag; ladle mixture into hot sterilized jars; seal. Makes 2½ pints.

WATERMELON-MARASCHINO PICKLE
2 pounds (about 2½ quarts) prepared watermelon rind
1 tablespoon powdered slaked lime (buy in drugstore)
Water
Cider vinegar
1 teaspoon salt
2½ pounds (5 cups) sugar
1 tablespoon each of whole allspice and cloves
6 small pieces of cinnamon stick
1 jar (4 to 6 ounces) maraschino cherries, drained

To prepare rind, pare and remove all green and pink portions from watermelon rind. Cut into 1-inch pieces and soak for 3 hours in lime dissolved in 1 quart water. Drain rind; cover with fresh cold water and cook, covered, for 1 hour, or until tender. Drain and cover with a weak vinegar (1 cup to 2 cups water) and let stand overnight. Drain. In preserving kettle bring to boil 3 cups vinegar, the salt, ½ cup water, the sugar, and the spices tied in a piece of cheesecloth. Cover and let stand for 1 hour. Add watermelon and simmer, covered, for 2 hours. Add cherries about 20 minutes before pickle is done. Discard spice bag and spoon pickle at once into hot sterilized jars; cover with boiling syrup. Seal jars. Makes 4 pints.

WATERMELON SHERBET
3 cups watermelon juice
½ cup sugar
⅛ teaspoon salt
1 envelope unflavored gelatin
Juice of 1 lemon

Mix first 3 ingredients. Remove about ¼ cup to small saucepan. Soften gelatin in juice in saucepan. Dissolve over hot water or very low heat. Add with lemon juice to first mixture. Freeze in crank-type freezer. Makes about 1 quart.
Note: To make juice, force watermelon pulp through a food mill or sieve. To get 3 cups juice, you will need about one-fourth of a good-size watermelon.

WATERMELON ALMOND SHERBET
1 watermelon
2 tablespoons cornstarch
1 teaspoon almond extract
⅓ cup sugar
½ teaspoon salt
1 teaspoon grated lemon peel

Remove the rind and 1 inch of white from melon and put red meat through food chopper, accumulating 4 cups pulp and juice. In saucepan over low heat cook the other ingredients. When well blended, stir in melon and restore to cooking temperature. Beat thoroughly and freeze. Makes 8 servings.

WEDDING CAKE—A white cake, often with spices and candied peel added, and flavored with almond extract, traditionally baked in tiered layers, covered with white frosting, and decorated. The first piece is supposed to be cut by the bride and groom together. This cake was formerly called the bride's cake. The groom's cake was a cake made with a dark batter, having molasses, raisins, candied fruits, nuts, and spices in it. Nowadays, the kind of cake served is a matter of choice. Formerly both bride's and groom's cakes were offered.

WEDDING CAKE
(Bride's Cake)
5¼ cups sifted cake flour
6 teaspoons baking powder
2 teaspoons salt
3 cups sugar
8 egg whites
1 cup shortening at room temperature
2 cups milk
1 teaspoon almond extract
1½ teaspoons orange extract
Ornamental Frosting

Mix flour, baking powder, salt, and 2 cups sugar. Beat egg whites in a large bowl until foamy. Gradually add remaining sugar, beating only until meringue will hold up in soft peaks. Stir shortening in mixing bowl just to soften. Sift in dry ingredients. Add 1½ cups of the milk and the flavorings. Mix until all flour is dampened. Then beat for 2 minutes at low speed in electric mixer. Add remaining milk and meringue and beat for 1 minute longer in mixer. Line bottoms of 1 square pan (10 x 10 x 2 inches) and 2 square pans (8 x 8 x 2 inches each) with paper. Pour batter into pans to equal depths. Bake in preheated slow oven (325°F.) for 45 minutes, or until done. Cool on racks. When cold, brush cakes to remove any loose crumbs. Trim one of the 8-inch cakes to make a 5-inch square. Put 10-inch cake on a large flat tray or plate. Spread top and sides with a thin layer of Ornamental Frosting. Cover top of cake smoothly with more Frosting.

Center 8-inch cake on top of 10-inch cake and frost. Center 5-inch cake on 8-inch cake. Frost. Then spread Frosting over entire cake to give a flat, even base for decorating. Force remaining Frosting through a pastry tube to make flowers, garlands, etc. Makes 50 servings.

Ornamental Frosting
½ cup soft butter or margarine
½ teaspoon salt
12 cups (3 pounds) sifted confectioners' sugar
5 egg whites, unbeaten
¼ cup light cream (about)
2 teaspoons vanilla extract

Cream butter. Add salt and part of the sugar gradually, blending after each addition. Add remaining sugar, alternately with the egg whites first, then with the cream, until of the right consistency for spreading. Beat after each addition until smooth. Add vanilla, and blend. (While frosting cake, keep bowl of frosting covered with a damp cloth to prevent excessive evaporation.) Makes 5 cups, or enough to frost one 10 x 10 x 2-inch cake and two 8 x 8 x 2-inch cakes and to decorate.
Note: Favors are occasionally put into the bride's cake: a thimble, tiny horseshoe, ring, button, or other favorite silver charms should first be wrapped in wax paper. Make small cuts at random in cake and insert charms before frosting cake.

WEDDING CAKE
(Groom's Cake)
4 cups sifted all-purpose flour
1 teaspoon baking powder
½ teaspoon each of ground cloves, cinnamon, and mace
2 cups butter or margarine
2¼ cups (1 pound) firmly packed brown sugar
10 eggs, well beaten
½ pound each of candied cherries and pineapple
1 pound dates, seeded and sliced
1 pound each of seedless raisins and currants
½ pound citron, thinly sliced
¼ pound each of candied orange and lemon peel
2 cups chopped nuts
1 cup each of honey and molasses
½ cup cider

Sift flour, baking powder, and spices together 3 times. Cream butter. Gradually add sugar; cream until light and fluffy. Add eggs, fruits, peels, nuts, honey, molasses, and cider. Gradually add sifted dry ingredients, beating after each addition until blended. Spoon into 3 loaf pans (10 x 5 x 3 inches each), greased, lined with heavy paper, and greased again. Bake in preheated very slow oven (250°F.) for 3½ to 4 hours. Makes 80 servings.
Note: Half of cake is often served at the wedding reception and the remainder put in gift boxes for the guests to take home.

WEIGH—In cookery to weigh means to calculate accurate amounts of required ingredients by the use of scales. The recipes in this Encyclopedia are based upon measurements rather than weights, and while household scales can be helpful in cookery, they are not absolutely essential. However, one of the areas in which they are almost a necessity is in canning, where amounts of ingredients in recipes are often given in weights. Scales are also helpful in the preparation of food for special diets.

EQUIPMENT

A number of different models of household scales are available. They are of two types generally: those which use weights, and the spring type. The first are the more accurate; and for this reason, weight scales are the ones used commercially. Both types of scales come in various sizes. Gram scales are a type of weight scale and are helpful for special diets. Weight scales which weigh both ounces and grams are now available.

AVOIRDUPOIS WEIGHT

Unit	Weight	Metric Equivalent
Pound	16 ounces or 7000 grains	0.453 kilograms
Ounce	16 drams or 437.5 grains	28.349 grams
Dram	0.0625 ounces or 27.343 grains	1.771 grams
Grain	0.0023 ounces or 0.036 drams	0.0648 grams

WELSH RABBIT or RAREBIT—A popular dish of melted cheese poured over toast. Beer, ale, wine, or even milk may be added to the rabbit. When topped with a poached egg it is called a Buck or Golden Buck.

WELSH RABBIT

½ pound sharp Cheddar cheese, diced or crumbled
⅓ cup milk
¼ teaspoon powdered mustard
1 teaspoon Worcestershire
   Dash of cayenne
1 egg, well beaten
   Toast or crackers

Put cheese in a heavy skillet and melt over very, very low heat, stirring constantly. As cheese melts, gradually add milk, stirring to blend. Add seasonings. Then add egg and cook, stirring, over very, very low heat until smooth and thickened. Serve on toast. Makes 4 to 6 servings.

WELSH RABBIT WITH BEER

2 tablespoons butter or margarine
1 pound sharp Cheddar cheese, shredded
½ teaspoon powdered mustard
   Dash of cayenne
½ teaspoon salt
1 teaspoon Worcestershire
½ cup beer, ale, or milk
2 eggs, slightly beaten
8 slices of toast
   Parsley

Melt butter in top part of double boiler or chafing dish over direct heat. Add cheese, and heat, stirring occasionally, until cheese is melted. Put over boiling water, add seasonings, and pour in the liquid mixed with eggs. Cook until thick, stirring frequently. Serve on toast with garnish of parsley. Makes 4 servings.

GOLDEN BUCK

½ pound sharp process American Cheddar cheese
¾ cup light cream or evaporated milk
1 teaspoon Worcestershire
½ teaspoon prepared mustard
   Toast
4 eggs, poached

Melt cheese in top part of double boiler over hot water. Gradually add cream, stirring constantly. Add seasonings. Pour over toast and top each slice with a poached egg. Makes 4 servings.

WEIGHTS AND EQUIVALENT MEASURES OF COMMON FOODS

BEANS, dried navy: 1 pound=2⅓ cups uncooked=6 cups cooked
BEANS, dried kidney: 1 pound=2½ cups uncooked=6¾ cups cooked
BEANS, dried Lima: 1 pound=2½ cups uncooked=6 cups cooked
BUTTER, unwhipped: 1 pound or 4 sticks =2 cups
BUTTER, whipped: ¼ pound or 1 stick =½ cup
CHEESE, cottage: ½ pound=1 cup
CHEESE, cream: 3 ounces=6 tablespoons
CHEESE, grated: 4 ounces=1 cup
CHESTNUTS: 1½ pounds in-the-shell= 1 pound shelled
CHICKEN: 3½ pounds drawn chicken= 2 cups cooked, diced
CHOCOLATE: 1 ounce=1 square
COCOA: 1 pound=4 cups
COCONUT, finely grated: 3½ ounces= 1 cup
COFFEE: 1 pound=5 cups
CORNMEAL: 1 pound=3 cups
DATES: 1 pound=2½ cups pitted, cut
FLOUR, all-purpose: 4 ounces=1 cup sifted
FLOUR, cake: 4 ounces=1 cup plus 2 tablespoons, sifted
FLOUR, whole-wheat: 7 ounces=1 cup
MACARONI: 8 ounces=2 cups uncooked =4 to 5 cups cooked
MEAT, beef: 1 pound=3 cups cooked minced
MEAT, beef: 1 pound uncooked=2 cups ground

MUSHROOMS: ½ pound sliced raw=2½ cups
NOODLES: 2⅔ ounces=1 cup uncooked =1 cup cooked
OATS, rolled, quick-cooking: 1 pound= 5⅔ cups uncooked
OIL: 2 cups=1 pound
PEANUTS: 1 pound in-the-shell=⅔ pound of nutmeats
PEANUTS: 1 pound shelled=3¼ cups
PEAS, dry: 1 pound, cooked=2½ cups
PEAS, split: 1 pound=5½ cups cooked
PEAS, split: 1 pound, uncooked=2 cups uncooked=5 cups cooked
PECANS: 1 pound in-the-shell=½ pound nutmeats
PECANS: 1 pound shelled=4¼ cups
POTATOES: 1 pound=3 medium
POTATOES: 1 pound raw, unpeeled=2 cups cooked, mashed
RAISINS, seedless whole: 1 pound=2¾ cups
RICE: 1 pound=2½ cups uncooked=8 cups cooked
SPAGHETTI: 8 ounces=2½ cups uncooked=4 to 5 cups cooked
SUGAR, granulated: 1 pound=2¼ cups
SUGAR, brown, firmly packed: 1 pound =2¼ cups
SUGAR, confectioners': 1 pound=3½ cups
WALNUTS: 1 pound in-the-shell=½ pound of nutmeats
WALNUTS: 1 pound shelled=4½ cups
YEAST: 1 package active dry yeast=¼ ounce or 2 teaspoons

CAN SIZES

Industry Term	Approximate Net Weight	Approximate Cups
6 ounce	6 ounces	¾
8 ounce	8 ounces	1
Picnic	10½ to 12 ounces	1¼
12 ounce	12 ounces	1½
No. 300	14 to 16 ounces	1¾
No. 303	16 to 17 ounces	2
No. 2	1 pound, 4 ounces or 1 pint, 2 fluid ounces	2½
No. 2½	1 pound, 13 ounces	3½
No. 3 cylinder	3 pounds, 3 ounces or 1 quart, 14 fluid ounces	5¾
No. 10	6½ to 7 pounds, 5 ounces	12 to 13

FROZEN FOOD PACKAGES

Vegetables	9 to 16 ounces
Fruits	10 to 16 ounces
Canned Frozen Fruits	13½ to 16 ounces
Frozen Juice Concentrates	6 and 12 ounces
Soups	10 ounces

WESTERN COOKERY

by Idwal Jones

The Pacific Coast, like ancient Gaul, has been divided into three parts: California, Oregon, and Washington. California's sea frontage runs upward for 780 miles, or roughly the distance from the toe of Italy to the heart of Sweden. Its lower zone, from the Mexican border up to Santa Barbara, is arid, but irrigation has long made it a copious producer of edibles of almost every variety. It yields oranges, lemons, grapefruit, olives, almonds, dates, avocados, and other subtropical fruits and vegetables.

The zone has had its own traditional cuisine that began with the settlement of the Spaniards in the late 1700's, and the planting of grapevines by friars in their mission gardens at San Diego.

The Spanish and Mexican influence on tastes in food are perceptible on every hand. The ubiquitous *frijoles,* and the beans' accompaniment, the hot chili peppers, red, green, or black, are grown in vast amounts. Also the inevitable tomato, which was widely eaten here when elsewhere in the country it was shunned as the "poisonous" love apple.

Southern Californians have a deep-rooted fondness for barbecues, with meat grilled outdoors, served with thin fried disks of cornmeal paste known as tortillas, and as enchiladas when rolled up with cheese and a fiery stuffing. These are the customary dishes for social gatherings of every kind even at fashionable Santa Barbara, where the *Visitadores* go a-riding in Spanish garb to meet at their annual fiesta. Barbecues, a reminder of the old pastoral days, are clung to with a persistence that gives rise to some wonderment, for they are held at night, and their survival does seem curious, for in southern California dusk is followed by a drop in temperature, and the steaks must be whisked from the grill on sizzling-hot plates.

But the barbecue is as enduring as folklore, and nowadays has been improved by the serving of lettuce dressed with lemon juice, olive oil, and a topping of grated cheese.

A singularity of California is that in its great central valley, a flat corridor running between two ranges of mountains and seldom more than an hour and a half from the ocean, the climate is uniform throughout. Around Sacramento oranges may even be picked a fortnight earlier than at Los Angeles, 500 miles to the south. A warm dry plain this, where a succession of grain, sugar-beet and red-bean fields, also fruit orchards, and vineyards, their lines wheeling as they open and close like the ribs of a fan, stretch onward to infinity. At intervals occur pasturages where cattle graze in the blue shadow of scrub oaks, a touch faintly reminiscent of deer parks in England. Beyond this irrigated domain with its sparse settlements lies the delta area, another country. Here the San Joaquin and Sacramento Rivers and a plenitude of lesser streams pour their waters into a chain of warm inland seas. And when the Pacific sends in its chill, punctual tides, the area is cloaked with a dense gray mist that here, as in San Francisco, is known as the tule fog.

In the Delta area food problems are unknown. Its repertory of foodstuffs is extravagant. In its 200 square miles exist folk of several backgrounds, each with their own type of cookery. Sikhs in turbans work the asparagus, rice, and artichoke fields. Chinese work the oyster beds, catch shrimps, and raise hogs, poultry, and fat white ducks for San Francisco's large Chinatown. Their eating houses are to be found at nearly every waterside wharf. The Italian and Portuguese fishermen are also hunters of feathered game that swarm in for the winter. Basques keep the area supplied with dairy stuffs, beef, and also marsh-bred lambs that forage in the bulrush tracts.

Ark dwellers, many of whom own a parcel of land on which they raise pigs and vegetables, especially the tomato, often pull up anchor to follow the "run" of some particular fish: shad, striped bass, salmon-trout, or a score of other varieties. Sturgeon, protected by law for many years, may again be caught, although angling for it is no gentle pastime.

Sturgeon has gone into the folklore of this area where the big fish was harried out of existence by the crews of rival fishing syndicates. At the city markets sturgeon could be bought for eight cents the pound, and its roe sold at fifty cents the bucketful. In the Delta it was salted down in barrels, and the ranch cooks braised cuts of it in red wine, or salted it down as if it were pork. Those were the lush days, still recounted by the older fishermen when they huddle around the stove in some waterside tavern until the fog has lifted.

The Delta is fortunate in having so close to it a market such as San Francisco. It is uniquely cosmopolitan. From its earliest days it has known every type of foreign cookery and adopted them all.

To procure seafood, its fishing fleet ranges the coast from Mexico where it catches abalone and tuna, visits Monterey Bay where fish of a hundred and fifty kinds abound, goes up to Alaska for the salmon, halibut, and so forth, and returns with this bounty to its base at Fisherman's Wharf. This is a congeries of fish bazaars and eating places, simple or elaborate, and a popular haunt of the citizens. They like shellfish, the Pacific crab, clams, and oysters, which are found nearer home. The native oysters, coppery and the size of a nickel, are sold not by the dozen but by the hundred. But above all reigns the favorite, the mammoth Pacific crab. On the wharf it is boiled outside in large iron pots that steam like so many geysers.

Dominant here are the crab fishermen, Italians of the third generation, who belong to an ancient guild hardly less devoted to the opera than to the netting and the cooking of crab. The local fish stew, the aromatic *cioppino,* and a much-fancied crab salad, are but two of their specialties. One story has it that *cioppino* was first made here by a Genoese captain who, deserted by his crew in the frenzy of the gold rush, turned his ship into a restaurant.

The Italians also introduced the artichoke, using it in dishes like the *frittata di carciofini* and also as a salad. They prefer their artichokes, which are of the globe kind, in young and tender bud. For eighty years San Francisco has been getting them from Colma, a village founded by Italians, a brief run southward on the "artichoke coast."

Colma came into renown when the champion athletes of the early 1900's, finding that the sandy rim made an agreeable run, chose the village as their training quarters. At its weather-beaten hotel they consumed artichokes in a variety of dishes, with a grating of hard cheese.

In cookery of this order, as in France where the soundest cookery is basically peasant, wine is indispensable. The culinary use of it is widespread, for the state has twenty-four districts where wine making is a hereditary craft. Three among them are Sonoma, a drowsy Spanish pueblo, and St. Helena, early settled by Germans, whose wineries seem like ancient châteaux. The winery of the classic vineyard at Livermore, however, has a plain workaday look, with a roof of galvanized iron.

Oregon is half forest, and for the rest valleys, small in the mountains and large in the central part, drained by wide rushing streams like the Willamette, the Rogue, and the Hood. Most Oregonians are country-bred, of New England descent, and their market towns have an old-fashioned air. In the Cascade Range, with its innumerable lakes and rivers, the coaching days endured longer than elsewhere, for the railroads came in late.

A typical farm in the Cascade uplands is a ten-acre forest clearing, fenced in to keep out the wild broom and rhododendrons, various deer, and the black bear. The cows amble wherever they choose, as do the goats, all of the silky Angora strain. Berries of every description, cultivated or wild, and the gooseberry which is extremely rare in California, grow wantonly, their branches sagging to earth. Oregon raspberries, peculiarly fragrant and of giant size, are prized above all. Raspberry jelly is made in almost every rural kitchen, and large amounts of it somehow turn up at luxury shops in the East.

Come winter, the cranberry, grown in the extensive bogs along the coast, makes its fitting appearance, for the game season has opened. Hunters bring in quail, wild pigeons, bobtailed deer, rabbits, and strings of pheasants, both of Chinese and Mongolian origin. These birds are prolific breeders, and myriads of them are turned loose from the state hatcheries.

To ward off any dearth in the flow of apple pies, the family orchard is customarily planted to apples of various kinds, like the Gravenstein, Gascoyne's Scarlet, American Mother, the quince-flavored Grieve, Egremont Russet, and other favorites, each with its own time for ripening. The daughter of the household is usually the guardian. She may have cut her teeth on apples, taken a course in pomology, and learned pastry making in her mother's kitchen.

One young lady, thus trained, entered a pie competition at a fair in the Rogue Valley. Apple culture is almost a religion and judges of apple pie regard as anarchic any departure from the fixed and ancient ways of making it. This modern young lady waited nervously for the verdict, one novice among the contestants, thirty-five in all. She won the blue ribbon, the judges lauding her pie for its old-fashionedness.

To achieve that was her intention. And she had used a recipe used by an ancestress who had cooked pies for President John Adams.

For all the popularity of the apple, it must yield to that of the pear, of which Oregon grows five times as many. Cherries also, especially the plump Ox-heart and Kentish cherries, which go into ambrosial tarts, are much grown. Bees thrive on their blooms and in the mountains, covered for months with wild sage, oregano, and the various thymes, beekeeping is much practiced. You look for bee farms in small nooks, shielded from rough winds, where rosemary grows magnificently and often makes a hedge. Country people prize rosemary honey and chunks of it in the comb, dark, glistening, and flavorsome, make part of their breakfast.

In the Northwest are secluded tracts of intensely green meadowland watered by innumerable brooks splashing down from the Cascade Mountains. Cows wade deep through fields of sorrel, cloves, and sown alfalfa. A dairy region is this, settled by German and Swiss farmers, whose homesteads are thriftily kept. They send their cream by truck to Astoria, on the Columbia River, and to the cheese factories in Tillamook.

Although their farms may be modern, womenfolk cling as tenaciously to old customs as do the Pennsylvania Dutch. Butter for their own use they make in the home dairy, a shed open to the breeze from the meadows. They form it into pats, stamped with a design of bees, a cow's head, or a maid in a sunbonnet.

In autumn the farmer presses apples to make cider, in which meat and ocean fish are generally braised. His garden supplies the white cabbage for the sauerkraut barrel; massive beets and turnips, always baked with cuminseed, and considerable red chard and fence-climbing spinach, destined for soup. What would the farm do without the plum tree? Its favorite dessert is raised dumplings, first boiled, then baked with plums in a heavily buttered sauce.

This cuisine has not spread much beyond the farms. The little pigs that live out with the cows are better known, especially at the innumerable villages on the Oregon coast. Smacks from California on their way to procure huge oysters at Tokeland on Willapa Bay in Washington pause at them to buy a hogshead cheese, an agreeable change in a diet that is largely fish. This hogshead cheese, prepared with old cider and herbs, is of a texture so firm that they often must hack it with jackknives.

Much fancied hereabouts is salmon, which comes largely from the estuary of the Columbia, the river that separates the state from Washington.

So abounding in large forests is Washington, and so thinly is it settled, that it is likely to retain its frontier character for decades to come. Its dwellers on the western side, almost wholly Nordic, have a strong awareness of the Pacific. The profusion of bays, sounds, estuaries, and gulfs, all packed with islands, has made this region a salt-water province. Here stand all its large ports and cities, growing with tomorrow in mind.

Deeper inland the axes ring, timbers fall, and in the wake of the loggers rise villages where life goes rustically forward. The early newcomers, except for the woodsmen who trekked in from Michigan and Wisconsin, were followed by settlers of the Down East strain, who arrived with their heirlooms, plows, and young trees from their home orchards.

The cookery here is still basically plain American, although modified by that of the later migrants and a food supply that lacked nothing in the way of fresh-water fish, deer and elk meat, greenstuffs, wild herbs, and salmon from the river and sea. Canadians have made popular their *Salmon tindish,* jugged hare, marinated deer and bear steaks, larded beef tongues, curried rabbit, and dishes involving the pigeon, pheasant, and partridge. Sausage, a viand that Canadians have never permitted to suffer in quality, are now found everywhere. Mostly they are of the highly spiced Oxford type.

In no roster of Washington foods should split-pea soup be omitted. Since the early days of the fur trade when it was introduced here by the French-Canadian voyageurs and trappers, it has been a country mainstay. Caldrons of this soup, laced with scraps of smoked pork, simmer at campfires in sixteen Indian reservations.

Along the western shore, where British people chose to settle, although not because of its moister air and fogs, one finds steak-and-kidney pudding and of course, plum pudding. Solidly planted here are the Germans, who brought with them their incomparable pancakes.

Latterly have come Finns, much devoted to cranberry-growing. But none have influenced Washington cookery more than the people from Sweden, who must be thanked for their ways of coping with lobsters and crabs, which they barbecue. To supply Seattle, the town on Puget Sound, which must consume nearly a million crabs each week, boats bring in loads of them from northern waters. The Alaskan crab, like its Japanese cousin, measures a foot and a half across the disc, and has legs three feet long.

Of all the customs in Washington none is of older usage than that of feasting at barbecues. The cook, in mackinaw and coonskin hat with tail, tends a grid on which succulent young pigs are roasting over a low fire of hardwood. With a bunch of twigs dipped into oil, he anoints the piglets until they are done and of a hue as golden as a sunset. When done, he sluices them with water from the brook, the skin instantly crackles, and the piglets are carved with the edge of a dinner plate. Applesauce, and plum tartlets are passed round, with mugs of chilled cider.

Merry occasions are these barbecues, evocative of the pioneer days, served in traditional style, and with foods eaten on the land from which they sprang.

APPETIZERS AND SOUPS

WINE PICNIC PÂTÉ

A wine picnic is a California institution. A glorious day planned for visitors from the East is often a trip to the Napa Valley vineyards (or the Livermore Valley or Santa Clara Valley) for a day of wine tasting and a picnic. A favorite bottle of wine purchased at the winery, a good cheese, and a loaf of French bread make a simple picnic.

    ¾ cup butter or margarine
    1 pound chicken livers
    ½ pound fresh mushrooms
    1 teaspoon salt
    ⅓ cup finely chopped green onions
    ½ cup of white wine
    1 garlic clove, mashed
      Pinch of dillweed
    4 drops of hot pepper sauce

Melt ¼ cup of the butter in frying pan. Add chicken livers, mushrooms, salt, and green onions; simmer for 5 minutes. Add wine, garlic, dillweed, and hot pepper sauce. Cover and cook slowly for 10 minutes more, or until chicken livers and mushrooms are very tender. Cool slightly and whirl in a blender until smooth, or press through a sieve. Blend in remaining butter. Taste and add additional salt if necessary. Pack into a crock; chill overnight. Makes about 3 cups.

SPLIT-PEA SOUP

    ½ pound salt pork, diced
    1 cup chopped onion
    2 garlic cloves, finely minced
    1 pound green split peas
    2 quarts water or broth
    1 bay leaf
      Few celery leaves
      Freshly ground pepper to taste

Cook salt pork in kettle until browned. Remove pork and reserve. In fat remaining in kettle, cook onions and garlic for 2 or 3 minutes. Add peas and remaining ingredients except pork. Bring to a boil, cover, and simmer for 2 hours, or until peas are mushy. Purée through sieve, food mill, or in blender. Add pork and reheat. Makes about 2 quarts.

CHERRY SOUP SCANDINAVIAN

Use either sweet or tart cherries for this soup and sweeten accordingly.

    1 cup water
      About ¾ cup sugar
    2 lemon slices
    ⅛ teaspoon each of ground cinnamon and cloves

    4 cups pitted fresh or frozen bing cherries
    1½ tablespoons cornstarch
    2 tablespoons water
      Red food coloring (optional)
      Heavy cream

Combine in a saucepan the water, sugar, lemon, cinnamon, and cloves. Bring to a boil and add cherries. Bring to a boil again and cook gently for about 2 minutes. Blend cornstarch and water and stir into cherries. Stirring gently, bring to a boil again. Cook until sauce thickens slightly and clears. Remove lemon slices. Add a few drops of food coloring if you wish. Chill. Serve as first course, or as dessert with cream. Makes 4 servings.

FISH AND SHELLFISH

There are innumerable "authentic" versions of this famous California dish, each with its adherents. This recipe is for a combination of fish, but it's basic enough to be used with lobster alone, or with crab, or just about any other denizen of the sea.

CIOPPINO

    1½ pounds fish*
    ½ pound raw shrimps
    1 large Dungeness crab
    12 clams
    ½ cup olive oil
    1 teaspoon minced garlic
    1 cup chopped onion
    1 cup chopped green onions
    ½ cup minced green pepper
    1 can (8 ounces) tomato sauce
    3½ cups (one 1-pound, 13-ounce can) tomatoes
    2 cups red table wine
    1 teaspoon salt
    ¼ teaspoon coarsely ground pepper
    ¼ teaspoon dried oregano
    ¼ teaspoon dried basil
      Parsley
      Hot garlic bread

*This fish should be a firm-fleshed one, like sea bass, rockfish, or even shark. Have it cut into good-size pieces. Have shrimps shelled and cleaned, the crab cleaned and cracked, the clams scrubbed. If there are no clams, use mussels, cockles, or oysters. To make the sauce, heat olive oil, next 11 ingredients, and ½ cup parsley together; then simmer for 5 minutes. Now arrange the fish, shrimps, and crabs in layers in a 3-quart kettle or casserole. Pour on the sauce, cover, and simmer over low heat or bake in preheated slow oven (300°F.) for 30 minutes, or until

the fish is done. Add the clams and as soon as they open up, sprinkle with more chopped parsley and serve with lots of hot garlic bread. Bibs are almost a necessity when eating Cioppino. Makes 6 to 8 servings.

SHRIMPS

Most of the shrimps eaten in the West these days come from somewhere else: the Gulf of California, the Gulf of Mexico, or even more remote places. We do eat lots of them: as appetizers, main dishes, first courses, and salads. Here is a popular way to serve them.

SHRIMPS VICTORIA

    1 pound raw shrimps
    2 tablespoons minced shallots
    ¼ cup butter or margarine, or more
    ½ pound mushrooms
    1 tablespoon all-purpose flour
    ½ teaspoon salt
      Pepper
    3 tablespoons sherry
    1½ cups dairy sour cream
      Hot cooked wild rice (optional)

Shell and clean the shrimps, and sauté them, along with the minced shallots, in the butter until shrimps are pink. Add the mushrooms and cook for 5 minutes, adding another tablespoon butter if needed. Sprinkle with the flour, salt, and some freshly ground pepper. Add sherry and sour cream and correct seasonings. Cook gently until hot and serve with wild rice if desired. Makes 6 servings.

PRAWNS IN CREAM

Generally speaking, there is no difference between a shrimp and a prawn, but Westerners title their largest shrimps (of several species) prawns.

    2 pounds raw prawns or large shrimps
      Boiling salted water
    ¼ cup butter
    ½ cup heavy cream
    ¼ cup dry sherry
    2 tablespoons finely chopped parsley
      Salt and pepper

Drop prawns into boiling water to cover and cook gently for 5 minutes. Drain, shell, and devein. Melt butter in large frying pan or chafing dish. Add prawns and cook them, turning gently, until lightly browned. Add cream, sherry, parsley, and salt and pepper to taste. Heat thoroughly. Spoon into crisp pastry cups or onto small toast points. Makes 6 servings.

CRABS

Westerners are unanimous in acknowledging that the Dungeness crab is the best

in the world, and many non-Westerners agree. It is sweet and meaty, and considerably larger than its Eastern cousins. Then there is the enormous King Crab from Alaska, which sometimes measures ten feet from claw to claw. When cooked and frozen, they are inclined to be a little stringy, but when frozen raw (they're *all* frozen, alas), they have a fine delicate flavor. Cracked Crab is a great favorite from San Diego to the Olympic Peninsula.

CRACKED CRAB

Dungeness crabs are cleaned, the legs and claws cracked open, the body cut into 4 sections. The pieces are heaped onto a bed of ice, and the participants shell out the meat and consume it simply with homemade mayonnaise, crusty French bread, and plenty of dry white wine. A good-size Dungeness crab will serve 2 not-too-hungry people.

HOT CRAB SALAD

On the West Coast the sweet Dungeness crab is used.

    1 pound flaked crabmeat (about 2 cups)
    1 cup sliced celery
    ½ cup finely chopped green pepper
    2 hard-cooked eggs, chopped
    1 cup mayonnaise
    1 tablespoon each of fresh lemon juice
        and Worcestershire
    ¾ cup fine soft bread crumbs
    2 tablespoons melted butter

Combine crabmeat, celery, green pepper, eggs, mayonnaise, lemon juice, and Worcestershire. Turn into buttered baking dish (about 1½ quarts). Sprinkle top with bread crumbs. Dot with butter. Bake in preheated slow oven (325°F.) for 30 minutes. Makes 4 servings.

BROILED KING-CRAB LEGS

If you can get uncooked King crabs, they're better. Use the large middle sections of the legs, one for each serving. Split the shells with a heavy pointed knife, the length of the leg (the shell is tough, not brittle, rather like heavy plastic), and make a cross cut in the middle. Lay back the shell just enough to allow the insertion of the sauce, which is a simple one: equal parts of melted butter and fresh lemon juice. Broil the crab legs over charcoal, cut side up, and baste several times with the sauce during the cooking. If crabs are precooked, this will take only long enough to allow the bottom side to become brown; if raw, the whole thing will turn red first. Serve in the shell.

OYSTERS

The West Coast abounds in oysters of all sizes, from the tiny Olympias, no larger than a shirt button, to the gigantic Willapas, which must be cut into two or four pieces to eat. Bluepoints from Eastern waters have been planted too, and flourish in some places. The little San Francisco Bay oysters, with their slightly greenish color and coppery taste, have all but disappeared because of overfishing and the pollution of the Bay, but once in a great while they are available. Since the days of the Gold Rush, Westerners have consumed oysters in large quantities and in every conceivable way, including this one.

PEPPER PAN ROAST

    ¼ cup minced onion
    ¼ cup minced green pepper
    1 garlic clove, crushed
    1 cup butter or margarine
    1 pint oysters

Cook onion, green pepper, and garlic in the butter for 2 or 3 minutes. Remove garlic, add drained oysters, and cook until plump, a very few minutes. Serve with toast. Makes 2 generous servings.

SALMON

Salmon is the king of fish in the Pacific Northwest, and the chinook is the king of salmon. Rich, moist, and delicious, it is good in all sorts of ways, but best simply broiled and served with lemon, butter, and parsley. The earliest settlers in the Northwest found the Indians roasting split salmon over open fires, and that is still a favorite method of cooking these magnificent fish.

BARBECUED SALMON STEAKS

When an event occurs that calls for feeding a crowd, a whole salmon outdoor barbecue is traditional. On the beach, the whole salmon is often butterflied and cooked on a plank. Any barbecue treatment of salmon should be simple; salmon and wood-fire flavors are full and almost sufficient.

    4 salmon steaks, about ¾ inch thick
    ⅓ cup fresh lemon juice
    3 tablespoons melted butter
    1 tablespoon each of brown sugar and
        grated onion
    ½ teaspoon powdered mustard
    1 teaspoon salt
        Pepper to taste

Wash salmon and pat dry. Combine lemon juice, butter, brown sugar, onion, mustard, salt, and pepper. Brush over surfaces of salmon. Allow to stand for 15

minutes. Place fish in a well-greased hinged wire grill or on a greased barbecue grill. Cook over moderately hot coals, turning once and basting with remaining marinating sauce, for about 4 minutes on each side, or until fish flakes easily when tested with a fork. Can be broiled, for 5 to 8 minutes on each side. Makes 4 servings.

SALMON MAYONNAISE

    5-pound piece of salmon
        Court Bouillon
    1 envelope unflavored gelatin
    ¼ cup water
        Mayonnaise
        Ripe olives, pimiento, almonds, and
        deviled eggs

Wrap the salmon in cheesecloth, leaving enough extra at the ends to make handling easy. Cook it in the Court Bouillon until it reaches an internal temperature of 160°F., about 10 minutes to the pound. Remove, unwrap, and allow to cool. Dissolve the gelatin in the water. Mix with 3 cups mayonnaise and cover the fish completely with the mixture. Garnish with rings of ripe olives, pieces of pimiento, and halves of blanched almonds. Surround with deviled eggs. Pass extra mayonnaise, made with lemon juice instead of vinegar. Makes 10 servings.

Court Bouillon

    3 quarts water
    1 quart white wine
    1 cup wine vinegar
    3 onions
    9 whole cloves
    4 carrots, finely diced
    2 celery stalks
    1 bay leaf
    1 teaspoon crumbled dried thyme
        Few parsley sprigs
    1 tablespoon salt

Put liquids in kettle. Stud onions with the cloves. Add with remaining ingredients to liquids. Cover and simmer for 1 hour. Strain.

 ## MEAT, POULTRY, AND GAME

LAMB SHANKS BAKED IN FRUITED WINE

Westerners, generally, use a lot of fruits with meats.

    4 lamb shanks
        Salt and pepper to taste
        All-purpose flour
    1 cup dry red wine
    1 cup each of dried apricots and pitted
        prunes, each cooked until just tender
    ½ cup each of golden raisins and sugar
    2 tablespoons each of vinegar, fresh
        lemon juice, and honey

Green Goddess Salad Dressing
on Romaine and Shrimp

Strawberries de Luxe

California Omelet

Lamb Shanks Baked in Fruited Wine

½ teaspoon each of ground cinnamon and allspice

Season lamb shanks with salt and pepper; dust with flour. Place in a baking pan. Cover and bake in preheated moderate oven (350°F.) for about 1½ hours, or until meat is tender. Meantime, combine remaining ingredients in a saucepan. Bring to a boil, then simmer for 5 minutes. Drain excess fat from lamb; pour fruit sauce over. Cover and bake in hot oven (400°F.) for 30 minutes more. Serve lamb with fruit sauce spooned over. Makes 4 servings.

Out of the Pyrenees, great numbers of Basques came to the West to be sheepherders here. Now almost every Basque settlement stages a grand early-summer festival—a Basque barbecue picnic. Tender spring lamb is grilled over great outdoor wood fires to be the *pièce de résistance.*

BASQUE BARBECUED LAMB
Ask your butcher to bone a leg of lamb, leaving seam open ("butterfly" it). During barbecuing, apply the baste with a brush of fresh parsley. Thin portions of the meat will be well done, thick portions slightly pink.

    Butterflied leg of lamb (5 to 6 pounds before boning)
 ¾ cup dry red or white wine
 ¼ cup each of olive oil and wine vinegar
 ¼ cup chopped parsley
 2 garlic cloves, minced or mashed
 1 teaspoon mixed dried herbs
 1 teaspoon salt
 ¼ teaspoon pepper

Brush meat all over with baste made by combining remaining ingredients. Place meat on grill, fat side up, over medium coals. Cook for 50 to 60 minutes, basting frequently and turning occasionally. To carve, start at one end and cut across the grain into thin slices. Makes 6 to 8 servings.

CALIFORNIA OMELET
 1 tablespoon minced green onion
 1 small garlic clove, minced or mashed
 2 tablespoons butter or margarine
 1 large tomato, peeled, seeded, and diced
 12 pitted ripe olives, halved
 1 ripe but firm avocado, peeled and diced
 6-egg French omelet

Cook onions and garlic in butter until just soft. Add tomato and olives and heat through. Add avocado, remove from

heat, and keep warm. Meantime, make omelet. Spread avocado filling down center of omelet, fold, and turn onto a warm platter. Makes 4 servings.

CHICKEN-AVOCADO TOSTADA
The Western *tostada,* borrowed from Mexico, has come to mean not just the tortilla fried crisp (as is the immediate Mexican translation), but a great hot and cold sandwich-salad, built upon a crisp fried tortilla and the West Coast's plentiful avocados.

 4 corn tortillas
    Cooking oil for frying
 1 can (15 ounces) chili with beans, heated
 6 cups shredded iceberg lettuce
 1 can (7 ounces) green chili sauce, chilled
 1 cup shredded or grated Parmesan cheese
 12 thin slices of chilled cooked chicken
 2 avocados, peeled and sliced lengthwise
    Radishes, tomato wedges, green onions, olives to garnish

Fry tortillas, one at a time, in hot deep or shallow fat until crisp and brown. Drain; place one on each serving plate. Spoon hot chili over top of tortillas. Toss shredded lettuce with about half of the green chili sauce; pile part of the lettuce in a stack over hot chili; arrange part in a bed around tortillas. Sprinkle about 2 tablespoons of the cheese over each serving. Arrange chicken and avocado slices on top of the center stacks of lettuce. Sprinkle with remaining chili sauce, then with remaining cheese. Garnish each serving with radishes, tomato wedges, green onions, and olives. Makes 4 servings.

SHERRIED ARTICHOKE CHICKEN
 1 frying chicken (about 3 pounds), cut into serving pieces
    Salt, pepper, paprika
 6 tablespoons butter or margarine
 2 cups (one 1-pound can) artichoke hearts, drained
 ¼ pound fresh mushrooms, sliced
 3 tablespoons finely minced onion
 2 tablespoons all-purpose flour
 ⅔ cup chicken bouillon
 ¼ cup sherry
 ½ teaspoon crumbled dried rosemary

Sprinkle chicken generously with salt, pepper, and paprika to taste. In a frying pan brown chicken pieces on all sides in 4 tablespoons of the butter; transfer to a casserole. Arrange artichoke hearts between chicken pieces. Add remaining butter to the drippings in frying pan; add mushrooms and onion and sauté until just tender. Sprinkle flour over mush-

rooms and stir in chicken bouillon, sherry, and rosemary. Cook, stirring, for a few minutes; pour over chicken. Cover and bake in preheated moderate oven (375° F.) for 40 minutes, or until chicken is tender. Makes 4 servings.

CURRIED RABBIT
 1 frying rabbit (about 4 pounds)
    Seasoned all-purpose flour
 ⅓ cup shortening
 2 cups chopped onions
 2 garlic cloves
 1 large apple, peeled and chopped
    Juice of ½ lemon
 1 tablespoon curry powder, or more
    Salt and pepper to taste
    Water

Have rabbit disjointed and cut into serving pieces. Dust generously with seasoned flour, and brown on all sides in hot shortening. Remove to a kettle. In drippings left in skillet cook onions, garlic, and apple for 2 or 3 minutes. When the mixture is wilted, add it to the meat, along with the lemon juice and curry powder. (Curry powders vary a good deal in strength, so use your own judgment.) Add salt, pepper, and water to cover (or part water and part canned tomatoes); cover and simmer for 2½ hours, or until done. Correct seasoning, and if necessary, thicken the sauce with a little flour-and-water paste. Serve with curry condiments. Makes 6 to 8 servings.

VEGETABLES

POTATOES IN PARSLEY SAUCE
This way with potatoes comes from the French side of the Basque population.

 3 tablespoons olive oil
 ½ cup each of finely chopped onion and parsley
 1 large garlic clove, minced or mashed
 4 medium-large boiling potatoes, peeled and cut into ¼-inch slices
 1½ cups chicken or beef bouillon
    Salt and pepper to taste

In olive oil in a large kettle slowly sauté onion, parsley, and garlic until soft, about 15 minutes. Add potatoes and cook, gently stirring, for a few minutes. Add bouillon and salt and pepper. Bring to a boil; reduce heat, cover, and simmer until potatoes are tender. Taste and correct seasoning. Makes 4 to 6 servings.

ARTICHOKE FRITTERS
Here only the bottoms *(fonds)* of the artichokes are used. The frozen or canned ones will do, but they won't be as good as

freshly cooked artichoke bottoms.

1 cup all-purpose flour
½ teaspoon salt
1 teaspoon baking powder
⅔ cup milk
2 teaspoons melted butter
1 egg, well beaten
12 large artichoke bottoms
     Fat for deep frying

Mix flour, salt, and baking powder in a bowl. Add milk and beat until smooth. Add butter and egg. If the batter seems too thick, add a little more milk. Cut the cooked artichoke bottoms into quarters, dip into the batter, and fry in deep hot fat (370°F. on a frying thermometer) until browned. Drain on paper towels and serve piping hot. Makes 6 servings.

CHILLED ARTICHOKES WITH GARLIC MAYONNAISE

6 large artichokes
  Fresh lemon juice
  Boiling salted water or salted water and dry white wine
1 cup mayonnaise
1 garlic clove, mashed
  Paprika
  Lettuce

Wash artichokes thoroughly in cold water; drain. Turn each artichoke on its side and cut straight across top, about one third of the way down, to slice off thorny tip. Cut off stem, making a flat base. Remove small leaves around base. With scissors, cut thorns from tips of outer leaves. Rub cut edges with lemon juice. Turn artichoke on cut end and press firmly to separate leaves slightly. With a small spoon or melon-ball cutter, carefully and thoroughly scoop out the center fibrous leaves and fuzzy core. Stand artichokes in 1 inch of boiling salted water, or 2 parts salted water, 1 part dry white wine, in large kettle. Cover and simmer for 40 minutes, or until tender. Drain; cover with clear plastic wrap; chill for 1 hour or more. Combine mayonnaise and garlic. Spoon into cored artichokes. Sprinkle with paprika. Serve on lettuce-lined salad plate. Makes 6 servings.

FRIED BEANS

Garlic, onions, or chili powder may be added for extra seasoning, but this is the basic way to fry *frijoles*. A small dish of beans is served at every meal in most Mexican cafés.

1 pound dried Mexican pink or pinto beans
6 cups water
1 tablespoon salt
½ cup lard, bacon fat, or ham fat

Wash the beans and put in kettle. Add the water. (Unless beans are very old and hard, soaking is not necessary.) Cook until tender but not mushy, for 2 hours or more; add the salt. Melt the lard in a heavy pot (the Mexicans use a *cazuela,* a large earthenware pot with sloping sides and rounded bottom). Then add the beans, a few at a time, mashing them with a spoon and adding a little of the bean liquid. Continue until all the beans and liquid are used; then cook and stir until the mixture becomes thick. Makes 6 servings.

■ **Variation**—Refried beans (*frijoles refritos*) are even better. The fried beans are reheated with more lard until hot and a little crispy around the edges; stir the crisp bits into the center.

SALADS

AVOCADO SALAD

Avocados are a welcome addition to many salads. They are often diced and added to a mixed green salad, sliced and served with sliced oranges, or used as edible containers for chicken salad. They are best, perhaps, simply served on the half shell, their centers filled with a dressing made with ½ cup each of wine vinegar and olive oil, and 2 tablespoons each of minced parsley, green pepper, and green onions, with salt and pepper to taste.

MEXICAN SALAD

Mexicans are partial to all sorts of salads, and as with us, the mixed green salad rates high. Sliced radishes, green peppers, and cucumbers are frequently added, and the dressing is apt to be a rather tart one: 2 parts oil to 1 part vinegar, with perhaps a little chili powder added for extra tang.

On Christmas Eve, however, there is a very special salad, the *Ensalada de Noche Buena,* which resembles somewhat the ambrosia of our Southern states.

ENSALADA DE NOCHE BUENA (Christmas Eve Salad)

6 beets, cooked
4 oranges, peeled
4 bananas, peeled
4 apples, peeled and cored
¼ cup sugar
3 limes
1 cup peanuts
1 head of lettuce
  Seeds of 2 pomegranates
1 cup tart French dressing

Dice the beets, oranges, bananas, and apples. Combine them and sprinkle with the sugar. Let stand for 30 minutes. Slice the limes very thin and chop the peanuts coarsely. Shred lettuce and line a bowl with it. Put diced fruits on top, spread over them the slices of lime, sprinkle with peanuts and pomegranate seeds, and pour French dressing over all. Bring to the table in all its glory, and mix well before serving. Makes 12 servings.

CAESAR SALAD

Numerous chefs and restaurateurs have claimed to be the originators of this popular salad, but the best guess is that it started in Tia Juana, during prohibition, at a restaurant called Caesar's. It's very good and filling, which is really all that matters.

1 garlic clove
¾ cup olive oil
2 cups croutons (made from stale Sourdough Bread, page 1932)
2 large or 3 small heads of romaine
  Pepper to taste
½ teaspoon salt
2 eggs
  Juice of 1 large lemon
6 or 8 anchovy fillets (optional), snipped into bits
½ cup grated Parmesan cheese

Crush garlic, add to olive oil, and let stand overnight. Brown croutons in ¼ cup of this garlic oil, stirring so that they will brown on all sides. Drain on paper towels. Break romaine into a large bowl. Add a generous grinding of fresh black pepper and the salt. Then dress with remaining garlic oil, turning so that every leaf is glossy with oil. Soft-cook the eggs for just 1 minute (do this ahead), and break them into the middle of the salad. Squeeze the lemon juice directly over the eggs, and mix so that there is a thick creamy look to the lettuce. Add anchovy if desired. Taste for seasoning, and add more salt, pepper, or lemon if it's needed. Add the cheese, and toss. Add the croutons last. Serve at once, so croutons remain crisp. Makes 10 to 12 servings.

GREEN GODDESS SALAD DRESSING ON ROMAINE AND SHRIMP

8 to 10 anchovy fillets
1 green onion
¼ cup each of minced chives and parsley
1 tablespoon crumbled dried tarragon soaked in vinegar, then strained, or 2 tablespoons minced fresh tarragon
3 cups mayonnaise
¼ cup tarragon vinegar

Chop anchovies and onion together until finely minced. Mix lightly but thoroughly with chives, parsley, tarragon, mayonnaise, and vinegar. Makes about 1 quart dressing. Store unused dressing in a covered container in refrigerator for a week or more.

Note: This dressing goes on a salad of broken romaine in a salad bowl rubbed with a cut clove of garlic, often generously embellished with chilled cooked tiny sweet San Francisco Bay shrimps, prawns, Dungeness (Pacific Coast) crabmeat, lobster, or chicken. Eastern counterparts or frozen or canned seafood can substitute for the western seafood. Prawns here are the very large shrimps.

BREAD AND PANCAKES

SOURDOUGH BREAD

There are dried sourdough starters on the market these days which take a good deal of work out of making this wonderful bread. However, it's fun to start from scratch, and if all goes well you'll have some of the best bread in the world.

      2 cups Sourdough Starter
      3 cups all-purpose flour
    1½ tablespoons butter or margarine,
         melted
      2 tablespoons sugar
      1 teaspoon salt
      ½ teaspoon baking soda
         Milk

Start mixing dough about 8 hours before bread is to be baked. Put Sourdough Starter in bowl. Add 2 cups of the flour and the remaining ingredients except soda and milk; mix well. Add enough more flour to make a dough that is fairly stiff. Shape into a ball and put in a greased bowl. Grease top of dough. Cover and let stand in a warm place for 4 to 6 hours. Dissolve soda in a little water and knead into dough, mixing thoroughly. Put in well-greased loaf pan (9 x 5 x 3 inches). Brush with milk, cover, and let rise until doubled in bulk. Bake in preheated hot oven (400°F.) for about 45 minutes.

Sourdough Starter

      1 teaspoon active dry yeast
      ¼ cup warm water
      2 tablespoons sugar
      1 tablespoon vinegar
      1 teaspoon salt
      2 cups all-purpose flour
         Potato water (or warm water)

Dissolve yeast in the warm water. Add next 4 ingredients. Then add enough potato water to make a creamy batter (about 2 cups). Put in a stone crock or bowl, cover and let stand in a warm place

for 2 to 3 days to ferment. It will become bubbly and have a sour odor. Makes about 2½ cups.

ORANGE RYE BREAD

Many Scandinavians settled in the Northwest. Their descendants there still maintain the delicious renown of Scandinavian home-baking.

      1 package active dry yeast or 1 cake
         compressed yeast
      ¼ cup water*
    1½ cups lukewarm water
      ⅓ cup sugar
      ¼ cup molasses
      2 tablespoons shortening
         Grated peel from 2 oranges
    1⅛ teaspoons salt
         About 2½ cups each of sifted rye
         flour and all-purpose flour

Sprinkle dry yeast or crumble cake yeast into warm water. *Use very warm water (105°F. to 115°F.) for dry yeast; use lukewarm water (80°F. to 90°F.) for compressed. Let stand for a few minutes, then stir until dissolved. In a large mixing bowl combine lukewarm water, sugar, molasses, shortening, orange peel, salt, and dissolved yeast. Gradually add flours, beating until smooth. On a lightly floured board knead dough lightly; turn into a greased bowl. Cover and allow to rise in a warm place until almost doubled in bulk. Punch down and shape into 2 loaves. Place each in a greased loaf pan (9 x 5 x 3 inches). Allow to rise again in a warm place until almost doubled in bulk. Bake in preheated moderate oven (375°F.) for 40 minutes. Makes 2 loaves.

SEATTLE DUTCH BABIES

These popoverlike eggy pancakes are still a Seattle specialty.

      3 eggs
      ½ cup each of all-purpose flour and milk
      2 tablespoons melted butter
      ½ teaspoon salt
         Melted butter
         Lemon wedges
         Confectioners' sugar

In a mixing bowl beat eggs with a French whip or fork until blended. Add flour to eggs in 4 additions, beating after each addition until just smooth. Add milk in 2 additions, beating slightly after each. Lightly beat in 2 tablespoons melted butter and the salt. Thickly butter two 9-inch pie pans. Pour half of the batter into each. Bake in preheated hot oven (400° F.) for 10 minutes. Reduce heat to moderate (350°F.) and bake for 5 minutes longer. Serve immediately. Offer melted butter, lemon wedges, and confectioners'

sugar for toppings. Makes 4 dessert servings, or 2 main-dish servings.

DESSERTS

WASHINGTON PLUM DUMPLINGS

There are two kinds of fruit dumplings. The old-fashioned variety was made by dropping spoonfuls of sweet dumpling batter into boiling stewed fruit, cooking until done, then serving with the sweetened fruit as a sauce. These, I think, are better.

      4 fresh plums
         Sugar
      ¼ teaspoon ground cinnamon or nutmeg
      2 cups sifted all-purpose flour
    2¼ teaspoons baking powder
      ½ teaspoon salt
      ⅓ cup butter or margarine
      ⅔ cup milk (about)
      1 egg white, slightly beaten

Cut plums into halves and remove stones. Mix 2 tablespoons sugar and the cinnamon. Sprinkle on cut sides of plums and put halves back together. Sift flour, baking powder, salt, and 2 tablespoons sugar. Cut in butter until mixture looks like coarse meal. Add milk, mixing until soft dough is formed. Knead on lightly floured board for 30 seconds. Roll dough out to ¼-inch thickness. Cut into four 4-inch squares. Put a plum on each square. Moisten edges of dough and bring corners up over the plums, pressing edges together. Put in a greased shallow baking pan. Prick with a fork. Brush with egg white and sprinkle with sugar. Bake in preheated moderate oven (350°F.) for about 30 minutes. Serve plain, or with cream. Makes 4 servings.

RASPBERRY JAM SCONES

Oven-fresh scones, dripping with raspberry jam made from the local crop of spicy raspberries, have long been a food treat at the West Washington State Fair near Seattle. The tradition extended to the Seattle World's Fair. In this home recipe, you bake the jam right into the scones. You could use any tart berry jam.

      2 cups sifted all-purpose flour
      1 tablespoon each of baking powder
         and sugar
      ¾ teaspoon salt
      ¾ cup butter or margarine
      2 eggs
      ¼ cup milk
      ½ cup thick jam
         Sugar

Sift together flour, baking powder, sugar,

and salt into mixing bowl. Cut in ½ cup of the butter until particles are fine. Beat eggs slightly with milk, add to dry ingredients, and toss with a fork to mix and form a soft dough. Divide dough into halves. On a lightly floured board, roll out each half into a 10-inch circle. Place one dough circle in a 10-inch layer-cake pan or on a cookie sheet. Spread with half of the remaining soft butter, then with the jam. Top with second circle. Spread it with remaining butter and sprinkle lightly with sugar. Bake in preheated hot oven (425°F.) for 20 minutes. Cut into wedges and serve warm. Makes 8 servings.

LIME-FROSTED PAPAYA

Usually Westerners serve papaya for a first course, a salad, or a dessert, simply chilled, halved (with the seeds scooped out), and with a slice of lime. Occasionally, for dessert, it is filled with a scoop of coconut or ginger ice cream or fresh lime sherbet.

    3 chilled ripe papayas, halved and
      seeded
      Washed fresh grape or fig leaves
      (optional)
    6 scoops of fresh lime sherbet
    6 thin slices of lime
      Light rum (optional)

Place each papaya half on a large grape leaf on a dessert plate. Put a scoop of sherbet in each half. Garnish each with a lime slice. Sprinkle lightly with rum if you wish. Makes 6 servings.

RED-WINE-BAKED PEARS

Washington, Oregon, and California account for about 80 per cent of the nation's commercial pear production, and the pear tree is a favorite in home orchards. Winter Bosc is considered the best variety for baking, but the summer Bartlett and other varieties work well in this recipe, too.

    6 medium-size pears, with stems
    6 whole cloves
 1½ cups dry red wine
    ¾ cup each of sugar and water

Pierce blossom end of each unpeeled pear with a clove. Place pears in a deep casserole, on sides or standing on end. Combine wine, sugar, and water, and pour over pears. Cover and bake in preheated hot oven (400°F.) for 30 minutes, basting occasionally. Uncover and continue baking, basting, for 15 minutes more, or until pears are tender. Serve hot or cold with remaining wine sauce. Makes 6 servings.

NORTHWEST HUCKLEBERRY (OR BLUEBERRY) BUCKLE

    ¼ cup butter or margarine
    ½ cup sugar
    1 egg
    1 teaspoon vanilla extract
    1 cup sifted all-purpose flour
    1 teaspoon baking powder
    ¼ teaspoon salt
    ⅓ cup milk
    2 cups fresh huckleberries or
      blueberries or 1 package (10 ounces)
      frozen blueberries, thawed and
      drained
      Spice-Crumb Topping

In a mixing bowl cream together butter and sugar. Beat in egg and vanilla. Sift together flour, baking powder, and salt. Add to creamed mixture alternately with milk. Turn into buttered 8- or 9-inch square baking pan. Sprinkle evenly with huckleberries, then with Spice-Crumb Topping. Bake in preheated moderate oven (375°F.) for 40 minutes, or until toothpick inserted in center comes out clean. Makes 8 servings.

Spice-Crumb Topping

Combine ½ cup sugar, ⅓ cup all-purpose flour, ½ teaspoon ground cinnamon, and ¼ teaspoon ground nutmeg. Cut in ¼ cup butter or margarine to make a crumbly mixture.

Serve these cakelike squares warm with butter as a coffeecake, or with heavy cream, a thin hot lemon sauce, or lemon or vanilla ice cream for dessert. Use frozen blueberries when fresh berries are out of season.

STRAWBERRIES DE LUXE

By drawing on the strawberries locally grown up and down the West Coast, strawberries are "in season" almost the whole year round.

      Large strawberries with stems
      Dairy sour cream
      Sifted light brown sugar

Arrange strawberries in a large crystal bowl (imbedded in ice, if you wish) in center of table. Provide each guest with a sectioned dessert plate or 2 small cups on a dessert plate, one section filled with sour cream, the other with brown sugar. Holding each strawberry by the stem, dip first into sour cream, then into brown sugar.

You could arrange this dessert so each person can reach to a central serving: Use a three-tiered stand with one item filled with sour cream, one with brown sugar, one with strawberries.

ALMOND DEEP-DISH APPLE PIE

 1½ cups all-purpose flour
    ½ teaspoon salt
    ½ cup butter or margarine
    ¼ cup lard
    ¼ cup finely grated almonds
      Water as needed
    6 to 8 medium apples, peeled and
      sliced
    ¾ cup sugar
      Juice and grated rind of 1 small
      orange
    3 tablespoons rum or brandy
      Heavy cream

Mix flour and salt. Cut in ¼ cup butter and the lard. Add nuts, and enough water to hold ingredients together. Refrigerate while you make the filling.

Put the apples in a shallow baking dish (about 2 inches deep). Combine ¼ cup melted butter, the sugar, orange juice and rind, and mix lightly with the apples. Now roll out the chilled pastry, not too thin, cut 2 or 3 tiny holes in it, and cover the apples, pressing the pastry against the edges of the dish; trim. Bake in preheated very hot oven (450°F.) for 15 minutes. Then reduce heat to slow (325°F.) and bake until the apples are tender. When done, pour rum into the holes, using a small funnel. Serve warm with heavy cream. Makes 6 to 8 servings.

SOUR-CREAM APPLE TORTE

    6 large firm apples, peeled and thinly
      sliced
    1 cup sugar
    6 eggs
    2 cups dairy sour cream
 2½ teaspoons vanilla extract
      Pinch of salt
    1 package (6 ounces) zwieback, crushed
      into fine crumbs (about 2 cups
      crumbs)
    ¼ cup sugar
    ½ teaspoon ground cinnamon
      About 1½ tablespoons soft butter

Place apples in a heavy pan, sprinkle with sugar (no water), and cook over very low heat until apples are tender. Beat eggs slightly; blend in sour cream, vanilla, and salt. Carefully stir egg mixture into apples, and continue cooking slowly, stirring gently, until mixture thickens slightly. Remove from heat. Mix zwieback crumbs with sugar and cinnamon. Coat bottom and sides of a 9-inch springform pan with soft butter. Press two thirds of the crumb mixture onto sides and bottom of pan. Carefully spoon in apple custard. Sprinkle remaining crumbs over top. Bake in preheated slow oven (325°F.) for 1 hour. Allow to cool. Chill if you wish. Makes 10 to 12 servings.

West Coast Salads

by Shirley Sarvis

There is a mystifying phenomenon in the order of courses in the West. The salad comes first. No one seems to know quite how this tradition got started, but for over a century now, Westerners have deviated from the continental example set by their eastern cousins and put the salad course before the meat course instead of after. Maybe the custom began in Spanish California where southwest barbecues and festival feasts offered an abundance of food, but in no particular order. Maybe it's a carry-over from Gold Rush days when a hotel or mining-camp cook could make a salad quickly to appease the appetites of hungry workingmen until the main part of the meal could be prepared. Perhaps it was the warm California climate that prompted people to want to eat something cool and refreshing first. It could have been the invention of early Westerners: a way to show off their wonderful variety of fresh fruits and vegetables to visitors from the East.

While we've been searching and sleuthing with food historians to try to find the reason for the first-course Western salad, we've come up with some theories of our own: the delicacy of a Western salad makes it deserving of a place at the forefront of a meal. The nuances of a wonderfully subtle salad can best be appreciated before tastes are dulled by spicier, richer foods. The goodness of a fine Western salad justifies its lead position; it deserves the total attention guests can give only to the first item served. There is opportunity for much more play and display in the serving of a salad early in the meal. Guests are concentrating on the food. The table is clear of other dishes and distractions.

Certainly commercial produce growers have promoted the emphasis the big salad gets by being first course; lettuce and other salad ingredients are important

crops in the Western economy; but the foremost theory put forth by food historians and popular conjecturers alike is that, in the early days of the West, the first-course salad simplified dinner and suited the necessarily casual style of living. We think that is a strong argument in favor of serving salad first today, and not just in the West. It is a simplification that meets the needs of today's casual living: it eliminates both a first course and a later salad course; it eases the task of the homemaker-hostess who has no help; yet it offers all the elegance of an introductory course at dinner.

A careful Western hostess takes great pride in the finesse of her salad, honoring the fine points of salad making. She capitalizes on her good fortune at having a profusion of fruits and vegetables to choose from. She arranges her greens and other ingredients to make the most of them.

Following are six salads, in themselves six reasons why a Western salad comes first. They are typical of the favorite first courses of Western hostesses. Different although they are, they all have in common certain essential qualities: delicacy, simplicity, some traditional first-course ingredients such as seafood, fruit, cheese, artichokes, and colorful attractive display.

BROWNED-BUTTER WILTED LETTUCE

Less familiar than wilting lettuce with hot bacon drippings and vinegar is wilting it with bubbling browned butter. More delicate is the result, and more suited to the role of a first-course salad. Select just the tender, light-colored leaves from the heart of butter (sometimes called Boston or butterhead) lettuce. Tear them into pieces slightly smaller than you would for most green salads to carry out the theme of delicacy. Prepare butter and dress the salad at the table so your audience can see the butter brown and then tenderly wilt the lettuce leaves. Over a candle warmer, heat the butter slowly, just until it turns a deep-golden color. Pour it, foaming, over torn lettuce and snipped chives. Toss, and serve at once.

    About 2 quarts torn and loosely
       measured hearts of butter or Boston
       lettuce
    2 tablespoons snipped chives
    ¼ cup butter

Place lettuce in salad bowl. Sprinkle with chives. Heat butter until it melts and foams and browns; watch carefully, do not let it burn. Pour hot butter over lettuce and chives. Toss lightly. Serve at once. Makes 4 servings.

CRAB AND GRAPEFRUIT SALAD WITH AVOCADO MAYONNAISE

In the West this salad no doubt derived from the local fondness for Pacific Coast crab. Inlanders and Easterners can substitute King crab, canned or frozen. Arrange crab and grapefruit individually, building each on a base of finely shredded iceberg lettuce.

    1 ripe avocado
    ⅓ cup mayonnaise
    4 teaspoons fresh lemon juice
    ¼ teaspoon garlic salt
       Finely shredded iceberg lettuce
    1 large chilled grapefruit, peeled and
       cut into sections, removing all
       membrane
    ½ pound chilled Pacific crab legs

Peel avocado and mash with a fork. Mix in mayonnaise, lemon juice, and garlic salt. Line chilled salad plates with the shredded lettuce. Arrange grapefruit sections and crab legs over lettuce. Spoon some of the dressing on top of each salad; pass remaining dressing. Makes 4 servings.

CALIFORNIA PARMESAN-WALNUT SALAD

Grate Parmesan cheese yourself and toast the walnuts slightly to taste this salad at its best. Your blender can speed the grating of hard cheese; to toast walnuts, place in preheated hot oven (400°F.) for just a few minutes. Use a combination of several of your favorite salad greens.

    ¼ cup salad oil
    3 tablespoons tomato juice
    1 tablespoon fresh lemon juice
    1 teaspoon grated or scraped onion
    ¼ teaspoon each of salt, pepper, and
       sugar
    ¼ teaspoon crumbled dried sweet basil
    1 quart coarsely torn and loosely
       measured salad greens
    ⅓ cup coarsely broken California
       walnuts, lightly toasted
    ¼ cup grated Parmesan cheese

Beat or shake together first 8 ingredients to make dressing. Place greens in chilled salad bowl and sprinkle with walnuts and cheese. Pour over salad just enough dressing to coat ingredients lightly. Toss; serve at once. Makes 4 servings.

SPECIAL MIXED GREEN SALAD

Its total simplicity is the beauty of this salad: the playing of one green against another in contrast. There is the bite of dark-green watercress brushing the icy crunch of romaine smoothed by suedelike petals of butter lettuce. Crumbles of blue cheese echo the peppery spice of watercress. Oil and vinegar dress it. Although loyal Westerners would choose a blue from an Oregon cheesery, you may use as well your favorite piquant blue-veined cheese or perhaps a Danish Bleu or Roquefort.

Make a simple oil and vinegar dressing seasoned with just salt and pepper—about ¾ cup salad oil to ¼ cup wine vinegar—

but taste! Proportions depend on the strength of the vinegar you use.

    3 cups each of butter lettuce hearts
      and romaine leaves, coarsely torn
      and loosely measured
    3 cups watercress leaves
    2 ounces blue cheese
      Oil and vinegar dressing

Place salad greens in chilled salad bowl. Crumble blue cheese over top. Pour on just enough dressing to coat each leaf lightly. Toss gently. Serve at once. Makes 6 servings.

GINGER CHEESE SALAD BOWL

This is a salad to begin in the kitchen and finish at the table. First, line a large salad bowl with torn mixed salad greens and top with some seedless green grapes, toasted almonds, and cheese cubes. Placing the arranged salad bowl before your guests, dress, toss, and serve.

    ½ cup salad oil
    4 teaspoons fresh lemon juice
    4 teaspoons dry sherry
    1½ teaspoons ground ginger
    1½ teaspoons wine vinegar
    ¼ teaspoon salt
    ⅛ teaspoon each of sugar and pepper
    4 cups coarsely torn and loosely
      measured salad greens
    1 small package (3 ounces) cream
      cheese
    4 teaspoons grated orange peel
    ¾ cup seedless green grapes or other
      seeded fresh grapes
    ⅓ cup diced almonds, lightly toasted
    1 tablespoon finely sliced green onions
      with tops (optional)

Shake together or beat with a fork the first 8 ingredients to make a dressing. Place salad greens in salad bowl. Press all sides of cream cheese block into grated orange peel until peel adheres; cut block into about ⅜-inch cubes; place together on salad greens. Arrange grapes and almonds in separate sections on top of greens. If you like, sprinkle all over with onions. At table, pour on just enough dressing to moisten ingredients; toss salad lightly. Makes 4 servings.

WESTERN ANTIPASTO SALAD

The Western Italian population influenced the eating of the marinated appetizer, or antipasto salad. Heating the marinade brings out the flavors of the vegetables it dresses.

    ½ cup salad oil
    ¼ cup red-wine vinegar
    ¼ teaspoon salt
    ⅛ teaspoon freshly ground pepper
    1 large garlic clove, minced or mashed
    1 package (9 ounces) frozen artichoke
      hearts, cooked just until tender,
      then drained
    ¼ pound fresh mushrooms, sliced
    ½ cup pitted black olives
    2 tablespoons each of chopped pimiento
      and freshly chopped parsley
      Romaine

Shake or beat together salad oil, vinegar, salt, pepper, and garlic. Pour into sauce-

pan and just heat through. Beat again to mix thoroughly and pour over artichoke hearts, mushrooms, olives, pimiento, and parsley. Cool, then cover and chill thoroughly for at least 2 hours; gently stir occasionally. At serving time, line individual salad plates with romaine leaves. Arrange marinated vegetables on top, spooning some of the marinade over romaine. Makes 4 to 6 servings.

WHALE—A mammal belonging to the order Cetacea. It lives in the deep sea and is valued commercially for its flesh and for its oil, which nowadays is used mainly in the manufacture of cosmetics, lubricants, and textiles.

Whales have been caught since the Middle Ages, but the emphasis on their products has shifted as civilization progresses. In the Middle Ages they provided food for Europe, and in the 17th, 18th, and 19th centuries they were caught chiefly for their oil, used for lighting and in the manufacture of soap. Whale meat today is a staple food item in Norway and other Scandinavian countries, where whale fishing and processing are important industries. During World War II, when food was extremely scarce in these countries, whale meat helped the people to survive. It is an inexpensive meat, of a rather brilliant, dark-red color. Since whale meat is tough, it has to be cooked like any tough meat, that is, marinated, pot-roasted, or otherwise tenderized.

Availability—Frozen whale steaks are available in specialty food stores.

Nutritive Food Values—Very high in vitamin A with traces of thiamine and riboflavin.

☐ Whale meat, 3½ ounces, raw = 156 calories

WHEAT—The grain of a grass of the genus *Triticum*. It is the most widely grown and prized of all the cereal grains, and the most important in all but the Asiatic countries. The little wheat kernels grow in beads at the top of stalks or straw. The harsh straw and chaff are winnowed off to leave only the tiny grains to which man owes so much. The flour made by grinding wheat grain is the best of all flours for breadmaking because of the presence of gluten, a form of protein which makes a soft and spongy dough.

A grain of wheat has three main parts. The outer covering is the bran, the inner part the endosperm, and the tiny nucleus within the endosperm is the germ. If the entire kernel is ground, the result is whole-wheat flour, graham flour, or entire-wheat flour. If just the endosperm is used, the result is flour—wheat flour—and plain flour.

There are hard and soft wheats used for making various kinds of flour. Hard wheats are made into bread and all-purpose flours; soft wheats are made into pastry, cake, and all-purpose flours. A special kind of hard wheat, durum, is ground to make the semolina used for making pasta. Besides flours, wheat is made into various ground products: semolina; farina, ground wheat with the bran and most of the germ removed; cracked wheat, cleaned wheat cracked into fragments; wheat cereals, made from the whole wheat or part of the wheat kernel.

Wheat is thought to be the oldest of man's grains and it has been cultivated for so many thousands of years that it is difficult to say exactly when the first wheat harvest was made. It was probably grown originally in the fertile plains of the Euphrates Valley. From there it spread east and west until now it covers the globe. We do know that it is largely to grains that we owe the initial transition from nomadic to settled life. When man stops long enough in one place to harvest his crops, a whole new way of life begins, differing from the wandering life of the earliest hunters and gatherers of wild foods. Grains are the chief of those "fruits of the fields" that sustain life. They need not be consumed immediately, they can be stored against need, and in themselves they bear the seed of their renewal.

Civilizations everywhere have long honored bread and wheat. In classical times, Demeter, goddess of the fields and fertility (the Romans knew her as Ceres, hence the word "cereal"), was at the heart of the Eleusinian mysteries, the secret cult that has been called the fountainhead of Greek culture. In ancient friezes she is pictured holding shafts of wheat. It was said that she gave the first grain to the hero Triptolemus, telling him to diffuse its blessing throughout the world. Triptolemus quite evidently followed her instructions; wheat is now, except in oriental rice-growing countries, the most widely eaten grain in the world.

In this country, the colonists of Virginia and Massachusetts brought the grain to our shores quite early. However, the climate of the eastern seaboard proved not so satisfactory for wheat as for the native corn, and the crop never became an important one. When the frontier expanded to what is now the middle and far west, the pioneers found the perfect home for their crop. The original wheat fields were considerably smaller than the vast expanses we know today. Old-fashioned methods of plowing, reaping, and winnowing made large production difficult. As mechanical progress made possible quick and efficient farming and harvesting processes, the wheat farmers expanded their crops. Such inventions as the reaper and efficient winnower have changed the food habits of Americans.

Availability and Purchasing Guide—
Wheat flour is available in the following forms:

Whole-Wheat, Graham, or *Wheat Flour* —These terms are synonymous for flour made from any cleaned, unrefined, unbleached wheat other than durum or red durum wheat.

Gluten Flour is a high-protein whole-wheat flour from which the starch has been removed.

Flour, White, Plain, All-Purpose, or *General-Purpose Flour*—These terms are synonymous for refined wheat flour. It is available bleached or unbleached.

Cake Flour—This is a highly refined bleached flour.

Self-Rising Flour—Refined bleached flour to which leavening ingredients and salt have been added.

Enriched Flour—This is refined bleached flour to which vitamins and minerals have been added.

Instant-Type Flour—This flour is in granular form, making it easier to pour and pack than other flours.

Other wheat products available are cereals, including hot cooked, quick-cooking, and ready-to-eat; bulgur or wheat pilaf (parboiled wheat); wheat germ, the rich embryo of the wheat grain; and a variety of crackers such as graham and shredded wheat crackers.

Since cereal products are not visible when purchased, select a brand in which you have confidence. Individually wrapped servings cost more than the large economy-size boxes. Cereals requiring long cooking are usually less expensive than the quick-cooking or ready-to-eat varieties. Select the cereal that is most convenient and economical for your use.

Storage—Flour should be stored at room temperature in tight containers. In hot weather, only small amounts should be kept on hand.

Cereals should be stored tightly covered in a cool dry place. Ready-to-eat cereals are packaged with an inner wrapping. Open carefully to keep this lining intact. The lining should be kept tightly folded to preserve the freshness of the cereal. Whole-grain cereals, even though unopened, should be refrigerated because of their fat content.

☐ Kitchen shelf, dry or uncooked cereal: 2 to 3 months
☐ Refrigerator shelf, cooked cereal: 2 to 4 days
☐ Whole-grain cereals, dry or uncooked, refrigerator shelf: 5 to 6 months

Nutritive Food Values—In white flour, starch is present in greater proportion and is more digestible than it is in whole-wheat flour. Therefore, it is higher in caloric value. If enriched, white flour contains added thiamine, riboflavin, niacin, and iron. Calcium and vitamin D may also be added. Whole-wheat flour, which contains all the nutrients available in the whole grain, is high in phosphorus, potassium, and has moderate amounts of protein, niacin, thiamine, and riboflavin. The caloric values of 3½ ounces of the most commonly available wheat flours are:

☐ Whole-wheat flour = 333 calories
☐ Flour, enriched or unenriched = 364 calories
☐ Self-rising, enriched = 352 calories
Wheat cereals are moderately high in

calcium, phosphorus, and sodium and contain good amounts of thiamine, riboflavin, and niacin. The amounts vary with the enrichment of the cereal. The caloric values of 3½ ounces of the most commonly available wheat products are:

☐ Bulgur, dry = 357 calories
☐ Bulgur, canned, unseasoned = 168 calories
☐ Bulgur, canned, seasoned = 182 calories
☐ Wheat germ = 363 calories
☐ Whole-wheat crackers = 403 calories
☐ Graham crackers, plain = 384 calories
☐ Graham crackers, chocolate-coated = 475 calories
☐ Graham crackers, sugar-honey-coated = 411 calories
☐ Cereal, rolled wheat, cooked = 75 calories
☐ Cereal, wheat, whole-meal, cooked = 45 calories
☐ Cereal, wheat and malted barley, quick-cooking = 65 calories
☐ Cereal, wheat and malted barley, instant = 80 calories
☐ Cereal, wheat-flakes, ready-to-eat = 354 calories
☐ Cereal, wheat germ, ready-to-eat = 391 calories
☐ Cereal, puffed wheat, ready-to-eat = 363 calories
☐ Cereal, puffed wheat with sugar and honey, ready-to-eat = 376 calories
☐ Cereal, shredded wheat, ready-to-eat = 354 calories
☐ Cereal, shredded wheat with malt, salt, and sugar, ready-to-eat = 366 calories
☐ Cereal, bran with sugar and malt, ready-to-eat = 240 calories
☐ Cereal, bran with sugar and wheat germ, ready-to-eat =238 calories
☐ Cereal, bran flakes, ready-to-eat = 303 calories
☐ Cereal, bran flakes with raisins, ready-to-eat = 287 calories

WHEY—The liquid part of milk which remains after the thicker part, or curd, is removed. The curd is used in making cheese. Whey contains sugar, minerals, and lactalbumin. Although some whey cheese is also made, most whey is further separated, with the fattier parts used in making butter and the remainder fed to livestock.

WHIP, TO—To beat an ingredient with an egg beater, a whisk, an electric beater, or a fork until it is light and puffy due to the air incorporated into it by the beating.

The secret of successful whipping is to do it quickly and thoroughly. Anything whipped should be used quickly, or the air incorporated in it will escape and the food will become limp.

WHISKEY or WHISKY—A spirit distilled from such grains as barley, rye, and corn, and subsequently refined, colored, and flavored by various processes. Each country produces a distinctive type of whiskey. There are differences in the method of production, the grains used, and of great importance, the character of the water. The water in Scotland, for example, rises through red granite, contributing to the flavor of Scotch whisky. Whiskey, by the way, is "whisky" in Scotland and Canada; in Ireland and the United States it is spelled with the "e."

The Latin term used to describe distilled spirits was *aquavitae*, "water of life." The Scotch and the Irish translated it to *usquebaugh* in Gaelic. The name was later contracted to *uisge* and still later anglicized to whiskey.

The four steps of whiskey production are malting, fermenting, distilling, and aging. First the grain is cleaned and then it is prepared for fermentation by a process called malting. During malting the grain is ground and then cooked with water to form a mash. Malt is added. Malt enzymes change the starch in the grain to sugar.

The next step is fermentation by yeast. In this process the grain sugars are converted to alcohol.

Distilling separates the alcohol from the waters. The vapors are caught, condensed, and drawn off as new whiskey which is colorless and harsh. Aging in wooden barrels is the final process, the one which provides the mellow beverage that is eventually bottled.

Whiskey, strictly defined by the United States Federal standards, is a grain spirit, distilled at less than 190 proof and one day old. Thirty-three whiskey variations are listed among the United States Standards, but general usage divides whiskey into two major sub-divisions, straight whiskey and blended whiskey. *Straight* whiskey is whiskey which is unmixed with other liquors or substances (except distilled water used for reduction of proof), such as straight bourbon whiskey and straight rye whiskey. Federal law requires that straight whiskey be aged in new charred oak barrels for at least two years. A *blended* whiskey is a balanced blending of straight whiskeys and neutral grain spirits (a high distillate, at least 190 proof, of any fermented mash), containing at least twenty per cent straight whiskeys and bottled at not less than eighty proof. The blend may combine several, or sometimes many, straight whiskeys with extremely light-bodied, almost flavorless, spirits (neutral grain spirits), and sometimes a blending agent such as sherry in very small amounts, resulting in a blended whiskey that is light in body.

The word *proof* applied to distilled spirits indicates the amount of alcohol in a liquor. Proof is twice the percentage of alcohol. Example: a 100-proof whiskey contains fifty percent alcohol. All whiskeys have a bottling proof between eighty and 110. Proof indicates potency, not necessarily quality.

A *bonded* whiskey is straight whiskey, produced and bottled in accordance with the Federal Bottling-in-Bond Act. It must be at least four years old, must be bottled at 100 proof, must have been produced in a single distillery, by the same distiller, and be the product of a single season and year. It must have been bottled at an internal revenue bonded warehouse under United States Government supervision.

Imported whiskeys come to the United States from Ireland, Canada, and Scotland. *Irish whiskey* (the Irish spell it with an "e" as do Americans) varies in the processing as well as in flavor depending on whether it is made in Northern Ireland or in the Republic of Ireland to the south. Both use barley malt and small cereal grains, and in the south these include oats and wheat with the unmalted barley and rye.

All *Scotch whisky* is a blend of malt whisky, made from malted barley, and grain whisky, made from malted and unmalted grains. These two types of whisky are distilled differently before they are blended. In addition there are four varieties of malt whisky, each coming from a different part of Scotland: Highland Malts come from the north of Scotland; Lowland Malts from the South; and Islay Malts and Cambeltown Malts from the Island of Islay and from Campbeltown on the Firth of Clyde respectively, both in western Scotland. Barley is the principal grain used, and the smoky flavor of Scotch is acquired in the process of drying the malted barley over peat fires, a process distinctive to Scotland.

Most *Canadian whisky* on the American market is a blend of heavy and light-bodied grain mashes and is similar to American whiskeys.

Caloric Values

- [ ] Bourbon, 1½ ounces, 86 proof = about 125 calories
- [ ] Irish, 1½ ounces, 86 proof = about 125 calories
- [ ] Rye, 1½ ounces, 86 proof = about 125 calories
- [ ] Scotch, 1½ ounces, 86 proof = about 110 calories

WHITEBAIT—A small salt-water fish, one and a half to four inches in length, which is the fry of the common herring or sprat. Whitebait are generally found in the Thames estuary in England and along the coast of the North Sea. The name is also given to various other small fish which are similar to the European whitebait, such as the smelts found off the California coast, to many silversides, and to some of the anchovies found in salt and fresh waters in the United States.

These little fish are generally fried in deep fat but they can be sautéed or broiled. They are available fresh in large eastern markets in November, December, and part of January. They should be stored in the refrigerator and eaten as soon as possible.

If whitebait is frozen, it should be frozen whole. Since they are so small, it is best to cover the fish with water in a small pan and freeze until ice is formed. Wrap the entire block of ice in moisture-vapor-proof material, excluding as much air as possible. Seal.

PANFRIED WHITEBAIT

Soak whitebait in ice water for 1 to 2 hours. Drain on a towel and roll in cornmeal. Panfry quickly in hot olive oil, shaking the pan often to move the fish about. Turn them carefully with a wooden spoon. Season with salt and pepper to taste and serve plain or with tartare sauce.

Chili Whitefish

WHITEFISH—A fatty fresh-water fish caught all year round in the Great Lakes in other North American lakes and streams, and in Alaska. Whitefish belongs to the salmon family. Some Arctic varieties live in salt water.

Whitefish can be prepared in almost any of the ways that fish is prepared: broiled, panfried, baked, baked stuffed, or poached.

Recipes occasionally call for white fish, two words. This does not mean the species of fish known as whitefish, but refers to any white-meated fish such as cod, flounder, sole, etc.

Availability—Whitefish weighs 2 to 6 pounds and is available year round fresh, whole or filleted. It is also sold frozen, in fillets, and smoked whole drawn.

Purchasing Guide—Fresh fish should have bright, clear bulging eyes; gills that look and smell clean; scales that are shiny and lie close to the skin; and firm flesh with some spring to it when pressed with a finger.

Storage—Fresh fish is very perishable. Wrap in moisture-proof paper or place in tightly covered container in coldest part of refrigerator.

Keep frozen fish solidly frozen until ready to use. Once thawed, use immediately. Do not refreeze.

- [ ] Fresh, refrigerator shelf, raw: 1 to 2 days
- [ ] Fresh, prepared for freezing; or frozen, refrigerator frozen-food compartment: 2 to 3 weeks
- [ ] Fresh, prepared for freezing; or frozen, freezer: 3 to 4 months
- [ ] Fresh, refrigerator shelf, cooked: 3 to 4 days
- [ ] Smoked, refrigerator shelf: 1 week

Nutritive Food Values—Very high in protein and vitamin A, phosphorus and potassium; has some thiamine, riboflavin, and niacin.

- [ ] Fresh, 3½ ounces, raw = 155 calories
- [ ] Fresh, 3½ ounces, baked and stuffed = 215 calories
- [ ] Smoked, 3½ ounces = 155 calories

Basic Preparation

- [ ] **To Broil**—Put split fish, skin side down, on oiled broiler rack. Dot with butter or brush with oil. Broil 4 to 5 inches from unit, basting occasionally with butter or oil, for 6 to 10 minutes, or until fish flakes easily with a fork. Do not turn. Season with salt and pepper.
- [ ] **To Panfry**—Cut fish fillets into serving-size portions. Sprinkle both sides with salt and pepper. Dip in a mixture of beaten egg and milk, using 1 egg to 1 tablespoon milk. Roll in fine dry bread crumbs, cracker crumbs, cornmeal, or flour. Put in ⅛-inch hot fat in heavy skillet and panfry over medium heat until browned on one side. Turn and brown on other side. Allow about 5 minutes for each side.
- [ ] **To Bake**—Cut fish fillets into serving-size portions. Sprinkle both sides with salt and pepper. For each 2 pounds of fish, mix 2 tablespoons fresh lemon juice

with ¼ cup melted butter or margarine. Dip fish into this mixture and put in shallow baking dish. Pour any remaining butter mixture over fish. Bake in preheated moderate oven (350°F.) for 25 to 30 minutes. Sprinkle with paprika.

□ **To Poach**—Cut fillets into serving-size portions. Put in a wire basket or on a plate. If plate is used, tie in a piece of cheesecloth. Lower the fish into salted boiling water or Court Bouillon (at right). Simmer for 10 minutes, or until fish flakes easily when tested with a fork.

□ **To Freeze**—Clean and eviscerate fish. Remove head and wash thoroughly. Dip pieces of fish in a solution of 1½ teaspoons ascorbic acid and 4 cups water for 20 seconds. Drain, and wrap pieces in moisture- vapor-proof wrapping, excluding as much air as possible. Seal.

BAKED WHITEFISH WITH BREAD STUFFING

1 large onion, chopped
Butter or margarine
1 cup soft stale-bread crumbs
¼ cup minced parsley
½ teaspoon crumbled thyme leaves
Salt
Dash of pepper
1 egg, well beaten
1 whole whitefish, about 4 pounds
Lemon wedges

Sauté the onion in ¼ cup butter until golden. Add next 3 ingredients, ½ teaspoon salt, the pepper, and egg; mix well. Fill cavity of fish with the stuffing, and sew up. Put in a well-oiled baking dish, sprinkle with salt, and dot with butter. Bake in preheated hot oven (400°F.) for 25 to 35 minutes. Serve with lemon wedges. Makes 4 to 6 servings.

CHILI WHITEFISH

1 pound whitefish fillets
1 tablespoon each of cooking oil and vinegar
2 tablespoons minced onion
1 teaspoon salt
2 teaspoons steak sauce
⅓ cup chili sauce
¼ cup water
1 tablespoon capers
1 cup cooked green peas

Cut fish into serving pieces. Bring oil, vinegar, onion, salt, steak sauce, chili sauce, and water to boil in top part of a double boiler. Add capers and fish. Cover and cook over boiling water for 25 minutes, stirring several times. Add peas; heat. Makes 4 servings.

COLD WHITEFISH

Poach a whole whitefish in Court Bouillon. Remove it from the broth, cool, and chill. Remove the skin but leave head and tail intact. Mask with a mixture of ½ cup each of mayonnaise and dairy sour cream to which you add 1 teaspoon prepared mustard, 2 tablespoons finely chopped onion, 2 tablespoons capers, 1

tablespoon finely chopped anchovy fillets, and 2 tablespoons tomato purée or strained chili sauce. Serve with vinegar, salt, and pepper to taste.

Court Bouillon

8 to 10 shallots, chopped finely, or 12 green onions
1 garlic clove, chopped
1 leek, chopped
2 or 3 carrots, scraped and sliced
¼ cup chopped parsley
1 teaspoon each of salt and pepper
1 bay leaf
Pinch of dried thyme
1 cup dry white wine
4 cups water

Mix shallots with garlic, leek, carrots, and parsley; add salt, pepper, bay leaf, and thyme. Cover with white wine and water. Put Court Bouillon on the range, bring to boil, and simmer for about 20 minutes. Strain through a fine sieve and use as directed in recipe.

SMOKED WHITEFISH AND RICE

½ pound smoked whitefish
¼ cup butter or margarine
½ cup light cream
4 hard-cooked eggs, diced
2 cups hot cooked rice
½ teaspoon curry powder
⅛ teaspoon pepper

Split whitefish and remove bones and skin. Flake fish with fork. Melt butter and stir in remaining ingredients. Add fish and mix lightly with fork. Heat gently. Makes 4 servings.

SMOKED WHITEFISH PLATTER

Remove the skin and arrange a whole smoked whitefish, with head and tail intact, on a bed of watercress. Garnish with lemon wedges and serve with strips of buttered pumpernickel for a smörgåsbord or with cocktails.

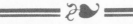

WHITE SAUCE—This term is applied to sauces which are light or blond in color, as opposed to the brown sauces which are made with brown stock. Some of the white-sauce group, such as Sauce Velouté, are made with white stock; that is, stock made with veal and/or chicken as opposed to beef stock, a brown stock. The term also applies specifically to a simple

sauce made with cream or milk and with a white *roux*: that is, a combination of butter and flour which isn't browned. This sauce is also known as béchamel. Béchamel sauce is available in jars.

First Aid for White Sauce

■ **Lumpy Sauce**—If the *roux* is hot and the liquid near the boiling point, the sauce should not be lumpy. However, if it is, strain it through a fine sieve or whirl it in a blender. Simmer over low heat for 5 minutes.

■ **Too-Thin Sauce**—Boil it down over moderate heat, stirring constantly, until it is of the desired consistency. Or thicken it with *beurre manié,* a paste of butter and flour which has been kneaded together. Blend ½ tablespoon butter with ½ tablespoon flour to a smooth paste. Remove sauce from heat and beat in *beurre manié.* Return to heat and boil for 1 minute, stirring constantly.

■ **To Store**—Scrape the sides of the pan with a spatula and add to sauce in pan. To prevent a skin from forming on the top, float a little milk or light cream or melted butter on top. Keep hot over hot water, but do not cover sauce. Or cool and refrigerate, or freeze.

To Make White Sauce

Melt the butter, stir in the flour, and cook it for two minutes without coloring. Then add hot milk and/or cream gradually or all at once. Cook sauce over moderate heat, stirring constantly, until thickened and smooth. It should be cooked for at least five minutes, or the raw taste of the flour will come through. Remove sauce from the heat and season with salt and white pepper. (Black pepper would mar its whiteness.) It is now ready for the addition of cheese and other ingredients, or to be served as is over fish, meats, and vegetables, or used as the basis for soups, soufflés, and creamed dishes.

White sauce comes in varying degrees of thickness, depending on the use. The table that follows gives the proportions of ingredients for different consistencies:

To Make White Sauce				
Consistency	Fat	Flour	Liquid	Use In
Thin	1 tablespoon	1 tablespoon	1 cup, hot	Soups
Medium	2 tablespoons	2 tablespoons	1 cup, hot	Sauces
Thick	3 to 4 tablespoons	3 to 4 tablespoons	1 cup, hot	Croquettes, souffles, pie fillings

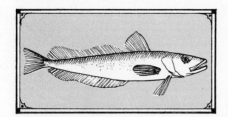

WHITING—A small gray and white salt-water fish sometimes called kingfish or silver hake. One variety is found along the Middle Atlantic coast, another variety off the New England coast. Whiting grow to an average length of twelve inches and weigh from one to four pounds. The fish has tender white flesh, fine in texture, flaky, with a delicate flavor. It can be broiled, panfried, baked, or poached.

Availability—Sold whole fresh or frozen, filleted, salted, or smoked.

Purchasing Guide—See Whitefish, page 1938.

Storage—See Whitefish, page 1938.

Nutritive Food Values—A good source of protein.

☐ Fresh, 3½ ounces, raw = 105 calories

Basic Preparation—See Whitefish, page 1938.

WHITING CREOLE

1 small onion, chopped
2 tablespoons butter or margarine
½ cup diced celery
½ cup chopped green pepper
2 canned pimientos, chopped
3½ cups (one 29-ounce can) tomatoes
1 tablespoon cornstarch
2 tablespoons water
  Salt and pepper
2 tablespoons chopped parsley
6 small whiting

Cook onion in the butter for 2 or 3 minutes. Add celery, green pepper, and pimiento and cook for 2 or 3 minutes longer. Add tomatoes, bring to a boil and simmer, covered, for 1 hour. Mix cornstarch and water and stir into mixture. Season to taste and add parsley. Put fish in the mixture and simmer for 7 minutes, or until fish flakes easily with a fork. Makes 6 servings.

MARINATED WHITING

1½ pounds whiting fillets
  ½ cup highly seasoned French dressing
  Paprika

Cut 1½ pounds whiting fillets into serving pieces. Refrigerate fish in ½ cup highly seasoned French dressing for several hours. Arrange fish on broiler rack; broil under medium heat for 5 minutes on each side, brushing with dressing used for marinating. To serve, pour drippings over fish; sprinkle with paprika. Makes 4 servings.

CREAMED SMOKED WHITING

1½ pounds boneless smoked whiting
 2 cups milk
 1 bay leaf
   Pinch of ground thyme
10 peppercorns
 1 slice of onion
¼ cup butter
¼ cup all-purpose flour
¼ cup light cream
   Dash of cayenne
 1 tablespoon chopped pimiento
 2 hard-cooked eggs, chopped

Soak fish in milk with bay leaf, thyme, peppercorns, and onion for 1 hour. Then put over very low heat, and simmer gently for 10 minutes. Flake fish. Melt butter and blend in flour. Add strained milk and cream slowly. Add fish and remaining ingredients. Makes 4 servings.

WILD RICE—A native American grass, *Zizania aquatica,* that bears a grain used for food. It is a tall plant that grows in water in the western Great Lakes area and has never been domesticated. The Indians have used it as a cereal for many centuries and today it is still gathered by local Indian tribes and marketed for consumption as a luxury food.

Wild rice should not be overcooked. It is more delicate than other rice, with a truly delicious flavor. It can be used like regular rice, but it is especially good with poultry and game birds.

Availability—Widely available packaged, uncooked, instant, or precooked, and in combination with white rice.

Storage—Store in covered container in a cool dry place. Will keep almost indefinitely.

Nutritive Food Values—High in protein, phosphorus, and potassium, with some riboflavin, thiamine, and niacin.

☐ 3½ ounces, uncooked = 353 calories

Basic Preparation—Wash ¾ cup uncooked wild rice in 3 or 4 changes of cold water, removing any foreign particles. Add 1 teaspoon salt to 3 cups boiling water. Add rice gradually so that water continues to boil. Cover and simmer, stirring occasionally with a fork, for 30 to 45 minutes, or until rice is tender and all of water is absorbed. Add butter to taste. Makes 2¼ cups.

HERBED WILD RICE

1 cup uncooked wild rice
1 teaspoon salt
¼ cup butter, melted
1 teaspoon grated onion
¼ teaspoon each of pepper and ground sage
⅛ teaspoon ground thyme

Rinse wild rice thoroughly in running water. Cover with water and bring to a boil. Drain and rinse. Cover with water again, add salt, and simmer until tender, about 30 minutes. Drain and rinse in hot water. Add remaining ingredients and mix thoroughly. Makes 6 to 8 servings.

SHRIMPS WITH WILD RICE

2 packages (10 ounces each) frozen shelled deveined shrimps
1 cup uncooked wild rice
1 garlic clove, minced
¼ cup olive oil
2 cans (8 ounces each) tomato sauce
1 sauce-can water
½ teaspoon ground oregano
½ teaspoon crumbled dried basil
1 large green pepper, seeded and cut into chunks
  Salt and pepper

Thaw shrimps. Cook rice according to package directions and put in 2-quart casserole. Sauté garlic in olive oil in a skillet for 5 minutes. Add all ingredients except shrimps and salt and pepper. Bring to boil and simmer for 10 minutes. Add shrimps; season to taste. Pour shrimp mixture over rice. Cover and bake in preheated moderate oven (350°F.) for about 30 minutes. Makes 6 servings.

WILD RICE STUFFING

1 cup wild rice
4 cups chicken broth
1 cup diced celery
¼ cup instant minced onion
½ cup butter or margarine, melted
1 can (4 ounces) mushroom crowns
½ teaspoon marjoram leaves
¼ teaspoon oregano leaves
¼ teaspoon pepper
1 teaspoon seasoned salt
¼ teaspoon thyme leaves
  Salt to taste

Wash wild rice well. Add to boiling chicken broth, bring to boil again, cover and simmer for 30 to 45 minutes, or until rice is tender, stirring occasionally with fork. All of broth should be absorbed. Sauté celery and onion in the butter for 2 or 3 minutes. Drain mushrooms, reserving 2 tablespoons liquid. Add mushrooms and liquid to rice with remaining ingredients, including celery mixture. Makes 6 cups, or enough to stuff a 10-pound turkey.

WINE

Produced in delicious variety in Europe
and America, wine adds flavor to a sauce or dish;
complements food as a refreshing drink;
and gives any meal that
extra gourmet touch.

Wine is the product of the natural fermentation of the juice of the grape. The term is also used to describe beverages made from other fruit juices or vegetable juices by adding sugar and yeast and fermenting the mixture. Examples are dandelion wine and elderberry wine. But strictly speaking wine is the product of the vine, for grapes contain naturally all the ingredients needed for a normal fermentation of the juice. No sugar nor yeast need be added.

The origin of wine goes back so far into the dim mists of the past that we have no records of when or where the first wine was made. There are evidences in archaeological discoveries that it was known in the Near East as long as 10,000 to 12,000 years ago. Ancient Egyptian frescoes depict scenes of grape harvesting and wine making. Excavators found winepresses in the Minoan ruins of Crete, and the palace of the Assyrian kings contained a huge wine cellar with a detailed record of its contents.

The Bible has many references to wine and to its ceremonial use, and no doubt from earliest times the fermented juice of the grape had been connected with religious rites. Primitive man must have thought that the natural phenomenon of the fermentation was magical, and certainly the joyous feeling that comes from drinking the beverage must have seemed magical too. This was indeed a divine gift.

Some of the complicated ways of treating wines were developed in ancient times. The Greeks of the classic age used pitch to seal their wine jars and this gave the wine a taste of resin. Today the modern Greeks still like the flavor and add resin to many of their wines to give them a distinctive taste. The Romans at their lavish banquets sipped wines that were strongly perfumed and spiced. The vermouths of today are versions of these aromatic drinks.

Early Phoenician merchants who ranged far afield, even into the Atlantic Ocean, spread the vine throughout the Mediterranean area. Wherever Roman legions went they took the vine and the knowledge of wine making with them —into France, Spain, Portugal, up the Rhine and Moselle valleys of Germany and even into southern England.

In more recent times, European colonizers have transported the custom around the earth—to Canada, Australia, New Zealand, South Africa, and South America. In our own country Spanish friars planted vineyards at their missions in what is now California, and later the settlers of the English colonies along our east coast experimented with the native wild grapes and also imported French vines. In the early years of the Republic, Thomas Jefferson was a noted wine enthusiast and brought many clippings from Europe for planting in Virginia.

To our ancestors wine was both a pleasure and a necessity. It was a pleasure, of course, because the fermented juice of the grape was—and is—a refreshing drink that enhanced food and cheered the soul; it was a necessity because the water supply was often tainted. Even milk sometimes brought serious illness or death. Wine was always safe.

The Characteristics of Wine

The characteristic qualities of a wine— its color, aroma, taste, body—are results of the soil, climate, grape variety, and finally of the vintner's art. In each wine region, through generations of experiment, growers have tended to concentrate on certain grape varieties that seem to do best in the soil and climate of the area. The vines are so sensitive to their environment that vineyards only a few yards apart will produce wines of entirely different qualities even when planted with the same grape variety. A slight change in the chemical content of the soil or the slant of the sun's rays can affect the wine's distinctive characteristics.

Strangely enough, the greatest wines come from soil that would seem most useless—sandy, chalky, or rocky—and from climates that are somewhat severe. France's great Burgundies come from the northern part of the region; Champagne is a northern district in France. In Germany, the farther north you go in the Rhine and Moselle valleys, the better the wine. It has often been said that vines that struggle for survival produce the best grapes.

Certainly the art of the vintner is important. He must decide just the right time for the harvest; he must supervise the fermentation; he must see that the new wine is properly stored in the right sort of container and at the right temperature to insure maturing.

With all these influences at work, it is not surprising that wine can vary from poor to great. The truly great wines—the big velvety Burgundies, the delicate Bordeaux, the rich whites of Germany—are, of course, limited in quantity because only small areas can produce such perfection. But there are many other fine wines that are not so important yet make delicious drinking, and there is a large supply of good honest *vin ordinaire* for everyday drinking.

People of wine countries, such as France and Italy, and wine lovers the world over enjoy the simple *vin du pays,* or regional wine, with their daily meals. Such wines are often called "gulping" wines, for their refreshing, thirst-quenching qualities hold no subtleties, no rich aroma to beguile the senses. They are good healthy accompaniments for family dinners or casual parties. The truly great wines are reserved for those very special occasions when time can be taken to savor each drop.

Types of Wine

Generally speaking, wines may be divided into four categories: *natural still wines*— red, white, and rosé (pink)—sometimes called "table" wines; *sparkling wines,* such as champagne; *fortified wines,* such as sherry and port; and *aromatic wines,* such as vermouth. Red table wines are dry and rosés are nearly always dry to dryish. White table wines and wines in the other categories vary from dry to very sweet.

The color of the wine does not necessarily reflect the color of the grape. Red wines, of course, are made from red grapes. The fruit is pressed, and the skins and pips are allowed to stay in the must to color it. Then the new wine is drawn off. White wines may be made in the same manner from white grapes, or they may be made from red grapes. In this case, the grape skins and pips are removed from the juice as the fruit is pressed. Some champagne is made by this method. Red grapes are used to make rosés, and the skins and pips are left in the must just long enough to turn it pink. Rosés are also made by mixing red and white wines, but the result is less satisfactory.

New wine is put in casks in the "caves" or cellar of the winery and left to age. Some wines stay in the cask only a few weeks or months before bottling; others are not bottled for years. Wine is a living, breathing thing even in the bottle, and the maturing process continues until the bottle is uncorked, or until it passes its prime, becomes old and flat and finally "dead."

In general white wines are drunk when they are young and fresh—within two to three years. The great whites of Germany and the sweet whites of Bordeaux last longer. Reds, with the exception of Beaujolais, which is drunk young, take longer to mature. Great reds, such as very fine Bordeaux and Burgundies, may take as long as ten to twenty years to reach their peak, and some Bordeaux have been known to live for sixty years.

In making champagne, the fermentation is halted by means of temperature control before all the sugar has turned to alcohol. The wine is bottled and the following spring, when the temperature rises, the remaining sugar ferments in the bottles, creating the bubbly effervescence. Some other sparkling wines are made by adding sugar to force a second fermentation or by adding carbon dioxide. The "manufactured" sparkling wines are not as fine.

Fortified wines are made by adding a dose of brandy to the wine to give it more strength. The brandy is usually distilled from the same wine. Aromatic wines, often also fortified, are flavored with various infusions—herbs, seeds, spices.

Storage of Wines

Remember, wine in the bottle is alive, and like all living things it is sensitive and should be handled with some care. It does not like being tossed about, does not like vibration, light, or temperature extremes. Store it in a dark, fairly cool spot away from heating units and drafts. A cool corner in the basement or an unheated closet are likely spots. The ideal temperature is 50 to 60 degrees or even a touch higher. The important points are that there should be no sudden fluctuations in "climate" and that the wine should rest undisturbed.

If you do not have such a spot, buy wine in small quantities and keep it in a dimly lit corner. Use it up within a few weeks.

Store wine bottles on their sides so that the corks are kept in touch with the liquid. If they dry out, they will shrink and let the air in to spoil the wine.

Older wines, like older people, dislike disturbances much more than young wines. If you are fortunate enough to find a bottle of fine aged Bordeaux or Burgundy, do not jiggle it home from the wine shop and serve it immediately. Give it a chance to rest quietly for several days or even weeks after you carry it home.

Once a living wine is opened it can not be recorked and returned to storage. Some table wines can be recorked and used again for one or two days, but older wines tend to die quickly and champagne loses its effervescence. If you have wine left over, it is wise to use it in cooking the next day. Fortified wines, with the exception of very dry (fino) sherry and a fine vintage port, will keep for a few weeks, although there is some deterioration. Fino sherries lose their brilliance within a week and a fine old port shows marked changes within a day or two. Opened bottles of aromatic wines will keep for a few weeks.

Wine with Food

Over the years much has been written about when to serve certain types of wine and which wines to serve with which foods. There are no strict rules. Even connoisseurs disagree and have indulged in many spirited arguments on the subject. Certainly customs vary from country to country. You may find that in a red-wine region you will be served red wine with fish, and you may dine in Spain and find sherry served throughout the meal.

Still some foods and wines do seem to complement each other, just as cheese goes with bread and bacon with eggs. Here are the most widely accepted rules:
Apéritifs: Dry sherry, dry champagne, a light dry white wine such as an Alsatian or a California Riesling, dry vermouth.
With fish: Dry white wine, dry champagne.
With beef, lamb, and mutton: Red wine, dry champagne.
With veal: Dry white wine, dry champagne.
With pork: Dry champagne, a light flowery white such as an Alsatian, a dry Moselle, or a California Riesling.
With chicken and turkey: Dry champagne, red wine, or dry white wine. There is disagreement among wine drinkers on whether to drink white or red with poultry. Your best guide is the method of cooking. A young chicken gently roasted on the spit goes well with a dry white wine. But a red goes with *coq au vin*. Some people like a light red with the Thanksgiving turkey, and others prefer a white.
With duck: Red wine, dry champagne.
With game: A good red wine, dry champagne.
With cheese: A good red wine.
With dessert and fruit: A sweet white wine, such as a rich German wine, a sauterne, or a slightly sweet champagne.
At the end of the meal: Port or other sweet fortified wine such as a sweetish sherry or Madeira.

Wine, with the exception of dry champagne, does not seem to go well with eggs, salads, or highly spiced dishes such as curries and chilies. Champagne is the one all-purpose wine that can be served with almost any food and throughout the meal. Rosés are at their best with picnic foods or informal buffets combining a variety of foods.

Serving Wines

Red table wines: With one or two exceptions, these should be served at room temperature. The exceptions—Beaujolais from France and (sometimes) the Italian Valpolicella—gain by being lightly chilled.

For all other reds, place the bottle in the room in which it is to be served a few hours in advance. An hour or so before serving, remove the cork to give the wine a chance to breathe. This will bring out the flavor and aroma.

Very old red wines, such as great Burgundies and Bordeaux, often develop sediment and must be handled with care. Remove them from their resting place to the dining room a day in advance and stand them upright to let the sediment slip to the bottom. Take out the cork several hours before serving and decant the wine. To do this, hold the bottle up to the light so that you can watch the liquid. Tip it slowly and let the wine slip gently into a decanter and keep your eye on the wine in the bottle. The minute you see cloudy sediment moving into the neck of the bottle, stop pouring. Let the decanter stand, upstoppered, until ready to serve.

Dry white table wines, champagnes, rosés: These should be lightly chilled. Do not let them get too cold. Between 50 and 55 degrees is right. The best method is to nestle the bottle in a bucket filled with ice for 15 to 20 minutes before serving. Or place it in the refrigerator for 2 to 3 hours. Open the bottle just before serving.

Dry sherries, dry Madeiras, and vermouths: Chill lightly. Vermouths may be served over ice.

Dessert wines: Sweet white wines, port, sweet sherries, and other dessert wines should be served at room temperature.

If you are serving more than one wine at dinner, serve the lesser before the greater and white before red. Of course you may follow a red wine at dinner with a sweet white or champagne at dessert.

One word of caution: do not serve your best wines after a prolonged cocktail party, but reserve them for true wine lovers and an occasion when they will be the sole stars. The other times, a pleasant table wine will serve the purpose.

Very tart salad dressings and sauces do not go very well with wine since they tend to kill the wine's delicate flavor. Decide which one you will feature, and match the other to it. Curry kills the taste of all wine, and beer, preferably imported, should be drunk with curries.

Also, do not have any highly scented flowers on your dinner table. Their sweet smell will overpower the wine's bouquet—and much of the pleasure of wine drinking is connected with the wine's own delightful aroma.

A question that is frequently brought up is how much money you should spend for a bottle of wine. The answer is: it depends on the occasion. Great wines are expensive, and unless you are an expert on recognizing them and their just price at the wine merchant's, have an idea of how much a specific kind or vintage is worth. You can do this by asking for the wine by name at different reputable stores and comparing the prices. But bear in mind that for a good bottle of table wine you should pay no more than $3.00 top price. Most likely, it will cost between $1.50 and $2.50 a bottle. Very often, you can pick up a pleasant wine for less, depending on where it comes from and its supply.

Wineglasses

Two or three generations ago, elegant families and fine restaurants and hotels had great arrays of different wineglasses. There was a special shape for each kind of wine: one for sherry, one for white wine, one for the great German whites, one for claret (red Bordeaux), one for red Burgundies, and so on. One needed the vast mansions of that era with the cupboard space and servants that went with them to care for such a collection.

Today's apartments and modern servantless homes do not permit such extravagance. Nor do we serve the elaborate seven-course meals with five different wines that were once fashionable. We have solved the problem with the all-purpose wineglass with a medium-size tulip-shape bowl. It serves equally well for whites and reds, for sherries, ports, champagnes, and vermouth on the rocks. It is nice to have a slightly larger-bowled glass for champagne if possible, for the larger bowl holds the bubbles better. But it is not necessary.

Wineglasses should be filled not more than two thirds full. This gives the bouquet (or aroma) a chance to fill the rest of the glass, and gives the drinker a chance to inhale the perfume as he sips the wine. Traditionally, the host pours a small amount of the wine into his own glass first and tastes it to be sure it is all right before he serves his guests.

A fifth bottle of wine or champagne should give you six to seven glasses, and a bottle of dessert wine eight to ten glasses. These are rough figures, of course, and depend on the size of the glasses. If you serve champagne throughout the meal, count on a half bottle for each guest.

Major Wine Regions and Their Products

FRANCE

Bordeaux — This area in southwestern France produces red wines, often called "clarets," that are famous for their clear jewellike color and for their delicate flavor and bouquet. The great Bordeaux wines are all château-bottled. That is, each is the product of an individual vineyard, bottled by the proprietor, and carrying the name of the château on its label. Among the famous names are Lafite, Latour, Haut-Brion, Margaux, Cheval Blanc, and Pétrus. These wines are scarce and expensive.

There are many less well-known châteaux in Bordeaux producing wines that range from excellent down to average or ordinary. The price generally reflects the quality. Other vineyards sell their grapes or bulk wine to shippers who bottle it under the label of the region or district, such as Médoc or St. Julien.

The principal grape variety used in red Bordeaux wines is Cabernet Sauvignon.

White Bordeaux wines are seldom dry. They vary from sweetish to very sweet. The Graves district produces the driest,

Champagne with canapés, olives, and chicken pastries   *Red Burgundy with broiled steak and tomato half*

although even these seem better with fruit than with a main course. Good vineyards in Graves are Olivier and Domaine de Chevalier.

From Sauternes in Bordeaux comes France's greatest dessert wine, Château d'Yquem. It is rich, perfumed, and round, and owes its special qualities to the fact that the grapes are gathered when over-ripe, even shriveled, and covered with mold called "noble rot." Other sauternes are less rich but still sweet. Rich white wines also come from the nearby district of Barsac. All go best with fruit or dessert.

Burgundy—This region of France also produces world-famed red wines. The big Burgundies come from the northern section, Côte de Nuits. They are noted for their full-bodied velvety texture, rich aroma, and deep-red color. The wines are bottled by the proprietors and carry the name of the vineyard or commune. Outstanding names in red Burgundies include Romanée-Conti, Le Chambertin, Le Corton, Le Richebourg, La Tâche, Musigny.

Among the less important vineyards,

many produce fine red Burgundies that make delightful drinking, although they may not have the deep velvety quality of the bigger wines.

The grape variety used in red Burgundies is Point Noir.

The best white Burgundies rank near the top as white dinner wines and they come from the section known as the Côte de Beaune. They are dry to dryish, full-bodied with fine bouquets. Among these are Le Montrachet, Meursault, and Corton-Charlemagne.

From the southernmost part of Burgundy come two very pleasant light wines, the red Beaujolais and the white Pouilly-Fuissé. These wines are often served *en carafe* in French restaurants.

A little to the northwest of Burgundy is the tiny Chablis district, home of the wine of the same name. Chablis is very dry, with a flinty taste and a faintly greenish tinge. It is the traditional drink with oysters, particularly on the half-shell.

Champagne—The world's most glamorous wine derives its name from this region in northern France where it is produced.

Champagne is a blended wine made usually from red and white grapes. A small amount made solely from white grapes is known as *blanc de blancs*.

Champagne producers buy grapes from various vineyards, and each company blends the resulting wines according to its own recipe. Nonvintage champagnes are blends of wines of various years—and a nonvintage from a fine house can be a good buy.

Champagnes range from dry to sweet and the labeling can be confusing. The dryest is labeled *brut; extra-sec* is dryish; *sec* is actually sweetish; *demi-sec* is sweet; and *doux* is very sweet.

Rhône Valley—This southern region of France makes both white and red wines, often unusually good. The sun is hot in the Rhône Valley and the red wines in particular often have a slightly scorched or earthy taste, making them rougher than the sophisticated reds of Burgundy and Bordeaux. But they have a hearty quality that goes well with hearty meats. The Hermitage and Côte Rôtie are robust; the reds from Châteauneuf-du-Pape are lighter.

White Bordeaux with broiled chicken and green beans　　**Port with dessert, a strawberry sponge roll**

Rhone white wines are light, dry, and slightly flinty in taste. White Hermitage and Chante-Alouette are the best known. The most outstanding rosé also comes from the Rhône valley—Tavel. It is drier than most pink wines and has a clear rosy color.

Loire Valley—Tourists flock to this picturesque valley to see the beautiful châteaux and while there they enjoy the delicious local wines. Reds, whites, and rosés are all produced but it is the whites that are the favorites. They are mostly light, delicate, and dry. Leading names are Pouilly-Fumé, Sancerre, and Muscadet. Vouvray is a white wine that ranges from dryish to sweet.

Alsace—This northeast corner of France borders on Germany and has many historical connections with that country. The same grape varieties are used here as in the German vineyards, and the wines resemble the lightest of the German whites. They are dry with a slightly flowery quality and go well with Alsatian foods, such as pork or sausage dishes. The wines are labeled with the grape names, the two best known being Riesling and Gewürztraminer.

French Vermouth—This is a dry vermouth with a flavor of herbs and seeds. In France it is drunk as an apéritif either plain or in a vermouth cassis: vermouth over ice with a touch of crème de cassis and a dash of soda. Crème de cassis is a syrup made from black currants.

GERMANY

Among the greatest and most costly wines in the world are the white wines of the Rhine and Moselle districts in Germany. The important Rhine wines are big and serious, full-bodied with deep perfumes. Moselles are lighter, more lively, and with flowery bouquets.

German wines range from dry to very sweet and even one vineyard may produce wines of varying sweetness. This is done by harvesting the grapes at intervals. Some are picked at the normal time to make a dry wine. Others are left to become overripe in order to make a sweeter wine. The final harvesting is of grapes that have shriveled and developed "noble rot." Bottle labels designate the ripeness of the grapes and amount of sweetness: *Spätlese* means dry to dryish; *Auslese* means sweetish; *Beerenauslese* means sweet; *Trockenbeerenauslese* means very sweet and rich.

Regional wines are labeled with the name of the village; wines bottled by the proprietor are labeled with the village name followed by the name of the vineyard. For example, Bernkasteler Doktor is wine from the Doktor vineyard in the village of Bernkastel. Three or four of the greatest vineyards omit the name of the village and use the vineyard name only. Among these are Schloss Vollrads, Schloss Johannisberg, and Steinberg. Some villages with outstanding vineyards are: *Rhine Valley*—Bodenheim, Oppenheim, Nierstein, Hochheim, Winkel, Erbach, Oestrich, Geisenheim.

Moselle Valley—Bernkastel, Piesport, Wehlen, Trittenheim, Wiltingen, Ockfen.

These are but a few of the many German towns and villages where fine vineyards are located.

ITALY

Italian wines do not include any "greats" but many of them are good, sound, agreeable wines. The reds are often earthy, even a little rough, and they go well with hearty Italian food and with barbecued meats. The best known is chianti, and the finest chianti comes in regular claret bottles, not the straw-covered round bottles. Other good reds are Valpolicella, Barolo, Bardolino.

Italian white wines are light and pleasing, and they can be dry, sweetish, or sweet. Soave is a soft dry white; Orvieto and Est! Est! Est! come either dry or sweet.

Italy also produces a sweet sparkling wine, Asti Spumante, and a well-known rich dessert wine, Marsala. Italian vermouths are dryish to sweet. The sweet vermouth is often served as an apéritif with a dash of Campari (Italian bitters) and a twist of lemon peel.

SPAIN

Spanish table wines are exported in very small amounts. It is the fortified sherries for which the country is famed. Sherry is not a vintage wine, but a blend of wines of various ages. By the *solera* system, as the method is called, young sherries are gradually, over a period of years, mixed with increasingly older sherries to give body, maturity, and flavor.

Sherries range from very dry to very sweet, depending on the grape varieties used. They are labeled as follows: *manzanilla,* light and dry; *fino,* pale and dry; *amontillado,* nutty and dryish; *golden,* medium sweet; *oloroso,* rich and sweet; *cream,* heavy and very sweet. Each firm puts out a variety of sherries.

PORTUGAL

Port is a fortified wine blended from many grape varieties and is always sweet. The finest ports, well aged, are very rich. *Vintage port,* a blend of great wines of an outstanding year, is matured in the bottle for 20 years or longer. These rare wines have a deep-red color and a deep aroma. They must be decanted. *Crusted port,* a little less fine than vintage, is aged in the bottle for about 10 years. It, too, must be decanted.

Ruby port is a young wine matured in the cask. It is light, with an agreeable fruity flavor. *Tawny port* is an older ruby port that has faded to a tawny color and become mellower. There is some white port made from white grapes.

As with sherry, the firms in Portugal each ship several wines and indicate the type on the labels.

UNITED STATES

California—Wine making in California dates back almost two hundred years, when the first vines were planted by Franciscan friars. For the past hundred years, California vintners have experimented with many different grapes and today most California wine is made from European grape varieties. The finest vineyards are located to the north, around the San Francisco Bay region, and most are planted with several kinds of grapes to produce a number of wines, both white and red.

The best wines are labeled with the name of the grape variety, although a few have specific names devised by the vintner or company producing them. Leading red table wines are labeled Cabernet Sauvignon, Pinot Noir, and Zinfandel. The Riesling is a good white table wine and Grenache a good rosé. Two sound wines for everyday drinking are labeled Mountain White and Mountain Red.

California vineyards also produce good champagnes and good fortified wines, such as sherries and ports.

New York—The New York Finger Lakes district has several outstanding wine companies producing wines from native grapes. These grapes, having been developed from the wild varieties found in this country, have flavors that are often called "foxy." The wines, as a result, are very different from those made from European grapes.

As with California wines, the best are labeled with the name of the grape, such as Elvira, Diana, Delaware. The whites are more successful than the reds.

Some European grape varieties are planted in New York but they are used mainly in blends.

Good champagne is made in this region and also some pleasant sherries.

Ohio—A small vineyard area in northern Ohio produces some interesting wines from native American grapes. These wines are labeled with the name of the grape variety.

Cooking with Wine

Cooking with wine is like cooking with any other flavoring, from onions through thyme or vanilla extract. The wine should be used to round out the flavor of a dish, and in some cases, as with meats, to tenderize it before cooking, in a marinade, or during cooking. Wine should always be used sparingly in cookery.

When wine is not part of a recipe, but you feel you would like to add some to the dish you're cooking, add a very little at a time, and taste as you go along.

The alcohol in wine and all spirits evaporates in cooking above the boiling point so that only the flavor remains. Preferably use a dry wine of good quality (a wine that you would like to drink) in your cooking since you will be tasting the wine's flavor.

Don't be hidebound about such rules as "white wines for white meats" and "red wines with red meats." Such dishes as chicken, veal, or beef are excellent with either wine. Fish is an exception. It is better cooked with white wine.

When cooking a sauce or other dish with wine, bring it to the boiling point to let the alcohol evaporate and do not cover the pan.

When cooking with fortified wines or spirits such as brandy, it is best to flambé the dish to let the alcohol evaporate completely. Pour the spirits into a heated spoon and then over the hot food, such as a meat. Set a match to it and let the flame burn down by itself. The alcohol will then have evaporated and only the flavor of the spirits remains.

Meats that have been marinated or soaked in wine to tenderize them must be well dried before cooking.

All meat to be cooked in wine must be well browned before the wine is added.

All dishes cooked with wine can be reheated successfully. A few slices of carrots mitigate the raw tartness of some red wines.

When sherry is used in cooking, especially in seafood dishes, it should be a dry sherry and used most sparingly.

SOLE IN WHITE WINE
¼ cup butter
2 shallots or 4 green onions, finely chopped
6 fillets of lemon sole or flounder
1½ cups dry white wine (about)
  Salt and pepper to taste
1 teaspoon crumbled dried tarragon
1 tablespoon chopped parsley
¼ cup all-purpose flour
1 cup heavy cream
  Buttered crumbs or grated cheese

Use 1 tablespoon of the butter to butter an oval or oblong baking dish (about 11 x 14 inches) or a fish poacher, which usually measures 12 x 16 inches, and a piece of paper cut to fit. Place shallots on bottom and arrange fillets on top. Barely cover with dry white wine. Season with salt and pepper. Add tarragon and parsley. Cover with the buttered paper and put in preheated moderate oven (350°F.)

for about 15 minutes, or until fish is just cooked through.

Remove paper; if you are to serve fish in the baking dish, pour off the liquid, but keep fish warm with the buttered paper over it. Measure liquid from the fish and reduce to 1 cup, if need be, over high heat. Prepare cream sauce by heating remaining 3 tablespoons butter and the flour together over low heat. Stir in fish liquid and the heavy cream. Correct seasoning. When sauce is thickened, simmer for 4 or 5 minutes. Pour sauce over fillets. Sprinkle with a few buttered crumbs. Put under preheated broiler for 3 or 4 minutes to glaze. Makes 4 to 6 servings.

DAUBE PROVENCALE
4 to 5 pounds chuck or rump of beef, rolled and tied
3 garlic cloves
1 onion stuck with 2 cloves
1 teaspoon crumbled dried thyme
½ teaspoon crumbled dried rosemary
1 teaspoon pepper
1 pig's foot, split
2 carrots
2 teaspoons salt (about)
  Coarse dry red wine
2 tablespoons tomato paste
1 cup stoned black olives
1 pound macaroni

Put all ingredients in a bowl except wine, tomato paste, olives, and macaroni. Add enough wine to cover. Let stand in refrigerator for 12 to 24 hours. Remove to casserole or Dutch oven. Cover tightly and either simmer on top of stove, or bake in preheated very slow oven (200° F.) for 4 to 6 hours, or until meat is tender. Add tomato paste and black olives (Italian or Greek type) and cook for another 30 minutes. Skim off excess fat.

Put meat and pig's foot on a platter and slice meat. Reserve sauce. Garnish platter with additional boiled onions and carrots if you wish. Cook macaroni in boiling salted water until done to your taste, and drain. Mix with thick luscious sauce and serve with the *daube*. This is called *macaronnade*. A *daube* is much better made one day and allowed to rest for 24 hours, when all fat can be removed. Then it can be eaten either cold in its own jelly or heated and served with *macaronnade,* as above. Makes 6 to 8 servings.

FILET OF BEEF WITH SHERRY
4 tomatoes, peeled, seeded, and chopped
5 tablespoons butter
  Salt and pepper
1 teaspoon sugar, if needed
12 mushroom caps
¼ cup water mixed with ¼ cup sherry
6 tournedos cut from the filet, about 1½ inches thick, each wrapped and tied with a piece of salt pork or bacon
¼ cup finely chopped beef fat or ¼ cup butter and 2 tablespoons cooking oil

1 teaspoon meat extract
6 pieces of fried toast, about the size of the tournedos
½ cup sherry

Cook tomatoes in butter until most of liquid has evaporated. Season with salt and pepper. Add sugar if needed. Set aside. Poach mushrooms in water and sherry mixture. Set aside. Using heavy skillet, sauté tournedos in hot beef fat until meat reaches desired state of rareness. Season tournedos with salt and pepper. Add meat extract to pan. Turn tournedos and cook for a few seconds longer to brown nicely. Remove to hot platter and put on fried toast. Top with a spoonful of tomato mixture and a mushroom cap. Add sherry to skillet and let it cook down very quickly with the pan juices. Pour over tournedos. Makes 6 servings.

CHICKEN BRAISED WITH WINE
7 tablespoons butter
3 tablespoons cooking oil
1 roasting chicken (3½ to 4 pounds)
  Salt and pepper to taste
1 teaspoon crumbled dried thyme
1 onion stuck with 2 cloves
1 small carrot
  Dry red wine
16 small white onions
1 teaspoon sugar
12 to 16 mushroom caps
  Beurre manié (butter and flour kneaded together)
  Chopped parsley

Melt 3 tablespoons of the butter and the cooking oil in a heavy skillet. Brown chicken over fairly high heat until nicely colored on all sides. Season with salt and pepper. Transfer to a casserole or baking dish which can be covered. Add thyme, onion with cloves, carrot, and enough full-bodied red wine to cover the chicken. Simmer, covered, in preheated slow oven (300°F.) for 1 to 1½ hours, or until chicken is just tender. Do not overcook. It may be that you will have to reduce temperature to slow (250°F.) if it seems to be cooking too quickly.

While casserole is cooking, sauté white onions in remaining butter. Cover pan or skillet and steam onions until tender. Add sugar at the last minute, to caramelize and give onions color. Sauté mushroom caps until lightly browned in the skillet in which you browned the chicken, adding more butter if needed. Season them with salt and pepper.

Remove chicken when it is tender, cut into serving pieces, and arrange on a hot platter. Reduce wine sauce over a high heat. Correct seasoning and thicken sauce with small balls of *beurre manié.* Pour sauce over chicken and top with chopped parsley. Garnish with glazed onions and mushroom caps and serve with boiled potatoes. Drink the same type wine used for Coq au Vin. Makes 4 to 6 servings.

Duckling Rosé

DUCKLING ROSÉ

1 duckling, about 5 pounds, cut in
  quarters
Salt
Paprika
Powdered ginger
1 tablespoon grated onion
1 cup rosé
⅓ cup brown sugar, firmly packed
⅓ cup granulated sugar
1 tablespoon cornstarch
1 teaspoon grated orange rind

Remove any excess fat from duckling
and put bird quarters in shallow baking
pan. Roast, uncovered, in preheated hot
oven (400° F.) for 30 minutes. Remove
from oven and drain off fat. Sprinkle
duckling pieces with salt, paprika, ginger,
and the onion. Pour ¼ cup of the wine
into pan. Cover tightly with foil and roast
for 45 minutes longer, or until duckling
is tender. Mix ¼ teaspoon salt, remaining wine, and other ingredients in saucepan. Cook, stirring constantly, until
thickened. Pour over duckling and roast,
uncovered, for about 10 minutes longer,
or until glazed, basting frequently. Makes
4 servings.

CABBAGE IN WHITE WINE

6 tablespoons goose fat, bacon fat, or
  olive oil
1 large head cabbage, coarsely
  shredded
Salt and pepper to taste
1 small onion, sliced
1 cup very dry white wine or vermouth

Heat fat in large heavy skillet or deep
pan over medium heat. Put cabbage in it
and cook, turning several times, until it is
lightly browned. Season with salt and
pepper. Add onion and white wine. Turn
down heat and simmer, covered, until
cabbage is soft and well blended, stirring
occasionally. Makes 4 servings.

PRUNES IN WINE

36 prunes
  Port
1 cup sugar
  Heavy cream, whipped

Soak prunes in enough good port to
cover them. Let stand for 24 hours. Heat
sugar with 1 cup port and stir until sugar
is dissolved. Add port from prunes and
cook for 3 minutes. Then add prunes and
cook until they reach the boiling point.
Cool prunes in the wine and put in refrigerator for 24 hours. Serve with port-
flavored whipped cream. Makes 6 servings.

WINTERGREEN—A trailing evergreen
plant, native to eastern North America,
which takes its name from the fact that
it keeps its foliage during the winter. Also
known as teaberry and checkerberry, it is
a low hardy shrub with white flowers and
small bright red berries.

The whole plant may be eaten, and

probably often was by the Indians of our
northeast coast. Wintergreen oil, an important flavoring material, used in medi-
cine and in candy, soft drinks, chewing
gum, and dentifrices, was once obtained
exclusively from the leaves of the plant,
but nowadays the twigs and bark of the
sweet birch are more used to give wintergreen flavor than the plant itself.

WOODCOCK—The name is used to describe two related birds, the European
woodcock, *Scolopex rusticola,* and a similar but smaller American bird, *Philohela
minor.* Both are migratory birds and are
considered the best of winged game.

The American woodcock is ten to
twelve inches long and weighs about ten
ounces, the female being the larger. It
has a rounded body, short legs, brownish-
gray feathers, and a bill that is extremely
sensitive at the tip.

Woodcock can be prepared or cooked
in the same way as other game birds.
When young, it can be roasted or broiled;
if of unknown age, it is best pot-roasted
and finished with a sour-cream gravy.
Frozen dressed woodcock is available in
specialty food stores and stores special-
izing in game.

BAKED WOODCOCK

Cut cleaned and drawn bird into serving
pieces. Dip into milk and flour seasoned
with salt and pepper. Brown on all sides
in hot butter. Place meat in casserole and
add enough sweet or sour cream to cover.
Add 7 or 8 crushed juniper berries for
flavor (optional). Bake, covered, in preheated moderate oven (350° F.) until
tender. Baking time depends on the age
and size of the bird, but it is tender when
easily pierced with a fork.

Note: If the bird is baked in sour cream,
the appearance of the sauce will be cur-
dled, but this is as it should be. If this
is objectionable, thicken the sauce with a
little flour mixed with water into a smooth
paste. Strain sauce before serving to remove juniper berries.

**WOODRUFF, SWEET (Asperula odo-
rata)**—A spreading plant with small white
flowers whose slim yellow leaves are used
to flavor beverages. The sweet woodruff
plant is a clumpy little one, growing only
about eight inches tall; it provides a good
ground cover. The characteristic odor of
its leaves is released when they are somewhat dried; they then smell like new-
mown hay. The leaves may be used to
flavor cold fruit drinks and wine cups.
Fruit cups, too, may be garnished with a
sprig. And the traditional May wine or
Maibowle is made by steeping woodruff
in Rhine wine.

MAIBOWLE

2 bunches woodruff
½ cup super fine sugar, or sugar to
  taste
½ cup brandy
3 bottles Moselle or Rhine wine
  Ice
1 bottle champagne
½ cup fresh strawberries (optional)

Wash woodruff and shake dry. Place in
deep bowl with sugar, brandy, and 1 bottle of the wine. Cover bowl; let stand
overnight at room temperature. Before
serving, strain mixture and pour over ice
in punch bowl. Add remaining still wine
and the champagne. Float strawberries in
punch bowl, for decorative appearance.
Makes 8 to 10 servings.

WORCESTERSHIRE SAUCE—A thin,
dark, pungent seasoning sauce, containing
garlic, soy, vinegar, anchovies, tamarinds,
onions, shallots, molasses, sugar, salt,
and spices. The sauce was originally made
in Worcester, England, and is used with
meats. It can also be used as a seasoning
ingredient in gravies, soups, tomato juice,
meat loaves, cheese rabbits, etc. Worcestershire is made in the United States but
is also available imported from England.

WORMWOOD (Artemisia absinthium)
—This spreading, shrubby perennial grows
to a height of four feet. It has lobed
gray-looking leaves covered with silky
hair. These leaves have some culinary
use, for they may be put on top of roast
goose to cut grease. A mixture of the
leaves and flowers is sometimes drunk for
colds, digestion, and even rheumatism.
Wormwood is best known, however, as a
flavoring ingredient in absinthe, a powerful spirit now illegal in this country.
Absinthe-type cordials made without
wormwood are available.

YAM—One of the various plants of the genus *Dioscorea,* a tropical group with twining or creeping stems and broad leaves. The yam is a thick tuber which develops at the base of the stem. There are more than 150 species of this widely used root growing in Central and South America, the West Indies, and tropical Asia. Some varieties grow up to 100 pounds; some are no larger than a small potato. The consistency varies from coarse and mealy to tender and mushy, with some crisp varieties.

There are as many ways of preparing yams as there are varieties of the tuber. They may be used in soup, like mashed potatoes, mashed and then fried or baked, boiled or baked in their jackets, cooked with meat in stews, or cut into slices and fried. Most yams have a bitter taste when raw, which disappears when they are cooked.

People often think that yams and sweet potatoes are the same thing, but although they resemble each other closely in taste, they belong to entirely different families of plants. For culinary purposes, yams and sweet potatoes are interchangeable and not even an expert with a refined palate would be sure to be able to tell the difference in a cooked dish.

Few true yams are cultivated in the United States, but certain moist-fleshed varieties of sweet potato are called "yams." The "air potato" or Asian species is grown to some extent for food and the cinnamon vine is cultivated as an ornamental plant for its cinnamon-scented white blossoms. But throughout the West Indies and most parts of Central and South America the yam is the principal food of the working class.

The name "yam" is a development from the Sengalese word *nyami,* to eat: African slaves named the strange sweet-potato-like tubers they saw for the first time in the West Indies. In the southern parts of this country sweet potatoes are often casually referred to as yams; although this is not accurate, in the kitchen it does not make any real difference.

Availability—Yams are available all year round in stores catering to people of Puerto Rican, South or Central American, or West Indian origin.

Purchasing Guide—Select firm yams with unwrinkled skins. Some yams have a white, yellow, or even purple flesh. Some are sold by the piece or by weight in pieces cut from the larger yams.

Storage—Uncut yams should be stored in a cool dark dry place. Cooked yams should be refrigerated.
- [ ] Kitchen shelf: 1 week
- [ ] Refrigerator shelf, cooked: 4 to 5 days
- [ ] Refrigerator frozen-food compartment, cooked: 3 months
- [ ] Freezer, cooked: 1 year

Caloric Value
- [ ] 3½ ounces, raw = 101 calories

Basic Preparation—Peel, wash, and slice

or cube. Can be cooked in any way potatoes are cooked.

ORANGE YAMS

4 medium yams
¼ cup firmly packed brown sugar
2 tablespoons butter or margarine
  Grated rind of 1 orange
¼ cup fresh orange juice
½ teaspoon salt
⅛ teaspoon pepper

Cook yams in small amount of boiling water until tender. Drain and peel. Mash while hot. Add remaining ingredients and beat until light and fluffy. Put in broiler-proof dish and brown lightly in broiler. Good with duck or other poultry, or with ham. Makes 4 servings.

PUERTO RICAN YAM AND CHEESE CRULLERS

2 cups grated peeled yams
½ cup sifted all-purpose flour
2 tablespoons cooking oil
1 teaspoon salt
¼ cup grated Cheddar cheese
1 egg, well beaten
3 tablespoons milk
  Fat or oil for deep frying

Combine all ingredients except fat. Beat until well blended. Drop mixture by teaspoonfuls into deep hot fat (375°F. on a frying thermometer) and fry until golden-brown on all sides. Drain on absorbent paper. Can be served with guava jelly if desired. Makes 4 dozen crullers.

YAM CUSTARD PIE

2 cups cold mashed cooked yams
3 eggs, separated
1 cup less 2 tablespoons sugar
2 tablespoons melted butter
½ teaspoon salt
1 cup milk
  Pastry for 1-crust 9-inch pie, unbaked
½ teaspoon vanilla extract
¼ cup shredded coconut

Beat yams and egg yolks together until light and fluffy. Beat in ½ cup sugar, the butter, salt, and milk. Pour into pastry-lined pie pan. Bake in preheated moderate oven (350°F.) for 40 minutes, or until set. Beat egg whites until foamy. Gradually beat in remaining sugar and continue beating until stiff. Add vanilla; pile meringue lightly on pie. Sprinkle with coconut. Bake in hot oven (425°F.) for 5 minutes. Cool. Makes 6 to 8 servings.

YAM SPICECAKE

2 cups sifted cake flour
¾ teaspoon salt
2 teaspoons baking powder
¼ teaspoon baking soda
1 teaspoon each of ground cinnamon and nutmeg
⅛ teaspoon ground cloves
½ cup soft butter or margarine
¾ cup sugar
2 eggs
1¼ cups cold mashed cooked or canned yams
½ cup milk
  Fluffy white frosting
¼ cup coarsely chopped nuts

Sift first 7 ingredients. Cream butter, add sugar, and cream until light and fluffy. Add eggs, one at a time, beating thoroughly after each addition. Beat in yams. Add sifted dry ingredients and milk, beating only until smooth. Line two 8-inch layer-cake pans with wax paper. Pour batter into pans. Bake in preheated moderate oven (350°F.) for about 35 minutes. Turn out on racks and peel off paper. Cool, and frost. Top with nuts.

Yeast

by Lucy Kavaler

Two thousand yeasts packed together would occupy barely the space required to write their name. Each of these tiny organisms has but one cell and reproduces in the most primitive way, by budding. Yeasts float unseen in the air around us, lie in the soil, fall onto plants and on our food. Although they could hardly be more different from mushrooms or truffles, they belong to the same group of living things, the fungi. Like all fungi, they require moisture and sugar or starch in order to grow, but unlike other fungi, the genus *Saccharomyces* changes the food it consumes into alcohol and carbon dioxide in a process known as fermentation.

A delicate goblet filled with champagne, a slice of soft white bread, a bottle of cold hearty beer are very different from one another, but all are linked by this single organism, the yeast. The carbon dioxide given off by the growing yeast pushes its way through flat heavy dough, lifting it into a light fluffy loaf. The alcohol imparts delightful and intoxicating qualities to grape juice and unappetizing grain mashes, transforming them into wines, whiskeys, and beer.

Mothers in ancient Egypt worried about their children's diet and sent jugs of beer to school. Their modern counterparts frown on alcohol for minors and so nowadays adults alone manage to down ninety-one million barrels of the foaming drink every year. Barley and corn malt provide the starch that nourishes the brewers' yeasts. Some beer

makers add fresh yeasts to each brew, while others save a little of the fermented liquid from one time to the next. Long before the true nature of fungi was understood, a scientist, forgotten now, observed that the same yeasts which fermented beer could also make bread and cakes rise. And the brewers handed their leftovers to bakers and housewives.

When America was young, it was the custom for a bride to receive a bit of a yeast starter from her mother. Each time she baked, she would keep some of the yeast-filled dough. Prospectors and trappers in the Northwest carried a similar lump of sourdough in their packs to make the tasty bread that bears its name. Today sourdough bread is a San Francisco specialty and only a few women still use starters handed down in the family for hundreds of years, but both home baked and commercially baked bread and coffeecake are as dependent on yeast as ever they were.

The brewers' yeast was sent back to the beer makers long ago, replaced by bakers' yeast, which is composed of strains specially selected for both their flavor and their ability to produce a lot of carbon dioxide and rather little alcohol. The yeast is compressed, with 3,500 billion yeast organisms going into a one-pound cake. Even this treatment does not quiet the active fungi, and they must be refrigerated or they will start to grow before being put into the dough. Yeast-makers have discovered that the organisms can be kept under control by further drying to send them into a resting stage. This active dry yeast cannot function, even without refrigeration, until it is revived with warm water.

The same packages of compressed or active dry yeasts are used by those who make their own wines. This sounds delightfully wicked and reminiscent of bootleggers and Prohibition, but actually the law allows the fermentation of 200 gallons a year for home use. Until recently the great wines of France were fermented only by the wild yeasts that settled on the grapes. Each vineyard, a Frenchman explains, has slightly different yeasts and these account for some of the subtle differences in wine flavor. Unfortunately, yeasts are scarce in dry seasons. Scientists, recognizing the uncertainties of nature, isolated the chief wine-making yeast strains and produced pure cultures in the laboratory. These are used exclusively in America and by a growing number of European vintners as well.

The question, what makes one wine sweet and another dry, would trap many a quiz program contestant. The answer has nothing to do with sweet or sour grapes. A wine is dry when the yeasts have been allowed to complete the fermentation process and to transform all the sugar in the juice into alcohol; when fermentation is incomplete, some sugar is left and sweetens the wine. The bubbles in champagne that tickle the nose arise when additional yeasts and sugar are placed in white wine and a second fermentation occurs. In order to make the gin for a martini and the Scotch for a highball, the yeasts must do their familiar work in a grain mash which is then distilled.

Quite another species of yeast, *Torulopsis* or *Candida utilis,* cannot perform the miracle of fermentation, but may become a miracle food of the future. In the hour it takes to prepare dinner, the population of the world increases by 3,600. It has been estimated that more than six billion people will be on earth by the year 2,000, many of them hungry unless new sources of food, such as torula yeast, are utilized. Torula reproduces at such speed that half a ton yields 6,000 to 7,000 tons of protein in a mere twenty-four hours. And these yeasts will thrive in mashes made of rotten fruits, sugar wastes, or molasses. During World Wars I and II there were unnerving reports that "the Germans are making steaks out of sawdust." The truth was nearly as strange. They were growing torula yeasts on the liquid left over when logs are made into wood pulp. Even today in the food-rich United States several paper mills are using their wastes in this way. Torula adds protein and vitamins to a number of canned soups, baby foods, pet foods, and TV dinners.

Although torula is really more a hope for the future than a food of the present, knowledge about this yeast can sometimes mean the difference between life and death. In World War II when Dutch prisoners of war were starving in a Japanese prison camp in Java, a botanist among them suggested growing torula yeast on scraps of rotten potatoes, spoiled fish, and ammonia distilled from urine. The yeast flourished on these repellent nutrients and provided more than 130 pounds of food a week, just enough to keep the men alive until liberation.

Availability—Packaged active dry yeast is widely available. Cakes of compressed yeast are also available, but are less widely distributed. The ⅔-ounce cake of compressed yeast is the equivalent of one package of active dry yeast. Since the dry yeast keeps much better than the compressed and equally good results are obtained with it, this type is much more in demand.

Storage

- ☐ Compressed, refrigerator shelf: 2 weeks
- ☐ Dry, kitchen shelf: until time dated on package

Nutritive Food Values—A good source of B vitamins.

- ☐ Baker's compressed, 3½ ounces = 86 calories
- ☐ Baker's dry, active, 3½ ounces = 282 calories
- ☐ Brewer's dry, 3½ ounces = 283 calories
- ☐ Torula, 3½ ounces = 277 calories

USING YEAST

There is a difference in compressed and active dry yeasts in that different temperatures of water are required for dissolving them. Lukewarm water (80°F. to 90°F.) should be used for the compressed. A drop of liquid which feels cool when placed on the inside of the wrist is lukewarm, or the right temperature for the compressed. Active dry yeast can be dissolved in slightly warmer water (110° F. to 115°F.). Compressed yeast will dissolve in milk but dry yeast should always be dissolved in water. If no water is called for in a recipe, ¼ cup water should be substituted for an equal amount of milk.

Some of the following questions are often asked about yeast:

Q. Is it possible to get yeast dough too warm?

A. Yes. If the rising place is too warm, some of the yeast will be killed. A temperature of 145°F. will kill yeast.

Q. How can one tell if compressed yeast is still good?

A. Fresh compressed yeast will "break clean" when crumbled into the water. If compressed yeast is old, it will be mushy.

Q. What is the purpose of salt in bread?

A. Salt imparts a pleasant flavor to bread and a small quantity also helps to point up other flavors. The main purpose, however, is to control the yeast action so the rising is not too rapid.

Q. How can one tell when enough flour has been added to the dough when a range is given?

A. Add one-half the flour amount specified, beat until smooth, then add more flour until it begins to clean the sides of the bowl and can be handled.

Q. How can one tell when dough has risen enough?

A. Press a finger deep into side of dough. If the dent remains, the dough has doubled or, in other words, it has risen enough. Be sure to check at minimum time given, so dough does not get *too* light.

How to Cook Superbly: Yeast Rolls and Buns

By Helen Evans Brown

Probably no experience so delights a cook as the feeling of yeast dough under her hands as she kneads it for bread or rolls. It seems alive, and that's because it is. Yeast is a plant, a living plant, and watching and feeling it grow as the dough rises is truly exciting. And then there's that wonderful aroma while it's baking! But most gratifying of all are the delectable results, achieved with so little effort. What a joy to produce light hot rolls for a family dinner, even though you've only been home an hour or two, or to make your own hamburger buns for the children. But when your miniature Parker House rolls are in such demand at the church fair, why should you announce that anyone could make them as well? Receipts for yeast rolls vary, but forming them into different shapes is the same. Some doughs stay in the refrigerator for several days, some can be baked as soon as they have risen. Dough can also be frozen for a short time, but it's more satisfactory to bake the rolls first, then freeze them.

EQUIPMENT

You'll need only the regular kitchen equipment: a large mixing bowl, a pastry board, cookie cutters, a rolling pin, cookie sheets, and muffin pans, as well as the usual measures, saucepans, spoons, and knives. It's also nice to have a heavy-duty electric mixer with a dough hook, if you have neither the time nor strength for kneading.

MIXING, KNEADING, AND RAISING

There was a time when milk for yeast rolls or bread had to be scalded, then cooled to lukewarm. This was to avoid any bacteria that might be in the milk and affect the yeast. As almost all of today's milk is pasteurized, this is unnecessary. However, the milk should be warm so that the yeast will work faster. I have found that the quickest way to mix the ingredients is to heat the water or milk to about as hot as the finger can stand, add butter, sugar, and salt to it, and stir until the butter is melted and the mixture is lukewarm. This won't take long if the butter is cold. The yeast is crumbled or sprinkled into warm water, then stirred until dissolved. Now add the beaten eggs, then beat in part of the flour. Vigorous beating at this point gets best results. Use a spoon or electric or hand beater. Add flour gradually until the mixture is too stiff to beat, then continue adding flour and mix until the desired consistency is reached, usually soft but not sticky. I use my hands for this, but a wooden spoon may be used. As the moisture content of flour varies, it is impossible to give the exact amount of flour needed. When making most rolls, sufficient flour has been added when the mixture leaves the side of the bowl, and is soft but not sticky. Now turn it out on a floured board, sprinkle with a little flour, and cover with a cloth. Let stand for 10 minutes, then start kneading if the recipe calls for it. To do this, fold the dough toward you, then, using the heels of your lightly floured hands, push it away. Give it a half turn, and repeat and repeat until the dough is smooth and shiny. While kneading, you may have to sprinkle a little more flour on the board to keep the dough from sticking. Now butter a large bowl; put the dough in it. Turn the dough in the bowl so that the top is greased, and cover. Put in a warm place—80°F. is ideal—to rise. (Refrigerator rolls do not require this raising period.) If you have an oven with a pilot light, put it in there with the door slightly ajar. When the dough has doubled in bulk, it is ready. If you are unsure, stick your forefinger into the dough. It is right if the imprint remains. Now knock down; this means to punch it in the middle with your fist. It will fall immediately. Give it two or three turns to smooth the dough (some recipes call for

a second kneading at this point); you are now ready to form and bake your rolls.

TO DISSOLVE YEAST

Use very warm water (105°F. to 115°F.) for dry yeast; use lukewarm (80°F. to 90°F.) for compressed.

EGG GLAZE

If you want your rolls beautifully shiny and browned, brush them, before baking, with a mixture of 1 slightly beaten egg and 1 tablespoon milk or water. The French call this gilding *dorure*.

SHAPING AND BAKING VARIOUS ROLLS

■ **Breadsticks**—Roll the dough about ½ inch thick, cut into ½-inch strips (use a ruler and pastry wheel), and cut each strip 8 inches long. Roll strips under the palms of your hands (really under the inside of your fingers) to make even sticks about 9 inches long. Arrange on a buttered cookie sheet (be careful not to stretch them when lifting), leaving space between them. Let rise until almost doubled, and bake in preheated hot oven (425°F.) for 5 minutes; reduce heat to slow (300°F.) and bake for 15 minutes longer, or until crisp.

■ **Butterfly Wings**—Roll dough ¼ inch thick and cut into strips 6 inches wide; roll like a jelly roll. Seal edge, cut into 2-inch pieces, and put on a buttered cookie sheet, sealed side down, and swirls at the sides. Using a round pencil, a wooden dowel, or the handle of a wooden spoon, press firmly across the center of each roll, parallel with cut sides. Cover and let rise until doubled in bulk. Bake in preheated hot oven (425°F.) for 10 to 15 minutes, or until nicely browned. In rising, the cut sides spread like wings, hence the name.

■ **Butter Rolls**—Roll dough very thin, about ⅛ inch. Brush with melted butter, then cut into 2-inch strips. Pile in stacks of six, and then cut each stack into 1-inch pieces. Put in buttered muffin tins, cut side up; cover and let rise until doubled in bulk. Bake in preheated hot oven (425°F.) for 10 to 15 minutes, or until nicely browned.

■ **Cloverleaf Rolls**—Form dough into smooth round balls of about ½ ounce each, and 1¼ inches in diameter. To form a smooth ball, work with fingers and thumbs, smoothing from top to bottom. Place 3 balls, smooth side up, in each buttered muffin tin; cover and let rise until almost doubled in bulk. Bake

in preheated hot oven (425°F.) for about 15 minutes, or until brown. If you use small muffin pans, be sure to make the balls smaller, or they'll pop right out of the pans.

■ **Crescent Rolls**—Roll dough into a circle about 8 inches in diameter, and cut into 8 pie-shape pieces. Or roll dough and cut into 4-inch squares, then cut each square into halves from corner to corner. Starting at the long side of the triangle, roll toward the tip, stretching the dough a little as you roll. Bend tips in to form a crescent and put on a buttered cookie sheet. Cover and let rise until doubled in bulk. Bake in preheated hot oven (425°F.) for 10 to 15 minutes.

■ **Dinner Rolls**—Form dough into balls, then roll under fingers to make cylinders with pointed ends. Put on buttered baking sheets, glaze, then slit lengthwise with a very sharp knife or razor blade. Let rise until doubled in bulk and bake in preheated hot oven (425°F.) for 10 to 15 minutes.

■ **Figure-Eight Rolls**—Roll dough ¼ inch thick and cut into ½-inch strips. Cut strips about 8 inches long, dampen one end, and form into circles. Or cut dough with a 3-inch round cutter, and remove center with a 2-inch cutter. Give circles of dough a single twist, forming a figure 8. Put on buttered cookie sheets and let rise until doubled in bulk; then bake in preheated hot oven (425°F.) for 10 to 15 minutes, or until brown.

■ **Bowknot Rolls**—Roll dough ¼ inch thick and cut into strips as for Figure-Eight Rolls. Tie in a knot and tuck one end under, then up through the center; tuck other end under. Put on buttered cookie sheets and let rise until doubled in bulk. Bake in preheated hot oven (425° F.) for about 15 minutes.

■ **Finger Rolls**—Roll dough about ⅓ inch thick and cut with a finger-roll cutter especially made for the purpose. Let rise until doubled in bulk and bake in preheated hot oven (425°F.) for 10 to 15 minutes, or until brown.

■ **Hamburger Buns**—Roll dough ½ inch thick, allow to rest for a few minutes, then cut with a round 4-inch cutter. Put on buttered cookie sheets, let rise until doubled in bulk, then bake in preheated hot oven (425°F.) for 10 to 15 minutes, or until brown.

■ **Pan Rolls**—Form dough into 1½- or 2-ounce balls. To have them uniform,

form dough into a long roll about 1½ inches in diameter, and cut into 1½-inch pieces. Form into smooth rounds, working from the top with fingers and thumbs. Put smooth side up in a buttered deep-sided square or round cake pan, almost touching if you want soft-sided rolls, about 1½ inches apart if you want browner sides. Let rise until doubled in bulk. Bake in preheated hot oven (425° F.) for 12 to 15 minutes, or until brown.

■ **Parker House Rolls**—Roll dough ¼ inch thick and cut with a round cookie cutter in any size you prefer. Brush with melted butter, and crease each round through the center with a round pencil or handle of a wooden spoon. Fold over at the crease and press edges gently together. Place close together if you want them to have soft sides, farther apart if you prefer the all-brown variety. Cover and let rise until doubled in bulk, then bake in preheated hot oven (425°F.) for 12 to 15 minutes.

■ **Pepper and Salt Sticks**—Make like Breadsticks (page 1953), but before baking brush with Egg Glaze (page 1953), and sprinkle with cracked black pepper and coarse salt. Bake like Breadsticks.

■ **Ring of Rolls**—Roll dough ¼ inch thick and cut into rounds with a cookie cutter. Dip rolls into melted butter and arrange in a ring in 9-inch pie pan, having each round overlap half the one next to it; a 9- or 10-inch pie pan takes about 20 rolls. Let rise until doubled in bulk, and bake in preheated hot oven (400°F.) for 15 to 20 minutes. Serve whole; guests break off their own portion according to their appetites.

■ **Salt Sticks**—Make like Pepper and Salt Sticks, but use caraway seeds with the coarse salt instead of the cracked pepper.

CRUSTY ROLLS

If you want a crust on your rolls, form as described above, but bake in preheated moderate oven (350°F.) for about 25 minutes, or until brown.

YIELD

It is difficult to tell just how many rolls you can get from the following recipes, as it depends upon the size and type you are going to make. Miniature rolls use about ½ ounce of dough (a 1¼-inch ball), regular-size rolls from 1½ to 2 ounces of dough (1¾- to 2¼-inch balls). I have given the approximate total weight of these doughs so that you can figure them out for yourself.

Cloverleaf, crescent, bowknot, figure-eight, and pan rolls: freshly baked and golden brown from the oven.

PLAIN YEAST ROLLS

These are not rich, but a good plain roll, lower in calories than most.

- 1½ cups milk
- ¼ cup butter or margarine
- 2 tablespoons sugar
- 1 teaspoon salt
- 2 packages active dry yeast or 2 cakes compressed yeast
- ½ cup water*
- 5 cups (about) all-purpose flour

Heat milk as described under Mixing, Kneading, and Raising on page 1953, add butter cut into pieces, sugar, and salt. Stir until lukewarm. Sprinkle or crumble yeast into water. *Use very warm water (105°F. to 115°F.) for dry yeast; use lukewarm (80°F. to 90°F.) for compressed. Let stand for a few minutes, then stir until dissolved. Stir in dissolved yeast. Beat in 4 cups of the flour as on page 1953, adding more flour until the dough is soft but not sticky; proceed as on page 1953 (kneading, rising, etc.). Form into any type of roll, let rise, and bake in preheated hot oven (425°F.) as described on page 1953. Makes about 2½ pounds of dough.

REFRIGERATOR ROLLS

A good recipe if hot rolls are wanted several days running, or if you want to mix them ahead and bake a few days later. The dough, when refrigerated, keeps for about 6 days if made with water, but only 3 days if milk is used.

- 1½ cups milk or water
- ½ cup butter or margarine
- ⅓ cup sugar
- 2 teaspoons salt
- 2 packages active dry yeast or 2 cakes compressed yeast
- ½ cup water*
- 2 eggs, beaten
- 6 cups (about) all-purpose flour

Heat milk as hot as your finger can stand. Add butter cut into pieces, sugar, and salt. Stir until the butter is melted and the mixture is lukewarm. Sprinkle or crumble yeast into water. *Use very warm water (105°F. to 115°F.) for dry yeast; use lukewarm (80°F. to 90°F.) for compressed. Let stand for a few minutes, then stir until dissolved. Add eggs and dissolved yeast to butter mixture. Add 4 cups of the flour and beat well. Add as much additional flour as is needed to make a soft dough. Turn out on a lightly floured board and knead until satiny and elastic. Butter a large mixing bowl, put in dough, turn over to grease top, and cover tightly. Put the dough in the refrig-

erator and remove as much as is needed at a time. Form into rolls, let rise until doubled, and bake in preheated hot oven (425°F.) for 12 to 15 minutes, as on page 1953. Weight is 3 pounds, 6 ounces.

NO-KNEAD FEATHER ROLLS

- 1 cup water
- ¼ cup butter or margarine
- 2 tablespoons sugar
- 1 teaspoon salt
- 1 package active dry yeast or 1 cake compressed yeast
- ¼ cup water*
- 1 egg, beaten
- 3 cups all-purpose flour

Heat water as hot as your hand can stand; add butter cut into pieces, sugar, and salt. Stir until butter is melted and the mixture is lukewarm. Sprinkle or crumble yeast into water. *Use very warm water (105°F. to 115°F.) for dry yeast; use lukewarm (80°F. to 90°F.) for compressed. Let stand for a few minutes, then stir until dissolved. Add dissolved yeast and egg to first mixture. Beat in flour to make a very soft dough; it will be too soft to knead. Brush top with melted butter, cover, and let rise until doubled in bulk. Stir down and spoon into buttered 2-inch muffin tins and allow to rise in a warm place until the dough has almost reached the top of the pans. Bake in preheated hot oven (425°F.) for 12 to 15 minutes. Makes about 18 rolls.

CORNMEAL ROLLS

- 1 package active dry yeast or 1 cake compressed yeast
- ¼ cup water*
- 1 cup milk
- ¼ cup butter or margarine
- 1 cup cornmeal
- 2 tablespoons sugar
- 1 teaspoon salt
- 2 eggs, beaten
- 3 cups (about) all-purpose flour

Sprinkle or crumble yeast into water. *Use very warm water (105°F. to 115°F.) for dry yeast; use lukewarm (80°F. to 90°F.) for compressed. Let stand for a few minutes, then stir until dissolved. Heat milk, add butter cut into pieces, cornmeal, sugar, and salt. Stir until butter is melted and mixture is lukewarm. Add yeast mixture, eggs, and flour; mix well, adding more flour if needed to make a soft but not sticky dough. Turn out on a floured board and knead until satiny and elastic. Cover and let rise until doubled in bulk. Knock down, form, and let rise until doubled. Bake in preheated

hot oven (425°F.) for 12 to 15 minutes. Dough weighs about 2¼ pounds.

WHOLE-WHEAT ROLLS

- 1 cup milk
- 2 tablespoons sugar
- ⅓ cup butter or margarine
- 1 teaspoon salt
- 2 packages active dry yeast or 2 cakes compressed yeast
- ½ cup water*
- 2 cups all-purpose flour
- 1½ cups (about) whole-wheat flour

Heat milk, add sugar, butter cut into pieces, and salt. Stir until lukewarm. Sprinkle or crumble yeast into water. *Use very warm water (105°F. to 115°F.) for dry yeast; use lukewarm (80°F. to 90°F.) for compressed. Let stand for a few minutes, then stir until dissolved. Add dissolved yeast and flours to first mixture. Beat well, turn out on a floured board, and knead until satiny and elastic. Cover and let rise until doubled in bulk. Knock down and knead lightly, then form into rolls; pan rolls, cloverleaf, parker house are good shapes for this dough. Bake in preheated hot oven (425°F.) for 12 to 15 minutes. Dough weighs about 2 pounds.

SQUASH ROLLS

- 1 cup water*
- ¾ cup sugar
- 1 package active dry yeast, or 1 cake compressed yeast
- Cooking oil
- 2 teaspoons salt
- 1 cup strained cooked winter squash
- ½ cup nonfat dry-milk solids
- 5 cups all-purpose flour (about)

*Use very warm water (105°F. to 115°F.) for dry yeast; use lukewarm (80°F. to 90°F.) for compressed. Put water and sugar into the large bowl of electric mixer. Sprinkle dry yeast or crumble cake into mixture. Let stand for 5 minutes; then stir until dissolved. Add 3 tablespoons oil, the salt, squash, and dry milk. Beat well at low speed. Gradually beat in 2 cups of the flour. (Or beat with rotary beater.) Scrape beaters, and add remaining flour by hand, mixing well. Let stand in a warm place until doubled in bulk, about 1 hour. Put on a floured board and knead gently. Roll to 1-inch thickness. Cut with floured 2½-inch cutter. Roll edges lightly in oil so that the baked rolls will separate readily. Put in greased baking pan (13 x 9 x 2 inches), and let rise until doubled, about 30 minutes. Bake in preheated hot oven (400°F.) for about 20 minutes. Makes about 15.

YOGURT—A semisolid milk product that has been made acid by the addition of bacterial cultures which have much greater acidifying power than natural ferments. Apart from being a refreshing and nourishing food, yogurt is said by many to have excellent medicinal qualities in keeping the intestinal system healthy, helping to clear up skin diseases, etc. Buttermilk, clabbered milk, kumiss, etc., are all dairy products related to yogurt.

Yogurt stems from the Balkans, and in the Balkans and the Near East it is consumed several times daily, either as is or used in cooking. It has been used there for so many centuries that no one knows how long, and the people of these regions claim that their unquestionable hardiness and longevity is due to the constant consumption of yogurt.

Yogurt can be made from any kind of milk, and although cows' milk is now most commonly used, it is still made from sheeps' and goats' milk wherever these animals are raised in the Balkans.

In America, yogurt is made commercially either plain or flavored with fruits and extracts. However, yogurt can also be made at home. Plain yogurt is an excellent ingredient in cooking, introducing an interesting flavor twist to familiar foods.

Availability—Yogurt made from whole milk or partially skimmed milk is widely available plain or flavored with vanilla or such fruits as prune, strawberry, pineapple, apricot, etc. The fruit-flavored yogurts are actually plain yogurt with the fruit in the bottom of the container.

Storage—Store in the coldest part of refrigerator.

☐ Refrigerator shelf: 2 to 3 days

Nutritive Food Values—A good source of vitamin B and calcium.

☐ Plain, 3½ ounces, made from whole milk = 62 calories

☐ Plain, 3½ ounces, made from partially skimmed milk = 50 calories

HOMEMADE YOGURT
¼ cup plain yogurt
1 quart non-fat milk (fresh or made from granules)

Let the yogurt stand at room temperature for 3 to 4 hours. Heat milk to 120°F. on a candy thermometer. Do not overheat. Cool to 90°F. Add the yogurt and mix thoroughly. Turn into a bowl or 4 individual containers. Do not stir or move containers. Cover and keep barely lukewarm until a curd has formed. Store in refrigerator. Makes 1 quart.

BULGARIAN COLD CUCUMBER SOUP
4 cups plain yogurt
½ cup chopped walnuts
2 cups diced cucumbers
Salt and white pepper to taste
2 garlic cloves, crushed

Beat yogurt until smooth. Combine walnuts, cucumbers, salt, pepper, and garlic. Add to yogurt and blend. Chill thoroughly. At serving time, you may add 1 ice cube to each serving. Makes 4 to 6 servings.

LAMB BARYANI
2 cups uncooked rice
Salt
4 onions
Butter or margarine
½ teaspoon ground coriander
½ teaspoon turmeric
1½ cups plain yogurt
1 pound boneless lamb, sliced
Seeds from 2 cardamom pods
¼ teaspoon ground cinnamon
3 whole cloves
¼ teaspoon chili powder
Water
2 hard-cooked eggs
Rosewater

Cook rice in boiling salted water. Drain. Slice 2 onions and cook until golden-brown in 2 tablespoons butter. Mix onion with coriander, turmeric, 1 teaspoon salt, and the yogurt. Rub mixture into lamb and let stand for 30 minutes. Pound remaining onions in a mortar with a pestle, or grind fine. Add lamb mixture and cook, uncovered, in skillet until some of the liquid has evaporated. Alternate layers of meat mixture and rice in a 3-quart casserole. Sprinkle top layer with cardamom seed, cinnamon, cloves, and chili powder. Pour 3 tablespoons butter, melted, over top. Add 2 or 3 tablespoons of water. Cover tightly and bake in preheated moderate oven (350°F.) for about 45 minutes. Garnish with eggs, cut into wedges. Sprinkle with a few drops of rosewater. Makes 6 to 8 servings.

STUFFED VEAL CUTLETS
2 pounds Italian-style veal cutlets
½ teaspoon crumbled dried rosemary
6 hard-cooked eggs, sieved
1 tablespoon minced onion
¼ cup minced fresh pineapple
¼ teaspoon ground cinnamon
¼ cup dry bread crumbs
¼ cup plain yogurt (about)
⅓ cup butter or margarine
1 cup rich beef bouillon
1 cup canned tomatoes

Pound meat until very thin. Sprinkle meat with rosemary and let stand for 2 hours. Mix eggs with onion, pineapple, cinnamon, crumbs, and enough yogurt to make a thick mixture. Put some of the filling on each cutlet. Roll up meat and skewer with toothpicks or fasten with a string. Brown veal in butter on all sides. Add bouillon and tomatoes. Cover and bake in preheated slow oven (300°F.) for 2 hours. Thicken liquid if desired. Makes 4 to 6 servings.

STEAK KABOBS
1½ pounds boneless tender steak, cut into 1½-inch cubes
½ cup plain yogurt
1 tablespoon minced shallot or green

onion
Pepper and salt to taste

In refrigerator marinate meat in remaining ingredients, except salt, for 1 to 2 days, turning occasionally. Thread on large skewers, and broil over hot charcoal for about 15 minutes, turning frequently. Season with salt. Makes 3 or 4 servings.

EGG AND TONGUE WITH YOGURT SAUCE
¼ cup butter or margarine
6 eggs
Salt and pepper to taste
6 slices of cooked tongue
6 slices of hot thin toast
1 cup plain yogurt
2 tablespoons soft butter
1 teaspoon paprika
2 tablespoons chopped fresh dill

Melt butter; slip eggs into butter and fry until whites are firm and yolks are still soft. Sprinkle with salt and pepper. Put a slice of tongue on a piece of toast. Top with hot fried egg. Beat yogurt until smooth and spoon yogurt over egg. Beat butter with paprika and put a small amount of butter and chopped dill on top of yogurt. Makes 6 servings.

CHICKEN TANDOORI
2 broiler-fryers, about 2½ pounds each
1 whole cardamom pod
1½ pints plain yogurt
1½ tablespoons fresh lime juice
1½ tablespoons butter or margarine, melted
1 garlic clove, crushed
1 teaspoon chili powder
½ teaspoon ground coriander
⅛ teaspoon ground ginger

Split chickens into halves, and discard backbones. Remove skin except from the wings. Cut small slits in meat in several places. Put in large bowl. Remove seed from cardamom pod, and crush. Mix with remaining ingredients, and pour over chickens. Marinate for at least 6 hours, or overnight. Broil slowly, covered with the marinade, for 25 to 30 minutes on each side, or until chicken is tender. Makes 4 servings.

EGGPLANT WITH YOGURT
2 medium eggplants
1 teaspoon minced garlic
1 cup plain yogurt
Salt and pepper to taste

Bake eggplants in preheated hot oven (425°F.) for about 40 minutes, turning occasionally. Peel off skin, and discard. Chop the pulp; add garlic, yogurt, and salt and pepper. Makes 6 servings.

YOGURT ONIONS
½ cup milk
3 tablespoons butter or margarine
8 onions, sliced
3 egg yolks
1 cup plain yogurt
Salt to taste
½ cup grated cheese
¼ cup whole-wheat cracker crumbs or wheat germ

In a saucepan combine milk, butter, and onions. Simmer for 20 minutes. Drain and put onions in a shallow casserole. Mix egg yolks with yogurt and salt. Pour mixture over onions. Sprinkle top with cheese and crumbs. Bake in preheated moderate oven (350°F.) for about 20 minutes, or until onions are tender. Makes 4 to 6 servings.

CARROTS À LA SULTANA
6 carrots, scraped and cut into thin slices
2 teaspoons fresh lemon juice
½ cup all-purpose flour
½ teaspoon salt
¼ cup chicken bouillon
1½ cups olive oil
1 egg white, stiffly beaten
1 cup plain yogurt
1 garlic clove, mashed
Thinly sliced unpeeled cucumber

Sprinkle carrots with lemon juice. Mix flour with salt. Gradually beat in bouillon and 1 tablespoon of the oil. When smooth, fold in egg white. Heat remaining oil until very hot. Dip carrot slices into batter and fry until brown and crisp. Drain on absorbent paper. Mix yogurt with garlic. Pour mixture over carrots. Serve at once with thinly sliced cucumber. Makes 6 servings.

AVOCADO SALAD WITH YOGURT DRESSING
3 large avocados
Fresh lemon juice
Salt to taste
2 cups fresh grapefruit sections
24 stuffed green olives
1½ cups cubed melon
1 cup drained mandarin orange sections
Yogurt Dressing

Halve avocados, remove pits, and cut into cubes. Sprinkle with lemon juice and salt. Toss all fruits together and chill until ready to serve. Just before serving mix salad with Yogurt Dressing. Makes 6 servings.

Yogurt Dressing
1 cup plain yogurt
2 tablespoons honey
1 teaspoon fresh lemon juice
1 tablespoon pineapple juice
1 teaspoon grated lemon rind
⅛ teaspoon salt

Beat yogurt until smooth and beat in remaining ingredients. Chill until ready to serve.

CUCUMBER YOGURT SALAD
1 cucumber, peeled
½ teaspoon salt
1½ cups plain yogurt
Cayenne, paprika, black pepper

Shred cucumber on coarse shredder. Sprinkle with salt. Let stand at room temperature for 1 to 2 hours. Drain, and squeeze out water. Beat yogurt and season with cayenne, paprika, and black pepper to taste. Fold cucumbers into yogurt. Chill. Makes 4 to 6 servings.

CHEESE, CUCUMBER, AND GRAPEFRUIT SALAD
2 cups creamed cottage cheese
1 tablespoon fresh lemon juice
¼ cup plain yogurt
¾ teaspoon salt
2 cups chilled fresh-grapefruit sections
1 cup coarsely grated cucumber
1 tablespoon chopped parsley
Salad greens

Gently mix cottage cheese, lemon juice, yogurt, and salt. Drain grapefruit sections, and chop coarsely. Fold grapefruit, cucumber, and parsley into cottage cheese mixture. Serve at once on salad greens. Makes 6 servings.

SPINACH-COTTAGE CHEESE SALAD
2 to 3 cups raw spinach, washed and well drained
6 radishes, thinly sliced
1 tablespoon minced onion
2 tablespoons French dressing
¼ cup plain yogurt
⅛ teaspoon marjoram
2 cups creamed cottage cheese
Stuffed-olive slices

Tear spinach into bite-size pieces. Add radishes, onion, and French dressing; toss lightly. Add yogurt and marjoram to cheese; blend. Arrange 6 mounds of cheese mixture on spinach. Garnish each mound with olive slices. Makes 6 servings.

SHRIMP AND CUCUMBER SANDWICHES
⅓ cup shredded cucumber, drained
1 cup cooked shrimps, chopped
2 teaspoons minced green onion
1½ teaspoons fresh lemon juice
⅛ teaspoon dried dillweed
¼ cup plain yogurt
Salt to taste
8 slices of white bread
Butter or margarine

Mix all ingredients except last 2. Cut crusts from bread, if desired. Spread bread with butter, then with first mixture. Makes 4 sandwiches.

YOGURT, CUCUMBER, AND RADISH RELISH
1 pint plain yogurt
¾ cup minced cucumber with skin
½ cup radish slices
½ teaspoon paprika
Salt and pepper to taste
1 teaspoon chopped parsley

Mix all ingredients except parsley. Chill well, and stir before serving. Sprinkle with parsley. Makes 4 to 6 servings.

YOGURT HONEY CAKES
3 cups water
2½ cups sugar
1½ teaspoons fresh lemon juice
½ teaspoon vanilla extract
1 cup plain yogurt
¼ cup light cream
2 eggs
2 cups sifted all-purpose flour
1 teaspoon baking soda
1 cup butter or margarine
Honey
Sweetened whipped cream

Mix water with sugar and lemon juice.

Bring to a boil, lower heat, and simmer for five minutes. Stir in vanilla. Keep warm.

Beat yogurt with cream and eggs. Sift flour with baking soda. Gradually stir flour into yogurt mixture. Heat butter and drop dough mixture by tablespoons into the hot butter. Brown on both sides. When cooked, drop dough into hot sugar syrup. Let stand in syrup for 5 minutes. Remove with a slotted spoon and arrange on a serving platter. When cool, split each cake into halves, spread with honey, and top with whipped cream. Makes about 20.

YOGURT FROTH AYRAN
2 cups plain yogurt
½ teaspoon salt
1 cup ice water
Mint leaves

Beat yogurt until frothy, about 5 minutes. Beat in salt and ice water and beat for another 2 minutes. Serve in tall glasses garnished with mint sprigs. Makes 4 servings.

YORKSHIRE PUDDING—A traditional British accompaniment for roast beef, consisting of a savory batter of eggs, milk, and flour baked in the beef drippings. Yorkshire pudding must be puffy, crisp, and golden-brown. It is sliced into squares and served at the same time as the meat, along with roast potatoes and a green vegetable, in the usual English way. The batter is usually baked in a shallow baking dish, but it can also be baked in muffin pans or other small baking pans of various shapes.

Yorkshire pudding takes its name from Yorkshire, a county in the north of England. The food in Yorkshire is excellent farm food, and anyone who has traipsed over the Yorkshire moors can never forget the bountiful farm meals served in this historic county.

YORKSHIRE PUDDING
2 eggs
1 cup milk
1 cup all-purpose flour
½ teaspoon salt
Beef drippings (about ¼ cup)

Beat together eggs and milk. Sift together flour and salt. Stir into the egg mixture. Beat batter until smooth and well blended. Pour about ¼ cup beef drippings into a baking pan (11 x 7 inches or 9 x 9 x 2 inches). If the beef was roasted in such a pan, remove meat and keep hot; discard all but ¼ cup drippings from the pan. Pour batter into pan. Bake in preheated hot oven (450°F.) for 10 minutes. Reduce heat to moderate (350°F.) and bake for 10 to 15 minutes longer, or until puffy and golden-brown. Makes 4 servings.

Bûche de Noël

YULE LOG—The Yule log is a huge piece of wood symbolically burned around Christmastime. It may be burned on Christmas Eve; some countries burn it a bit every day for the twelve days of the Christmas season. In some places it is kept until the next year to light the new Yule log. In parts of France a bit of the log is kept throughout the year to insure a good season of crops and help cattle bear their offspring easily.

In all Christmas celebrations, light plays an important part, as a symbol of hope and deliverance from spiritual and physical darkness. The candles on our Christmas trees and the burning Yule log are symbols of our desire for light. So is a cake in the shape of a Yule log, which is traditional in England and in France, where it is known under the name of *Bûche de Noël*. The cake is made like a jelly roll, filled with a creamy filling, and decorated to resemble the bark of a tree.

BÛCHE DE NOËL
(Yule Log)

5 eggs, separated
¼ teaspoon cream of tartar
1 cup granulated sugar
1 tablespoon grated orange rind
2 tablespoons sherry
1 cup sifted cake flour
¼ teaspoon salt
   Confectioners' sugar
   Coffee Cream Filling
   Chocolate Frosting
   Grated pistachio nuts
   Marzipan (optional)

Beat egg whites until foamy. Add cream of tartar and beat until stiff. Gradually beat in ½ cup sugar, 1 tablespoon at a time. Beat egg yolks until thick and lemon-colored. Beat into egg yolks remaining ½ cup sugar, the orange rind, and sherry. Fold egg-yolk mixture into egg whites. Sift flour with salt. Fold gradually into egg mixture. Pour into foil-lined jelly-roll pan (1 x 15 x 10 inches). Bake in pre-heated moderate oven (375°F.) for about 20 minutes. When baked, turn out on towel sprinkled with confectioners' sugar. Carefully remove foil from cake. Roll up cake in the towel from the 10-inch end and let stand until cold. Unroll carefully and spread with Coffee Cream Filling.

Reroll and spread the entire roll with Chocolate Frosting. Run tines of fork the length of the cake to resemble bark. Cake can also be iced using a star tip on a pastry bag and running lengthwise lines of frosting over the sides and top of the entire cake. Sprinkle grated pistachio nuts along the "bark" of the cake and trim with marzipan leaves. Makes 8 to 10 servings.

Coffee Cream Filling

Chill 2 cups heavy cream with ¼ cup confectioners' sugar and 1 tablespoon instant coffee powder. When chilled for 2 or more hours, whip until thick enough to spread. Spread on cooled cake.

Chocolate Frosting

Melt 3 ounces (3 squares) unsweetened chocolate and 3 tablespoons butter or margarine. Mix 4 cups confectioners' sugar, ⅛ teaspoon salt, 7 tablespoons milk, and 1 teaspoon vanilla extract. Add chocolate mixture and blend well. Let stand, stirring occasionally, until of spreading consistency.

ZABAGLIONE or ZABAIONE—A dessert

ZABAGLIONE or ZABAIONE—A dessert of Italian origin, made of eggs, sugar, and wine beaten until thick over boiling water and served either warm or cold in dessert or parfait glasses. It is also used as a sauce for fruit.

ZABAGLIONE

4 egg yolks
¾ cup sugar
¾ cup Marsala

Combine ingredients in top part of a double boiler. Cook over simmering, not boiling, water, beating constantly with a wire whip or an egg beater, for about 10 minutes, or until very thick. Serve immediately in glasses or small coffee cups. Makes 4 to 6 servings.

Cold Zabaglione

Proceed as above. Set pan in a basin filled with cracked ice. Beat zabaglione until thoroughly cold. Pour into glasses or cups and keep refrigerated. Unless the zabaglione is beaten until thoroughly cold, it will not remain frothy but will collapse and separate. Makes 4 to 6 servings.

ZEPPOLE—A doughnutlike pastry of Italian origin. It consists of pieces of dough which may be filled with bits of cooked cauliflower, anchovies, etc., before frying. The dough can also be fried plain and sprinkled with salt, or with sugar and cinnamon.

ZEPPOLE

1 teaspoon active dry yeast
¾ cup warm water
1 egg
2 cups all-purpose flour
½ teaspoon salt
  Cooking oil

Sprinkle yeast into water. Let stand for a few minutes; then stir until dissolved. Beat in egg, flour, and salt. When smooth, cover and let stand in a warm place until doubled in bulk. Beat down and let rise again until doubled. Drop by tablespoonfuls into 1 inch of hot oil (375°F. on a frying thermometer). When browned on one side, turn and brown on the other. Drain on absorbent paper. Serve as a bread with butter or sprinkled with sugar and cinnamon as a dessert. These are also good dipped in honey or syrup. Makes about 20.

Note: For variety, flour hands and shape tablespoonfuls of dough around a small piece of cooked cauliflower or an anchovy before frying. Cubes of Mozzarella or a teaspoonful of Ricotta can be used in the same way.

ZUCCHINI—A variety of summer squash developed in Italy. It is also known as vegetable marrow or Italian marrow. Zucchini is cylindrical in shape but larger at its base than at its top. The skin has a lacy pattern of green and yellow that concentrates to give the appearance of stripes. It grows to be ten to twelve inches long and two to three inches thick, and has pale-green flesh and a delicate flavor.

Availability—Fresh zucchini is available in some food stores year round with the peak season from May to July. Frozen zucchini is available.

Purchasing Guide—Look for zucchini that have tender rinds, are glossy in appearance, and free from blemishes. They should be fairly heavy for their size. Choose zucchini that are small with a narrow diameter. They are best when 6 to 7 inches long and 1 to 1½ inches thick.

Storage—Buy in small amounts. Keep in the vegetable compartment of the refrigerator.

☐ Fresh, refrigerator shelf or vegetable compartment, uncooked: 3 to 4 days
☐ Refrigerator shelf, cooked: 4 to 5 days
☐ Fresh, prepared for freezing; or frozen, refrigerator frozen-food compartment: 2 to 3 weeks

□ Fresh, prepared for freezing, or frozen, freezer: 6 to 12 months

Nutritive Food Values—Provides fair quantities of vitamin A and C, and small amounts of other vitamins.

□ 3½ ounces, cooked and drained = 12 calories

Basic Preparation—Wash but do not peel. Remove stem and blossom ends. Cut into ½-inch slices or cubes.

□ To Cook—Have about 1 inch of water boiling in a saucepan. Add zucchini and salt to taste. Cook, covered, for 10 to 15 minutes, or until tender. Drain, and season to taste.

Zucchini may also be baked, creamed, or used for fritters. Young zucchini can be sautéed in butter until tender. Season to taste with salt, pepper, and garlic.

□ To Freeze—Use young zucchini. Wash and cut into ½-inch slices. Blanch in boiling water for 3½ minutes. Chill in cold water for 5 minutes. Drain. Pack into containers, allowing ½-inch headspace. Seal.

ZUCCHINI CHICKEN

- 1 broiling-frying chicken (about 2½ pounds), quartered
- 11 tablespoons olive oil
- 1 pound tomatoes, finely chopped
- 2 green peppers, finely chopped
- 2 medium zucchini, coarsely chopped
- 1 small onion, coarsely chopped
  Bouquet garni (mixed herbs in cheesecloth bag)
  Salt to taste
  All-purpose flour to thicken

Brown chicken pieces in 3 tablespoons of the oil. Remove pieces from pan and add remaining oil and all other ingredients except *bouquet garni,* salt, and flour. Fry briefly, stirring constantly. Add chicken and *bouquet garni* and simmer, covered, until chicken is done, about 30 minutes. Remove *bouquet garni.* Season with salt. Thicken with a flour and water paste if desired. Makes 4 servings.

LAMB-STUFFED ZUCCHINI

Here's a fine way to use up leftover lamb. Select 6 small zucchini, 6 or 7 inches long and about 1½ inches in diameter, and remove pulp with an apple corer; or split lengthwise and scoop out some of the pulp. Mix 1 cup minced cooked lamb, 1 cup cooked rice, 2 tablespoons minced onion, 1 tablespoon minced parsley, ¼ teaspoon ground oregano, and enough gravy, mayonnaise, cream sauce, or sour cream to moisten. Add salt to taste and stuff zucchini. If any stuffing is left over, form it into small balls and put with zucchini in a baking dish. Pour over 3 cups of tomato sauce seasoned with oregano, basil, or dill. Bake in preheated moderate oven (350°F.) for 30 minutes, or until the zucchini are tender. Makes 3 servings.

Zabaglione

ZUCCHINI ZITI

½ cup minced onion
½ cup butter or margarine
½ cup minced green pepper
1½ to 2 pounds zucchini, sliced
3 cups peeled, seeded, and chopped tomatoes
1 teaspoon salt
½ teaspoon pepper
1 can (4 ounces) sliced mushrooms, undrained
1 pound ziti or other short pasta

Sauté onion in hot butter for 2 minutes. Add all other ingredients except ziti. Cover and cook over low heat for about 30 minutes, stirring frequently. Zucchini slices should be tender, but still preserve their shape. Serve on hot cooked ziti. Makes 6 servings.

BAKED ZUCCHINI AND CORN

3 ears of corn
1 pound unpeeled zucchini, thinly sliced
1 medium onion, thinly sliced
¼ cup butter or margarine, melted
1 teaspoon salt
¼ teaspoon pepper
1 teaspoon chili powder, or to taste
1 can (8 ounces) tomato sauce

Grate corn kernels from cobs. Mix corn and remaining ingredients except sauce. Put in shallow 1½-quart baking dish. Pour sauce over top. Bake, uncovered, in preheated moderate oven (350°F.) for about 45 minutes. Makes 6 servings.

ZUCCHINI AND PEPPER STEW

1 can (6 ounces) tomato paste
1 cup water
1 stalk celery, sliced
1 carrot, sliced
½ cup cooking oil
4 large green peppers, sliced
2 medium zucchini, diced
4 small potatoes, peeled and diced
1 large onion, chopped
1 garlic clove, minced
Salt and pepper
Grated Parmesan cheese

Put first 4 ingredients in saucepan, bring to boil and simmer, covered, for about 1 hour. Heat oil in skillet and add next 5 ingredients. Cook until slightly browned. Add to first mixture and simmer for 10 minutes, or until vegetables are tender. Season with salt and pepper to taste and serve with the cheese as a main dish. Makes 6 servings.

SAUTÉED ZUCCHINI ITALIAN STYLE

1½ pounds zucchini, each 5 to 6 inches long
3 tablespoons olive oil or butter or margarine
½ teaspoon salt
⅛ teaspoon pepper

Wash zucchini. Do not peel. Cut into crosswise slices ⅛ inch thick. Heat oil in a 9- to 10-inch skillet. Add zucchini. Cook until slices are translucent and the edges are lightly browned, turning with a spatula to cook uniformly. Add more oil if needed. Sprinkle with salt and pepper. Makes 6 servings.

ZUCCHINI OMELET

2 tablespoons olive oil
1 small zucchini, diced
1 celery stalk, diced
2 fresh tomatoes, peeled
½ teaspoon salt
Dash of pepper
4 eggs, beaten
2 tablespoons grated Parmesan cheese
½ teaspoon crumbled dried thyme

Heat oil in skillet and sauté zucchini and celery until celery is tender. Add tomatoes, salt, and pepper. Cook, covered, for 10 minutes, stirring frequently. Mix beaten eggs, cheese, and thyme and pour over vegetables. Cook over low heat for 8 to 10 minutes on each side. Makes 4 servings.

ZUCCHINI AND CUCUMBERS IN SOUR CREAM

2 zucchini, about 8 inches long
1 cucumber, 8 inches long
½ inch of boiling water
¾ teaspoon salt
½ cup chopped green onions
2 tablespoons butter or margarine
½ cup dairy sour cream
⅛ teaspoon pepper
Chopped parsley

Wash zucchini and cucumber. Cut into crosswise slices ¼ inch thick. Put zucchini slices in a saucepan with boiling water and salt. Cover, bring to boiling point, reduce heat, and cook for 15 minutes, or until almost tender. Add cucumber slices and cook only until crisp-tender, about 3 minutes. Drain if necessary. In the meantime sauté green onions in butter. Add to zucchini and cucumber along with sour cream and pepper. Mix lightly. Heat, but do not boil. Sprinkle with chopped parsley. Makes 6 servings.

ZUCCHINI WITH CREAMY CHEESE TOPPING

12 zucchini, about 5 inches long
Salt
2 eggs
All-purpose flour
Margarine
2 cups dairy sour cream
1 cup shredded sharp Cheddar cheese

Wash and trim zucchini. Cook in small amount of boiling salted water until tender, about 10 minutes. Drain and cool. Beat eggs with ¼ teaspoon salt. Roll zucchini in flour, then dip into egg, and fry in hot margarine until browned on both sides. Put in shallow broiler-proof baking dish and pour sour cream over top. Sprinkle with cheese. Put under broiler until golden-brown. Makes 6 servings.

ZUCCHINI PICKLES

2 pounds zucchini
½ pound onions
¼ cup salt
2 cups sugar
2 cups cider vinegar
1 teaspoon celery seeds
1 teaspoon ground turmeric
½ teaspoon prepared mustard
2 teaspoons mustard seeds

Wash zucchini and cut into thin slices. Peel and quarter onions and cut into thin slices. Cover with water and add salt. Let stand for 2 hours, then drain. Bring to a boil the sugar, vinegar, and spices and pour over the vegetables. Let stand for 2 hours. Boil for 5 minutes and pack in 4 hot sterilized pint jars. Seal. Makes 4 pints.

ZWIEBACK—A sweet biscuit or rusk which is first baked and then sliced and toasted in the oven to make it into a kind of dry toast. The word comes from the German, and means "baked twice." Commercially made zwieback is available.

Caloric Value

☐ 3½ ounces = 423 calories

ZWIEBACK

1 package active dry yeast or 1 cake compressed yeast
¼ cup water*
1 cup milk
4 cups all-purpose flour
1 egg, beaten
½ cup granulated sugar
¼ cup melted butter
1 teaspoon vanilla extract
½ teaspoon salt
Confectioners' sugar
Fresh lemon juice

Sprinkle dry yeast or crumble cake into water. *Use very warm water (105°F. to 115°F.) for dry yeast; use lukewarm (80°F. to 90°F.) for compressed. Let stand for a few minutes, then stir until dissolved. Scald milk and cool to lukewarm. Add milk and 2 cups of the flour to yeast. Beat thoroughly. Stand in warm place for about 1 hour, or until light and bubbly. Beat in remaining ingredients except confectioners' sugar and lemon juice and remaining flour; if necessary, add a little more flour to make a medium-stiff dough. Stand in warm place and let rise until doubled in bulk. Punch down and turn out on lightly floured board. Knead for about 5 minutes. Shape dough into 2½-inch round buns. Place buns on greased cookie sheet, about 1 inch apart. Allow to rise again in warm place until doubled in bulk. Bake in preheated hot oven (400°F.) for 10 minutes. Lower heat to moderate (350°F.) and bake for 15 minutes longer. Cool buns. Slice into ¾-inch slices. Return to slow oven (300°F.) and bake for 40 minutes, or until the slices are lightly browned on both sides. Mix confectioners' sugar with lemon juice to prepare a thin icing. When zwieback are cold, frost with lemon icing. Makes about 2 dozen.

Zucchini Chicken

150 ways to be a better COOK

SEASONING

1. Pep up the same old mayonnaise (1 cup) with 1 teaspoon curry powder; 1 tablespoon chutney; 1 tablespoon prepared horseradish; 1½ tablespoons tart jelly; 2 tablespoons of the juice from sweet pickles (a delightful marinade for coleslaw, too); or 1 tablespoon dill-pickle juice for an interesting variation.

2. Make a *bouquet garni* to flavor boiled beef, fish, stews, hearty soups. Merely tie sprigs of celery, parsley, a bay leaf in a square of cheesecloth and throw into the pot; remove after cooking. Other herbs and vegetables, such as fennel, leek, marjoram, tarragon, can be added.

3. Experiment with the clean-cut flavor of dried dill: sprinkled on a green salad; dusted on top of creamed vegetables; as an interesting zip to delicate meats like veal and poultry; added to the butter sauce for Lima beans, green beans, fresh peas.

4. Be cautious with strong herbs and spices. Remember you can always add more. Start with pinches and build up to taste, particularly with bay leaf, sage, or garlic.

5. Try to cook on the day before you serve it anything with multiple spices, herbs, or onions. It's twice as good the second day if the flavors are allowed, as the French say, "to marry."

6. Toss a dash of vanilla extract into recipes containing chocolate.

7. Invest in a vanilla bean. Keep it in the sugar canister you reserve for baking.

8. Serve hot chocolate or cocoa with cinnamon stick as a stirrer. It looks and tastes wonderful.

SOUP SLEIGHT OF HAND

Two soups are better than one. Served hot or cold, they start the most mundane meal with a bang. These are interesting:

9. One can split pea with ⅓ can tomato and ½ can cream-of-asparagus; add water to make proper thickness.

10. One can cream-of-celery, ⅓ can tomato, 1 cup cooked celery, and 1 can crabmeat make a beautiful bisque; thin to desired consistency with water.

11. One can black-bean soup added to chili or stew shortens the cooking time and produces that desirable deep-brown, days'-long-cooking taste.

12. Rice with a difference: Mix about 3 cups consommé with 1 cup rice that has been browned for about 3 minutes in the skillet with 1 tablespoon butter or oil. Bake, covered, in preheated moderate oven (350°F.) for about 30 minutes.

HOT BREADS, BISCUITS, AND PANCAKES

Hot breads give an everyday family meal a company touch. Try these for rave reviews: For the average-size loaf of bread (French or Italian style or any with a crisp crust), use 1 cup butter or margarine and add:

13. The juice and grated rind of 1 lemon.

14. The heads from a package of frozen broccoli.

15. Two tablespoons of any of these: celery seed, dried dill, chopped fresh parsley, poppy seed.

16. Five tablespoons sugar, 1 teaspoon ground cinnamon, a shake or two of ground nutmeg or mace. Spread thickly on each slice (not cut completely through), wrap in foil, heat thoroughly in oven.

Saltine crackers, too, make delightful accompaniments for salad and soup meals. Try these:

17. Top about 2 dozen crackers with a mixture of 1 cup grated Cheddar cheese, the whites of 2 eggs, 1 tablespoon chili powder. Spread and brown in hot oven for about 3 minutes.

18. Spread crackers with peanut butter and dab of mayonnaise; put under broiler for quick toasting.

Canned biscuits are wonderful time-savers, special treats when used with imagination. Here are some ideas:

19. Split into halves, dip into melted butter, roll in sugar-and-cinnamon mixture. Bake.

20. Cut each biscuit into three portions, deep fry, and roll immediately in grated Cheddar or Parmesan cheese flavored with a little garlic salt. Great appetizers.

21. A delicious teatime or coffee-break goodie! Split biscuits and spread between the layers a mixture of chopped walnuts, dates, candied orange peel, enough honey to moisten; top with brown sugar and dots of butter or margarine. Bake.

22. Make quick snacks by splitting and filling unbaked canned biscuits with chopped peanuts, crisp bacon, and mayonnaise. Bake.

23. Serve piping-hot buttered biscuits on top of warm stewed fruit; cover with thick sweet cream, dash of ground cinnamon.

Use pancakes as a base for unusual main dishes. Here are some ways:

24. Spread with a cooked mixture of hamburger, onions, green pepper, and a spicy barbecue sauce.

25. Cover with chili, onions, and cheese; brown in oven.

26. Use as a base for creamed eggs, with slivers of ham, bacon, and mushrooms.

27. Serve with tuna or chicken à la king topped with Parmesan cheese and slivered almonds; put under broiler.

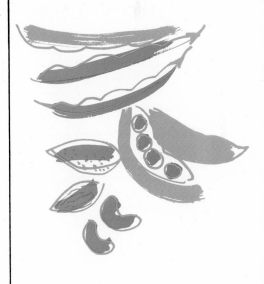

Make pancakes a party dessert.

28. Use them as a base for a shortcake: Butter them while hot, spread with fresh or frozen berries, cover with whipped cream.

29. Spread them while hot with cream cheese and heated maple syrup. Top with chopped salted nuts.

MEAT, POULTRY, FISH

30. Add a cooked-meat filling to split, unbaked canned biscuits. Bake and serve as individual meat pies for cocktail-party hors-d'oeuvre.

31. Rub inside of any poultry with ground thyme before roasting.

Serve seafood or meat salads in wedges of melon:

32. Crabmeat in honeydew, for instance, or chicken in cantaloupe.

33. Mix a good amount of crisply fried onion bits into a crust and as a topping for meat pies.

34. Marinate chicken in a mixture of lemon juice and onion slices before broiling.

35. Stud a small onion with whole cloves to use as flavoring for beef stock or stews. (Remove whole after cooking.)

36. Add green grapes to chicken salad, crabmeat salad.

37. Broil a few seedless grapes on seafood casseroles; add for the last few minutes of broiling to chicken or fish.

38. Make a sauce of black cherries for roast pork. Mix 1 can (1 pound) of pitted black cherries, 2 tablespoons brown sugar, 1 tablespoon soy sauce, and a couple of tablespoons of the drippings.

39. Serve broiled chicken with peaches or apricots added for the last few minutes of broiling.

40. Marinades are magic for turning inexpensive cuts of meat into really superb dishes. There are a number of possible combinations for this miraculous liquid, but here is one of the best:

1 cup French dressing, red wine, or wine vinegar, 2 teaspoons mixed spices (cloves, bay leaf, garlic), 2 tablespoons mixed chopped onion, parsley, chives, fresh dill or dillseeds, 1 teaspoon powdered mustard.

Mix all ingredients together; soak meat in the marinade for at least 2 hours before cooking. Use excess liquid for gravy, basting, or sauce. Fish also benefits from the marinade. Soak the fish for 1 to 2 hours in 1 part vinegar or dry white wine to 2 parts oil. Lemon juice may be substituted for the vinegar or wine.

41. Do not overcook fish, for most of it takes only a few minutes provided it is at room temperature. To test doneness, use a toothpick inserted in thickest part (usually near bone). Separate meat from bone; when meat is no longer transparent, fish is done.

42. Try this for two-dish, one-operation broiling: When broiling hamburgers, small steaks, or ham on the broiler racks in the oven, put, in the drip pan underneath, a dish that will be all the better for catching the juice and drippings. Canned spaghetti or Spanish rice, as examples, with hamburger or steak; canned corn with ham. Be sure the meat is not too fat. Trim if necessary.

43. To separate excess fat from meat drippings, quickly pour into a tall cup and place immediately in cold water. The fat will rise to the top and can be skimmed off easily, leaving the substance for use in the gravy.

44. A surprise center in cocktail meatballs is a pitted ripe olive stuffed with Cheddar cheese and cooked right along with the meat.

SAUCES AND GRAVIES

Thicken gravies and sauces and add unusual flavor at the same time with:

45. A couple of slices of crumbled stale rye bread to about 2 cups gravy.

46. One cup herb-flavored bread crumbs to 2 cups gravy.

47. Don't throw away that ketchup, mustard, chili sauce, or relish bottle if there's the least bit left. Rinse them out with a small amount of vinegar and water and add to gravies, meat sauces.

48. Try leftover coffee to add richness to beef, ham, or pork gravies. About 1½ cups coffee to 3 to 4 cups gravy does the trick.

49. Slip a square of unsweetened chocolate into a brown sauce or gravy to add south-of-the-border richness.

50. Try easy-does-it mustard sauce with ham, cold meats, on sandwiches. Add 2 tablespoons powdered mustard to 1½ cups mayonnaise, 1 tablespoon sugar, 1 teaspoon vinegar or lemon juice. That's all there is to it.

51. Substitute horseradish for the mustard and you have another marvelous sauce. Perfect for boiled beef and cold cuts.

52. Instead of using water for thinning gravies and stews, try using canned consommé, bouillon, concentrated beef cubes, or homemade meat or chicken stock.

53. Make a quick sweet-and-pungent sauce for pork, tongue, or beef with 10 gingersnaps, 1 tablespoon vinegar or lemon juice, ½ cup water, 2 tablespoons brown sugar, and 1 tablespoon grated lemon rind added to 3 to 4 cups gravy.

54. Make a glaze for roast pork or ribs with ½ cup honey, ½ cup soy sauce, and 1 tablespoon powdered mustard.

55. Brush barbecued ribs, hamburgers, frankfurters with French dressing.

56. Browned flour adds more flavor and color to gravies. Make it by stirring it in a dry skillet over very low heat. Remember it has about ½ the thickening power of unbrowned flour. In addition to its other virtues, browned flour doesn't lump or thicken beyond control.

57. Thicken sauces only partially with flour. Try egg yolks for finishing the job. Use 1 egg yolk to about 2 cups basic cream sauce. A wonderfully delicate sauce for pork, ham, or chicken is made by adding 1 tablespoon tarragon vinegar and 1 egg yolk to basic cream sauce.

VEGETABLES

58. Add ground nutmeg (a couple of shakes for unexpected interest) to eggplant, spinach, squash, and also, for a surprising spiciness, to beef gravies and stews.

59. Use sugar as a seasoning. A pinch or two in vegetables gives them a fresher taste, never makes them sweet.

60. Add a pinch of ground oregano and basil to any recipe that includes tomatoes, and don't forget that pinch of sugar.

Put the baked potato in high society by:

61. Adding bits of cooked pork sausage;
62. Stuffing mealy baked ones with leftover beef ground up and mixed with browned onions and a dash of Worcestershire;
63. Adding a delectable mixture of diced celery, green pepper, and crisp bacon;
64. Switching to Swiss cheese instead of Cheddar and adding snips of scallions.

For all above suggestions, bake potatoes in usual way: oil skins, place in hot oven (400°F.), and bake until you can pierce skin easily with a fork. Remove from oven and cut into halves immediately. Scoop out potato and mash thoroughly, adding ½ to ¾ cup liquid for additional moisture (use milk for vegetables and cheese, beef stock or consommé with meats). Put mixture back into skins and broil for additional brownness and crusty tops. Try something new with new potatoes, such as:

65. Quick-fry them, after parboiling in own jackets.
66. Broil them in the oven. First scrape; put into broiler with ample butter or margarine, shaking them frequently for overall brownness; they're done in about 15 minutes. Serve piping hot, dredged with paprika and parsley.
67. Mix them with fresh green peas in a sauce made of melted butter or margarine and crisp bits of bacon. Add lemon juice just before serving.
68. For deliciously dry boiled potatoes, drain off all water. Dry potatoes on a clean cloth and put them back into pot over low heat for a few minutes. Always remove the lid from the pot after they are done.
69. Snap up green beans with sliced water chestnuts, a few cashew nuts, almonds, bean sprouts. Mix with equal amount of fresh peas and a few of the pea pods.
70. Fry yourself a reputation with French-fried vegetables. Dip the following into egg-and-milk batter and fry quickly in deep fat: tender sprigs of parsley, cauliflower, okra, green beans, slivers of eggplant, and fresh green tomato slices. Dip individual pieces into batter (for 6 servings: 2 egg yolks, ½ cup milk, ¾ cup cake flour, ½ teaspoon salt) and drop into fat that is hot enough to brown cube of bread immediately. Fry until golden-brown and drain on paper towels. Serve immediately. To keep large quantities warm, place pieces on cookie sheet in warm oven, with space around each.

Give the hard-working onion a raise like this:

71. See what it does to ordinary summer squash when fried in golden bits and added, along with a handful of diced hard-cooked eggs. To brown onions, use half olive oil and half butter or margarine. The olive oil lends flavor and will not brown or burn as quickly as butter. This method is also good for sautéing mushrooms and green peppers.
72. Bake boiling-size onions with a glaze of honey and soy sauce. Broil them on skewers with the same sauce for company service.
73. Add a couple of tablespoons of browned minced onions to fresh spinach.
74. Parboil large, sweet onions, hollow out the middles, and stuff with corned-beef hash. Top with bread crumbs and Parmesan cheese and bake quickly until brown.

75. Add a few browned onions to macaroni and cheese, scalloped potatoes.

Be experimental in mixing vegetables as an attention-getter. Perfect partners:

76. Green peas with canned or fresh mushrooms.
77. Okra, tomatoes, green peppers, corn.
78. Baked eggplant, tomatoes, green peppers, and onions: boil eggplant for 12 minutes, dice pulp, mix with other raw vegetables. Put them all back in eggplant skin and bake in the oven for about 20 minutes. The seasonings: salt, pepper, oil, ground basil, and oregano.
79. Hominy with ripe olive slices, butter, margarine, and a little cream.
80. Whole vegetables, stuffed, make hearty, delicious main courses. In addition to the perennial pepper, here are a few other ideas:
81. Stuff tomatoes with Cheddar cheese, chips of crisp bacon, some of the tomato pulp. Top with more bacon and cheese; pop into broiler.
82. Try eggplant, boiled or baked, mixed with cooked lamb, browned onions, a tomato, dashes of ground nutmeg, and rosemary, salt, and pepper, stuffed into eggplant skin, topped with bread crumbs and grated cheese, and baked in oven.

83. Stuff flat pattypan squash with cooked hamburger, green pepper, hard-cooked egg, mixed with a little French dressing, and bake.

84. Use cornmeal as a thickener for corn pudding, using about half as much as you would of flour. You can also use fewer eggs.

85. Cook a couple of lettuce leaves (outer ones preferably) with either fresh or frozen peas. Use no, or almost no water; the lettuce furnishes the necessary moisture. Add a sprinkle of sugar and a few boiled onions if desired.

86. Never boil vegetables vigorously. Always cook them at low heat, just at boiling point. Cook them in tightly covered vessels (the tighter the cover the less water you use), with never more than the minimum amount of water (you can always add more if necessary). They are always at their best when crisp and should never be soft and mushy. It is much better to add seasonings and herbs after cooking.

87. Crisp reminders for salad: Never cut the greens. Tear them into desired size. Cutting makes them limp and bruises them. Always wash salad greens in very cold water. Shake off excess water very gently and place in a bowl that is large enough so that they won't be crushed or bruised. Place in refrigerator for about 1 hour before serving.

88. Marinate potatoes for salad in French dressing for about 1 hour before mixing with mayonnaise or other dressing.

89. Try stuffed olives with rice for a taste treat.

90. Green peas with rice, served hot or cold with a French dressing, are good.

EGGS

91. Scramble eggs in the top of a double boiler. You'll have fluffier ones. Here's the way to do it: Put 4 eggs, lightly beaten, into top part of double boiler. Add 3 tablespoons water and 2 tablespoons butter. Stir slightly. Place over boiling water and stir gently until done.

92. Add ½ cup diced Swiss cheese, ¼ cup diced scallions.

93. Add 1 cup cubed liverwurst or salami slices with 3 tablespoons minced browned onions.

94. Add 1 cup chopped parsley, ½ cup diced green pepper.

95. Add 1½ cups diced boiled potatoes, ½ cup finely chopped raw onions. The amounts given above are for each 4 eggs used.

96. Try the covered-skillet method for frying eggs. Lightly grease skillet, break eggs into it, and cook, covered, for about 5 minutes for the most beautiful and delicious fried eggs you ever tasted. Remember: use lowest possible heat.

97. Add 1 tablespoon cold water to 2-egg omelet; never use milk.

98. Flavor a cream sauce for hard-cooked eggs with curry powder. Serve over noodles mixed with browned bread crumbs flavored with salt, coarse-ground black pepper, and a dash or two of ground nutmeg.

99. Add excitement to deviled eggs with canned sardines, tuna fish, a few capers, chopped-up green olives, a slice or two of liverwurst, ham or bacon chips.

100. Use the yolks of 2 mashed, hard-cooked eggs for thickening in a delicious salad dressing. Add ½ cup oil, ¼ cup vinegar, 1 tablespoon sugar, 1 teaspoon celery seeds. Mix well. This is a semi-thick, delightful dressing.

101. Hard-cooked eggs mixed with unpeeled fresh apple chips and mayonnaise make a marvelous salad.

102. Heat deviled eggs in the broiler under a sauce of mayonnaise mixed with the juice of ½ lemon.

103. Try this change for scrambled eggs: Break 6 eggs into a bowl. Do not beat, whip, or stir. Into a cold skillet put 3½ tablespoons butter, 3 tablespoons heavy cream, and the eggs. Turn heat up to the highest temperature and stir the eggs very slowly, watching them carefully, as they cook very fast. Add salt and pepper when served.

104. Don't ever boil eggs. Always start them in cold water and bring water slowly to boiling point. When water reaches this point, lower heat. This method takes about 5 minutes longer than boiling method, but you'll rarely have a cracked shell or a misshapen egg, and never a tough, rubbery one.

105. Poached eggs are usually better than hard-cooked eggs in many recipes, because the degree of doneness can be determined visually. One method that takes a little practice, but usually works, is to put a drop or two of vinegar into the water; when the water is gently boiling, with a spoon stir a little well in the water and drop the egg into it immediately. Another method: Fill a skillet ⅔ full of water. Allow ½ teaspoon salt to 4 cups water; add vinegar. Bring water to the boiling point, then reduce heat. Break egg into saucer and gently slip into the water. As eggs cook, dip some water from the sides and pour it over the tops. When film forms over the yolks, and whites are firm, remove with a buttered skimmer or pancake turner. Eggs can also be poached in milk or stock for added flavor.

FRUITS

Use fruits unexpectedly with vegetables, meats, such as:

106. Add slivers of orange rind and the juice of the fruit to a pan of baked beans.

107. Orange juice instead of lemon juice on carrots, or mixed in with mashed sweet potatoes or squash.

108. Color a green salad with crescents of unpeeled red apple.

109. Add delightful tang to green salad with wedges of orange, grapefruit, cantaloupe, fresh pineapple.

110. For a delicious cold-weather dinner, try stuffing hollowed-out apples with pork sausage and baking slowly.

111. Use leftover frozen fruit juices instead of water in gelatin salads or desserts.

112. Hollow out large, tart apples; stuff with mincemeat topped with honey and nuts. Bake as usual.

113. Use leftover canned fruit juices for glazes for ham, pork.

114. Add thick wedges of raw apple to canned kraut; bake in oven or stew over low heat.

115. Bananas crushed through a sieve add wonderful flavor and texture to packaged custards, gelatin desserts, ice creams, and sherbets. Use 1 banana for every 3 servings.

116. Use a can of purple plums (pit them) and juice for an exotic pot-roast sauce.

117. Use brown sugar for stewing fresh fruits. Add the peel of ½ lemon, the juice of 1 whole lemon, 1 cinnamon stick. Delicious with peaches, plums, cherries, apples, similar fruits.

118. For added zip to a fruit cup, add a few drops of vanilla and a pinch of salt.

119. Cooked fresh fruits can be more delicious with half the amount of sugar if you add it after the fruit has cooked until tender or after it is done.

120. Make a really savory compote of fresh or canned fruits by adding 2 tablespoons powdered mustard and 1 cup sugar to 1 quart fruit and syrup.

121. Heat canned fruits to serve with hot cereals. Canned peaches or pineapple dusted with brown sugar and warmed in broiler are delicious.

DESSERTS AND DESSERT SAUCES

122. Try adding a dash of almond extract to peach-pie and cherry-pie fillings.

Here are some grand ice-cream sauces that turn plain vanilla into a glorious concoction!

123. White raisins, walnuts, honey, and rum flavoring.

124. Apricot preserves, lemon juice, and crushed mint leaves, well blended.

125. Packaged caramels melted in 1 cup hot strong instant coffee.

126. Whip 1 large package (8 ounces) cream cheese with 3 tablespoons milk and 1 tablespoon sugar for a dreamy topping for stewed fruits, hot fruit pies, fruitcakes.

127. Make individual upside-down cakes in custard cups.

128. Try this quick, delicious glaze for cookies, coffeecakes, or simple pound-cake: 1 cup confectioners' sugar, enough water to make it spreadable, a generous handful of mixed glazed fruit.

129. Add any of these to piecrust for interesting flavor and texture: chopped nuts, ground cinnamon or nutmeg, grated lemon rind. For meat pies, add herbs such as ground thyme or dill.

130. Plain toast becomes a treat when spread with peanut butter, honey, and a crunchy topping of Grapenuts. Put it back in hot oven just long enough to brown and heat through.

131. Toast your bread and butter it before making bread pudding.

132. When using a brand-new aluminum pie pan, punch several small holes in the bottom to insure a completely browned bottom crust.

133. Always preheat the oven thoroughly before baking any pie if you want perfect results.

134. Put a pinch of salt in all desserts, whether the recipe calls for it or not.

135. For apple pie with a difference, try slicing a few dates over the apples before putting on top crust.

TRICKS, TREATS, SHORTCUTS

136. Tomatoes cut vertically instead of horizontally tend to bleed less.

137. Sprinkle lettuce for salad with lemon juice while crisping in the refrigerator.

138. Keep simple syrup on hand for making mixed drinks, flavoring iced tea or coffee. It's more economical and makes a better blend with vegetables, too. Use about equal parts sugar and water until sugar dissolves into a smooth liquid.

139. Add 1 teaspoon butter and 1 tablespoon cocoa to an 8-cup coffee brew for a delicious Dutch variation.

140. Use yogurt or buttermilk instead of oil or sour cream for salad dressing. Delicious and a delight to dieters.

141. Keep a ready-to-use shaker of sugar and cinnamon on hand at all times for cookie, coffeecake, toast toppings. Try a little instant coffee in the mixture for a change.

142. Toast cold rice cereal for quick croutons. Use with soups or tossed into green salad at the last minute.

143. Add 1 tablespoon oil, butter, or margarine to rice before boiling. Makes grains separate and glossy and rice will never stick to pot.

144. No cook should ever be caught without stock. It is the liquid resulting when meat or fish is simmered in water and is a fine seasoning for soups, sauces, gravies, aspics. Keep a closely covered jar (make it a big one) in your refrigerator to collect it. Good, vitamin-rich foods that otherwise might be wasted can be used; celery tops and parings, ends of green beans, pea pods, carrot skins, parsley stems, bits of onion. Cover these with water and simmer for about 30 minutes; strain and store, or freeze in ice-cube pans and store. You can also combine with these the juices from fresh or canned vegetables such as green beans, asparagus, peas, or any delicately flavored ones. Juices from strong-flavored vegetables, such as cabbage, Brussels sprouts, turnips, are too potent for this purpose.

145. To any basic recipe for dumplings to be served with meat or chicken, add

any of the following for added interest: ¼ cup finely chopped parsley; 2 tablespoons grated cheese; ½ teaspoon raw onion, 3 tablespoons minced parsley and green sweet pepper, mixed. To keep dumplings light and fluffy as they should be, always cook them in a covered pot and never lift the lid. A glass pie plate makes a heavy, tight cover.

146. Use drawn butter for sautéing veal or chicken, also as a sauce for asparagus, cauliflower, fresh peas. Here is a way to do it: Gently melt butter in vessel that is deeper than it is wide. Skim off foam that rises to top, then pour the melted fluid off slowly and carefully, leaving in the vessel the whitish or cloudy substance that has settled. The clear liquid is the drawn butter, and has a flavor that is delicious and altogether different from regular butter.

147. Try this for quick cookie shaping and for a lighter, crisper yield: Drop the cookie dough in teaspoon-size bits about 2 inches apart on the cookie sheet. Press down with the bottom of an ordinary drinking glass which has been covered with a cloth dampened in cold water. Do not bear down; gently does it.

148. Think of food coloring in a new light. The tiniest bit of red, for instance, added to chocolate puddings or icings makes a richer, brighter brown. The merest dash of yellow food coloring added to white sauces makes them much more attractive and looks as if egg yolks have been added.

149. Use frozen-fruit-juice ice cubes for punches and cold drinks, so that the flavor will not become diluted. Apple juice is one of the best, because of its clearness and its ability to blend with other flavors. Just pour juice into trays and freeze.

150. For the most delicious iced coffee you ever tasted, try this: freeze extra-strong coffee in ice-cube trays. Put frozen cubes in tall glasses (enough to fill), then pour warm milk over them and top with 1 tablespoon whipped cream.

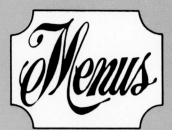

100 Menus
to help you plan
more varied meals
for your family with
the recipes in this volume

*Recipes for all starred dishes found in this volume.

BREAKFASTS

Brook Trout Meunière*
Cheese Waffles*
Fresh Peaches and Cream

———

Orange and Banana Pieces
Crisp Breaded Tripe*
Home-Fried Potatoes
Tomato Wedges

Welsh Rabbit*
Toast
Canadian Bacon
Frozen Mixed Fruit

———

Strawberries and Cream
Seattle Dutch Babies*
Pork Sausages

Grapefruit and Orange Slices
Egg and Tongue with Yogurt
Sauce* on Toast

———

Tomato Juice
Creamed Smoked Whiting*
Corn Waffles*
Honey Butter*

Melon Slices
Rainbow Trout, Rocky
Mountain Style*
Hashed-Brown Potatoes
Melba Toast

———

Broiled Grapefruit
Golden Buck*
Crisp-Fried Sausage
Cakes
Buttered Toast
Grape Conserve

LUNCH OR SUPPER

Raspberry Applesauce
Mottram Kidney in
Cream* on Biscuits
Poached Eggs
Hot Biscuits
Prune Butter

———

Cranberry Juice
Tuna Fritters*
Raisin Muffins
Tangerine Marmalade

Poached Mixed Dried
Fruit
Venison Sausage*
Waffles*
Butter   Maple Syrup

———

Rhubarb and Strawberries
Batter-Fried Tripe*
Chili Sauce
Corn Muffins

Turkey Salad*
Watercress Sandwiches*
Apricot-Prune Upside-
Down Cake*

———

Tuna and Potato Tart*
California Parmesan-
Walnut Salad*
Breadsticks*
Butter

Double-Boiler Tuna
Soufflé*
Braised Lettuces*
Yogurt, Cucumber, and
Radish Relish*
Crescent Rolls*
Orange Sherbet

———

Trout, English Style*
Carrots with Dill*
Raspberry Jam Scones*

Turkey Chow Mein*
Soy Sauce
Broccoli
Jellied Tomato Salad
Apple Cobbler

———

Ham Waffles*
Blueberry Jam
Gratin of Eggplant*
Raisin-Orange Turnovers*

Veal Brains in Mushroom
Sauce*
Green Noodles
Artichoke-Heart, Mandarin-
Orange, and Almond
Salad
Zwieback*   Butter

———

Frosty Watermelon Soup*
Bacon Waffles*
Maple Syrup
Guava Jelly

Jellied Veal Slices*
Anchovy Vinaigrette Sauce
Potato Salad
Sliced Tomatoes
Serbian Walnut Strips*

———

Duck Hash*
Baked Zucchini and Corn*
Crusty Bowknot Rolls*
Whipped Butter
Watermelon Sherbet*

Cuckoo's Eggs*
Chopped Spinach
Orange Yams*
Toasted Sesame Seed Rolls
Lemon-Lime Ice

⸻

Tripe Creole*
Batter-Fried Broad
Noodles
Stuffed Zucchini*
Marmalade Turnovers*

Stewed Tripe with
Vegetables*
Toasted Rolls   Black Bread
Herb Butter
Chocolate Butterscotch
Bars*

⸻

Tuna Coleslaw with Grapes*
Open-Face Broiled
Cheddar Sandwiches
Fruit Gelatin   Cookies

Split Pea Soup*
Sweetbread and Cucumber
Salad*
Crackers and Crisp Breads
Yam Spicecake*

⸻

Cream-of-Corn-and-Cress
Soup*
Crab and Grapefruit Salad
with Avocado Mayonnaise*
Pepper and Salt Sticks*

Pot-Roasted Turkey,
Jamaica Style*
Herbed Wild Rice*
Buttered Broccoli
Whole-Wheat Rolls*
Butter
Almond Deep-Dish
Apple Pie*

⸻

Cream Vichyssoise
Glacée*
Breast of Veal with
Sausage Stuffing*
Classic Ratatouille*
Sherry Tortoni*

Chicken and Watercress
Soup*
Tuna-Noodle Casserole*
Okra and Tomatoes
with Lemon*
Almond Brandy Torte*

⸻

Lamb Shanks Baked in
Fruited Wine*
Wild Rice Stuffing*
(in a casserole)
Watercress Salad*
Mocha Torte*

Roast Boneless Turkey
Roll*
Potatoes in Parsley
Sauce*
Braised Leeks, Nicoise*
Raw Vegetable Sticks
(Carrots, Cucumbers)
Strawberries de Luxe*

⸻

Jellied Herb Veal Loaf*
Potato Chips
Vegetable Salad
Bread   Chive Butter
Yam Custard Pie*

Commander's Palace Trout
Alexander*
Gratin of Greens*
Orange Rye Bread*
Parsley Butter
French Chocolate Torte*

⸻

Hot Crab Salad*
Ensalada de Noche
Buena* (Christmas
Eve Salad)
Sourdough Bread*
Herb Butter
Baked Bonbons*
Black-Walnut Brittle*

Tomato Juice Cocktail
Turkey and Broccoli
Amandine*
Peas and Mushrooms
Pan Rolls*   Butter Balls
Apricot Torte*

⸻

Bulgarian Cold Cucumber
Soup*
Individual Tuna Pies*
Broccoli alla Piemontese*
Blueberry Upside-Down
Cake*

Roast Pork with
Chinese Vegetables*
Yellow Rice
Butterfly Wings*
Sweet Butter
Prunes in Wine*

⸻

Marinated Whiting*
Ginger Cheese Salad
Bowl*
Hot Buttered Rye Bread
Swedish Sans Rival Torte*

Pinwheel Turkey Pie*
Avocado and Orange Salad
Assorted Crisp Breads
Swedish Varmlandstärta*

⸻

Veal Saumoné*
Rice Salad
Whole Baby Carrots
à la Grecque*
Avocado Salad*
Syrup-Poached Orange
Slices

Roast Leg of Veal*
Roasted Potatoes
Buttered Asparagus Stalks
Special Mixed Green
Salad*
Vacherin à la Suisse*
(Meringue Shell)

⸻

Chicken-Liver Turnovers*
Caesar Salad*
Cornmeal Rolls*
Sour-Cream Apple Torte*

Pressed Turkey*
Mayonnaise
Onion or Shallot Soufflé*
Romaine Hearts and
Radishes
Apple Pie and Cheese

⸻

Veal and Peppers,
Italian Style*
Zucchini and Cucumbers
in Sour Cream*
Crusty Dinner Rolls*
Almond Cookies
Orange Sherbet

Sherried Artichoke
Chicken*
Duchess Potatoes
Marinated Tomatoes
Pineapple Upside-Down
Cake*

⸻

Marinated Veal Steak*
Fettuccine
Zucchini and Tomatoes
Italian Bread
Coffee Tortoni*

Tuna en Brochette*
Stewed Tomatoes
French-Fried Onion Rings
Lima-Frosted Papaya*

⸻

Western Antipasto Salad*
Filet of Beef with
Sherry*
French-Fried Potatoes
Brownie Waffles*
Vanilla Ice Cream
Fudge Sauce

Menus

Turtle Soup*
Pilot Crackers
Prawns in Cream*
Pastry Cups
Cucumber and Onion
Salad
Pecan Pie

———————

Sole in White Wine*
Caponata*
Italian Bread
Garlic Butter
Watermelon-Almond Sherbet*

Broiled Turkey Salad*
Zucchini in Tomato Sauce*
Parker House Rolls*
Herb Butter
Lemon Meringue Tarts

———————

Curried Tuna*
Hot Cooked Rice
Pear Chutney*
Breadsticks
A True English Trifle*

Veal Chops Soubise*
Duchess Potatoes
Herbed Green Peas
Seeded Breadsticks
Washington Plum Dumplings*

———————

Turtle Steak with Sour-
Cream Sauce*
Home-Fried Potatoes
Succotash
Spiced Raisin Relish*
Northwest Huckleberry
Buckle*

Chicken Braised with
Wine*
Parsley Boiled Potatoes
Sautéed Zucchini,
Italian Style*
Ripe Watermelon
Pickle*
Sherry Gelatin

———————

Sweet-and-Sour Tuna*
Chow-Mein Noodles
Avocado Salad with
Yogurt Dressing*
Opera Torte*

Ho T'ao Chi Jing
(Walnut Chicken)*
Fried Noodles
Radish-Garnished Chinese
Cabbage Slaw
Red-Wine-Baked Pears*

———————

Veal Cutlets, Sicilian
Style*
Green Noodles
Tossed Salad
Hot Crisp Italian
Bread
Biscuit Tortoni*

Veal Shoulder with
Cheese Sauce*
Baked Potatoes
Braised Onion Slices*
Bibb Lettuce
French Dressing
Jaegertorte
(Hunter's Torte)*

———————

Samosas (Curried Meat
Turnovers)*
Zucchini and Pepper Stew*
Sour-Cream Watercress
Sauce* on Salad Greens
Fruit and Cheese

Cioppino*
Hot Garlic Bread
Old Colony Gingerbread
Waffles*
Orange Hard Sauce*

———————

Lamb Baryani*
Fluffy Turnips*
Zucchini Pickles*
Zeppole*
Honey

Fresh Tangerine and
Turkey Salad*
Puerto Rican Yam and
Cheese Crullers*
Guava Jelly
Walnut Crescents*

———————

Italian Tuna Frittata*
Mayonnaise-Spread Toast
Molded Watermelon Salad*
Ginger-Mince Upside-
Down Cake*

Zucchini Chicken*
Cucumber Yogurt Salad*
No-Knead Feather Rolls*
Butter
Vanilla Fresh-Fruit Cup*

———————

Tuna Green-Bean Casserole*
Spinach-Cottage Cheese
Salad*
Crisp Breads
Cherry Soup Scandinavian*

Baked Turkey and Rice*
Zucchini and Sliced Tomatoes
Breadsticks*
Cherry Upside-Down Cake*

———————

Tuna Tetrazzini*
Cheese, Cucumber, and
Grapefruit Salad*
White Corn Tortillas*
Blueberry Turnovers*

Vitella Tonnato
(Veal with Tuna)*
Hot Rice Salad
Green Peas   Carrot Strips
Cold Zabaglione*

———————

Trout en Papillote*
Shoestring Potatoes
Green-Bean Soufflé*
Tossed Salad
Green Goddess Salad
Dressing*
Black-Walnut Wafers
Ice Cream

Stuffed Veal Rolls*
Fried Green-Tomato Slices
Browned-Butter Wilted Lettuce*
Cherry Torte with Cream*

———————

Hunter's Chili*
Turnip Salad*
Toasted Split
Hamburger Rolls*
Plain Cake with
Whipped-Cream Topping*

Turkey Curry*
Fluffy Rice
Sautéed Bananas
Cashews   Chutney   Raisins
Lemon Bread Pudding

◆

Fresh Tuna Tarragon*
Herbed French-Fried Potatoes
Chilled Artichokes with
Garlic Mayonnaise*
Old Colony
Gingerbread Waffles*
Mock Devonshire Cream*

Veal Chops Paprika*
Madame Fraize's Cabbage
and Zucchini Skillet*
Refrigerator Rolls*
Herb Butter
Fresh Fruit and Cheese

◆

Chili Whitefish*
Braised Chinese Cabbage*
Haricots Verts Maillanoise
(Green Beans,
Maillane Style)*
Chocolate Cake
Raspberry Gelatin

Sherried Turkey with
Potatoes*
Brussels Sprouts with
Almonds
Fresh-Pear-and-Orange
Salad
Walnut Shortbread*

◆

Daube Provençale*
Boiled Onions   Carrots
Macaroni Salad
Sherry Custard

Breaded Veal Cutlet
(Wiener Schnitzel)*
Braised Red-Cabbage
Dumplings
Viennese Torte*

◆

Corned-Beef Turnovers,
Mushroom Sauce*
Green Peas
Waldorf Salad
Chocolate Soufflé

Hawaiian Veal Stew*
Patty Shells
Red-Cabbage Slaw
Yogurt Honey Cakes*
Honey   Whipped Cream

◆

Broiled King Crab Legs*
Zucchini Ziti*
Braised Celery*
Apple Crisp

Turkey with Welsh-Rabbit
Sauce* on Toast
Frozen Mixed Vegetables
Sliced Cucumbers with
French Dressing
Fresh Plums

◆

Truite au Bleu*
Parsley Buttered Potatoes
Artichoke Fritters*
Avocado Salad
Mocha Torte*

Stuffed Veal Cutlets*
Fluffy Turnips*
Braised Endive*
Bowknot Rolls*
Garlic Butter
Chocolate Cream Pie

◆

Tripe à la Lyonnaise*
Cauliflower Sauté with
Lemon
Pan-Browned Potatoes
Stuffed Tomato Salad
Apricot-Prune Upside-
Down Cake*

Turkey Pie with
Corn-Bread Topping*
Spinach Soufflé*
Bibb Lettuce and Radishes
Hungarian Walnut Bars*
Fresh-Fruit Slices

◆

Venison Meatballs*
Parmesan Noodles
Stuffed Baked Eggplant*
Lemon Meringue Pie

Old-Fashioned Veal Loaf*
Creamy Mashed Potatoes
Carrots à la Sultana*
Poached Pears with Kirsch

◆

Lamb-Stuffed Zucchini*
Fried Beans*
Tostadas*
Ambrosia Upside-Down Cake*

Turkey Paprika*
Saffron Pilau*
Cabbage in White Wine*
Italian Dinner Rolls
Sherry Tortoni*

◆

Turkey Soup*
Shrimps Victoria*
Hot Wild Rice
Braised Celery*
Cranberry-Apple Pie

Simmered Breast of Veal*
(with Bacon, Sausage,
Carrots, Onions,
Potatoes, Cabbage)
Tomato and Cucumber Salad
Zabaglione*

◆

Basque Barbecued Lamb*
Potatoes and Onions
(Cooked with seasoned
butter in foil)
Tomato and Lettuce Salad
Strawberry Shortcake

Barbecued Turkey Steaks*
Broccoli Soufflé*
Braised Fennel*
Pan Rolls   Herbed Butter
Angel-Food Cake
Ice Cream

◆

Venison Ragout*
Water-Chestnut and Rice
Stuffing* (Baked in
casserole)
Tomato and Cucumber Slices
Blueberry Cobbler

Braised Leg of Veal*
Tangerine Sweets*
Onions in Onions*
Cloverleaf Rolls
Sweet Butter
Cherry Torte with Cream*

◆

Barbecued Salmon Steaks*
Finnish Stuffed Turnips*
Buttered Frenched
Green Beans
Toasted Cheese Rolls
Blueberry Pie

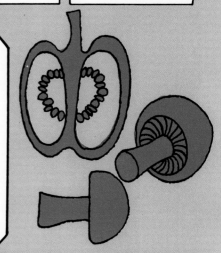

*Recipes for all starred dishes found in this volume.

GENERAL INFORMATION

The Ingredients and Measurements Used in Recipes

All recipes in this book have been tested in the Woman's Day Kitchens with standard American measuring cups (8 ounces = 16 tablespoons), measuring spoons (1 tablespoon = 3 teaspoons), and other standard kitchen equipment. All measurements are level. Liquids are measured in standard 8-ounce glass measuring cups, at eye level.

All sugar is granulated white sugar unless otherwise specified.

All flours, cake and all-purpose, are sifted before measuring unless otherwise specified. No self-rising flour is used.

All baking powder is double-acting baking powder.

All brown sugar is firmly packed when measured.

All confectioners' sugar is sifted before measuring.

All pepper is ground black pepper unless otherwise specified.

Fats and shortening are measured at room temperature, packed firmly into measuring cup and leveled with a straight knife. They are scraped out with a rubber spatula.

Salted butter or margarine, packed in ¼-pound sticks, is used unless otherwise specified. 1 stick = ½ cup = 8 tablespoons = ¼ pound.

1 tall can evaporated milk (14½ ounces) contains 1⅔ cups undiluted evaporated milk. Sweetened condensed milk is an entirely different product, and cannot be used interchangeably with evaporated milk.

⅓ to ½ teaspoon dried herbs can be substituted for each tablespoon fresh herbs. Crumble herbs before using to release flavor.

Before starting to cook or to bake, read the recipes carefully. Assemble all ingredients and equipment. Follow recipe exactly. Do not increase or decrease recipe unless you are a skilled enough cook to recognize what adjustments must be made as to ingredients, pan sizes, and/or cooking time.

Cooking Temperatures and Times

Cooking temperatures and times are approximate for meat. They depend not only on the weight and kind of meat, but also on its shape, temperature, and its bone and fat contents. A meat thermometer was used in testing.

Cooking times for meats are as recommended by the National Live Stock and Meat Board, 36 Wabash Avenue, Chicago, Illinois 60603.

Oven Temperatures

TEMPERATURES (Degree F.)	TERM
250 to 275	VERY SLOW
300 to 325	SLOW
350 to 375	MODERATE
400 to 425	HOT
450 to 475	VERY HOT
500 to 525	EXTREMELY HOT

Important—Preheat oven for 10 to 15 minutes before placing food in it. Many a cake has been spoiled by being placed in a barely heated oven. Baking times are based on the assumption that the oven is already at the stated temperature.

Check the oven temperature control frequently, especially if baking times vary from those given in recipes. (This can be done with a portable oven thermometer.) If a control is consistently off, call your public utility. They should be able to reset the oven temperature control.

Caloric Values

The caloric values, where mentioned, for each food are based on 100 grams, about 3½ ounces edible portion, as mentioned in Composition of Foods, Agriculture Handbook No. 8, Agricultural Service of the United States Department of Agriculture, Washington, D. C., revised December 1963.

WOMAN'S DAY
Encyclopedia of Cookery

Complete Recipe Index
for Volumes 1 to 12

In this cross-index of all the recipes in the twelve volumes of the Woman's Day Encyclopedia of Cookery the reader will find each recipe listed alphabetically under the name of its principal ingredient, as Chicken, Eggplant, Orange, etc. Recipes are also listed under menu categories or kind of preparation, as Appetizer, Soup, Salad, or Croquette, Meatball, Tamale, etc. Recipes with foreign names are listed by those names as well, and those recipes which have a geographical or personal description, as Danish Kringle or Kentucky Burgoo, will be found alphabetically under such descriptive names.

Immediately following each recipe is the number of the volume in which it appears (printed in bold face) and its page number (printed in light face). Those recipes which appear in Volume 10 under the entry Quantity Cooking are indicated by the symbol (QC) following the recipe.

A

Aal i Gelé (Jellied Eel), **4**-539
Aardappel-Purée met Ham en Uien (Purée of Potatoes with Ham and Onions), **4**-592

Abalone, 1-5
Chowder, **1**-5
Sauté, **1**-5
Achivades Pilafi (Clam Pilaf), **5**-818

Acorn Squash, 1-6; **11**-1759
Apple-Stuffed, **11**-1762
Baked, Supreme, **1**-7
Baked, with Whipped Potato Rosettes, **11**-1762
Grapefruit- and Tangerine-Stuffed, **11**-1762
Sausage-Stuffed, **1**-7
Slices, French-Fried, **11**-1762
Steamed, **1**-7
Adobong Manok at Baboy (Chicken and Pork), **9**-1369
Aeblekage (Apple Cake), **4**-543
Aebleskiver (Danish Doughnuts), **4**-542
Aeggestand (Cold Scrambled Eggs), **4**-538
African Style Peanut Soup, **8**-1322
Agnello alla Cacciatora (Lamb Cacciatora), **6**-954
Agourontomatosalata (Tomato and Cucumber Salad), **5**-822
Aguacates Batidos (Whipped Avocado), **11**-1709
Agurkesalat (Cucumber Salad), **4**-542
Agurkesuppe (Cucumber Soup), **4**-538
Aigo-Sau (Fish Stew), **2**-216
Aïoli, Aïoli Sauce (Garlic Mayonnaise), **1**-7; **5**-740; **10**-1614, 1621
Alabama Fruitcake, Old, **5**-759
à la King Leftovers, **7**-1050
Alaska Duck Salad, **1**-23
Alaska Pie, Mincemeat, **7**-1164

Albacore, **1**-8
Broiled Fresh, **10**-1560
Divan, **1**-8
Fresh, Sauté Amandine, **1**-8
Pickled, **1**-8
Albóndigas (Meatballs), **11**-1705
Alcachofas Rellenos con Sardinas (Sardine-Stuffed Artichokes), **11**-1741
Ale, **1**-10; see also Beer
Alentejo Style Fish (Peixe a Alentejana), **9**-1455

Alewife, **1**-10
Alewives Baked with Lemon, **1**-10
Algerian-Style Eggs, **5**-775
Allemande Sauce, **1**-10; **10**-1613, 1619
Allspice, **1**-11
Almásrétes (Apple Strudel), **6**-921

Almond(s), **1**-11
Amandine Butter, **10**-1615, 1624
(for appetizers), **1**-89
Bacon from Heaven (Toucinho-do-Céu), **9**-1457
Bavarian Cream, **1**-15
Blanched, Blanching, **1**-13; **5**-780
Bouillon, **1**-75
Brandy Torte, **12**-1853
Bread Cookies, Brussels (Pain d'Amandes), **2**-200
Bread (Mandelbrot), **6**-992
Brittle, **1**-16
Burnt, **1**-13
Burnt-Almond Soufflé, **11**-1688
Butter Cake, **5**-783
-Butter Strips, **3**-473
Carrot Conserve, **2**-309
Celery-Almond Stuffing, **11**-1781
Cheesecakes (Queijadinhas de Amêndoas), **9**-1457
-Chicken Salad, **1**-14
Chocolate Torte (Rehruecken), **11**-1804
Coleslaw, **10**-1586
Cookies, **2**-250
Cookies, Chinese, **4**-635
Cookies, Glazed, **1**-16

Cookies (Hsing Jen Ping), **3**-404
Cream Filling, **8**-1320
Croquettes, **4**-518
Cucumber-Almond Salad, **10**-1586
Custard, Thomas Jefferson's, **1**-14
Deep-Dish Apple Pie, **12**-1933
Diamonds, **5**-709
Extract, **1**-13
-Filled Coffee Ring, **1**-15
Filling, **1**-15, 69; **8**-1308
Florentines, **8**-1272
Fondant-Dipped, **5**-708
Four Specie Dollars (Fire-Speciedaler-kaker), **8**-1243
Hearts, Nonsweet, **1**-15
Ice Cream, **6**-929
Lebkuchen, Dropped, **7**-1046
Linzer Torte, **4**-635
Macaroons, **1**-15
Marzipan, **8**-1243
Mazurka (Mazurek Migdałowy), **9**-1431
Meringue Cookies, **7**-1135
Meringues, Rich, **7**-1135
and Mushroom Sauce, **7**-1152
Noodles, **1**-14
Nougat, **2**-288
-Olive Spread, **2**-279
Paste, **1**-13, 15
Pea and Cheese Salad, **8**-1315
Pfeffernüsse, **9**-1367
Popovers, **2**-238; **9**-1437
Poppy-Seed Noodles, Hungarian, **8**-1233
Praline, **9**-1480
Red Snapper Amandine, **10**-1540
Salted, **1**-14
Sauce Amandine, **1**-14
Sherry Snow Pudding, **9**-1492
Slices, **1**-74
Slivers, **5**-780
Soufflé, **1**-15
Soufflé Sandwiches, **10**-1610
Soup, **1**-14
Soup (Sopa de Almendras), **11**-1742
Soyed, **11**-1734
Spinach with, **11**-1756
Spritz Cookies, **11**-1758

Aveiro Mussels (Mexilhões de Aveiro),
    9-1455
Avga Gemista (Stuffed Eggs), 4-639
Avgolemono (Egg-Lemon Sauce),
    5-819
Avgolemono Soupa (Egg-Lemon Soup), 5-818
Avkokt Torsk (Boiled Cod), 8-1236

Avocado(s), 1-128
    Chicken-Avocado Tostada, 12-1930
    Chicken Salad, 1-130
    -Chicken Soup, 11-1690
    -Citrus Dessert, 1-130
    and Corn Salad (Ensalada de Aguacate y
        Maíz), 7-1142
    Crabmeat Salad à la Ritz, 1-130
    Crabmeat-Stuffed, 1-130
    Cream, 1-130
    with Creamed Shrimps, 10-1658
    Cream, Frozen, 1-59
    Dip, 1-130
    Dressing, 10-1588
    Drink, Iced (Es Advokat), 11-1714
    Frankfurter-Avocado Dip, 5-718
    and Fresh Pineapple Salad, 9-1408
    Gelatin, Salad, 1-130
    -Grapefruit Dessert, 5-814
    Guacamole, 1-130
    Halves with Spiced Shrimps, 10-1581
    and Ham with Cauliflower Salad
        (Ensalada de Coliflor con Aguacate),
        7-1142
    Hors-d'Oeuvre, 6-913
    Ice Cream, 1-24
    Lime Pie, 1-130
    Lobster-Avocado Sandwiches, 7-1081
    -Melon Salad, 6-911
    Olive-Avocado Appetizer, 8-1256
    Paste (Guacamole), 7-1138
    Pineapple-Avocado Spread, 9-1403
    Ring with Strawberries, 11-1776
    Romaine-Tomato Salad, 4-566
    Salad, 12-1931
    Salad (Ensalada de Aguacate), 11-1709
    Salad with Yogurt Dressing, 12-1958
    Sandwiches, 4-635
    Shrimp Boats, Puerto Rican, 1-130
    Soup, 11-1727
    Soup, Chilled, 1-130
    Soup (Sopa de Aguacate), 7-1138
    Stuffed with Veal, 12-1896
    Tomato-Avocado Hors-d'Oeuvre, 6-913
    Tomato-Avocado Salad, 10-1586
    -Tomato Cocktail, 3-455
    -Tomato Salad, 2-300
    and Tuna Salad, Molded, 5-787
    Vegetable-Avocado Salad with Paprika
        Dressing, 10-1586
    Whipped (Aguacates Batidos), 11-1709
Awayuki-kan (Snow Gelatin), 6-978

B

Baba, 1-131
    Baba au Rhum (Rum Cake), 1-131; 5-748
    Baba au Rhum, Quick, 1-132
Babi Ketjap (Braised Pork in Soy Sauce),
    11-1714
Babka, Easter (Wielkanocna Babka),
    9-1431
Babka, Polish, 7-1156
Babki Śmietankowe (Cream Tarts), 9-1431
Bacalao Veracruzano (Codfish in Spicy
    Tomato Sauce), 7-1140
Bacalao a la Vizcaína (Basque Salt-Cod
    Casserole), 11-1743

Bacon, 1-132
    Bacony Beans, 1-132
    Batter Bread, 2-231
    and Bean Casserole, 7-1066
    Bean, and Onion Chowder, 11-1691

and Beef Succotash, 1-133
Biscuits, 1-134
-Buttermilk Waffles, 2-238
-Cheese Toast, 11-1825
Chutney and Bacon Fingers, Hot, 1-86
-Corn Fritters, 8-1224
Cured, 4-523
Dip, 11-1697
Bacon (and) Egg(s)
    and Corn Cakes, 1-134
    with Noodles, 8-1233
    Pie, 4-626
    Skillet, 1-133
with Fresh Mustard Greens, 8-1204
Fried Apples with, 1-45
and Green-Bean Salad, 4-565
Island Toast with, 11-1826
and Liver Sandwiches, 7-1076
Muffins, 2-237
with Mushrooms, Broiled, 8-1200
Nutburgers, 6-869
and Olive Rolls, 7-1089
and Peanut Butter Sandwich, 1-134
Peanut-Butter Spread, 8-1324
Peanut Sandwiches, 8-1325
and Potato Pudding (Peruna ja Pekoni
    Laatikko), 5-681
Potato Salad, Hot, with, 1-134
Relish, Sweet-and-Sour, 2-191
Rolls, 2-281
Sauce with Peas, 1-134
Slaw (Spekkie Sla), 4-592
with Succotash, 3-484
-Topped Macaroni and Cheese, 7-1093
and Veal Terrine, 12-1894
Waffles, 12-1914

Bacon, Canadian
    Baked, with Port-Wine Sauce, 7-1151
    with Currant Jelly (Hamburgryg med
        Ribsgelé), 4-540
    -Kraut-Potato Skillet, 1-133
    and Veal Terrine, 12-1894
Backhendl (Fried Chicken), 1-122
Badun (curry), 4-527
Bagels, 1-134
Bagna Cauda, Piedmontese (Hot Bath),
    10-1627
Bahamian Tomato Canapés, 1-86
Bahia Style Shrimps (Camarões a Bahia),
    11-1704
Baked Alaska, 1-136
Baked Alaska, Grapefruit, 5-814
Baked Products, To Freeze, 5-737
Baking Powder, To Measure, 7-1117
Baklava (Filled Pastry), 5-823; 8-1216
Balachong, Fresh Tomato (Pazundok Ngapi
    Gyaw), 11-1716
Balinese Spiced Eggs (Telur Masak Bali),
    11-1714
Balkan Stuffed Eggplant, 4-616
Balm, 1-137

Bamboo Shoot(s), 1-138
    Pork with (Tung Sun Ch'ao Jo), 3-399
    Salad, Chinese, 10-1583
    Sautéed, 1-138

Banana(s), 1-138
    and Apricot Cup, 1-107
    Baked, in Fresh Orange Juice, 1-139
    Baked (Maia Kalua), 9-1435
    Black-and-White Marshmallow Delight,
        7-1114
    Butternut-Banana Bread, 8-1225
    and Cantaloupe Salad, 1-142
    Chiffon Pie, 9-1397
    Christmas Tarts, 11-1812
    Coffee-Banana Bavarian, 6-980
    in Cream, 5-758
    Cream Pie, 1-139
    in Currant Jelly, Baked 1-139
    Curry, 4-527
    -Filled Orange Layer Cake, 1-142
    Foster, Brennan's, 4-513
    Fried, 1-35

Fritters, 1-139
Fritters (Empanadas de Plátanos), 11-1708
Frosted, 7-1160
Fruits and Roots, Sweet (Ginatan), 9-1370
-Ham Rolls, Glazed, 6-856
and Ham, Spiced, 6-853
Heavenly (Maduros en Gloria), 11-1709
with Honey, Baked, 1-139
Ice Cream, 6-929
-Mace Whipped Topping, 7-1100
Meringue Pie, 9-1392
Meringue Pudding, 1-142
-Nut Bread, 1-139
Nut Pie, Creamy, 5-801
Orange, and Walnut Salad, 10-1588
Paste with Cheese (Bananada con Queijo),
    11-1709
Peanut Salad, 8-1323
Pie, 9-1393
Plantain(s), 9-1414
    Baked, 9-1414
    Balls Soup, 9-1414
    Chips, 9-1414
    Curry, 4-527
    with Pork Cracklings, 9-1414
    Turnovers, Jamaican, 9-1414
Pudding (Pudim de Bananas), 9-1457
au Rhum, 5-701
in Rum Custard Sauce, 2-304
Shake, Slim, 7-1088
-Shrimp Curry, 1-139
Soufflé, 7-1098
Split, 6-934
Split Salad, 5-755
Stoba, 2-301
Toast, 11-1825
Bananada con Queijo (Banana Paste with
    Cheese), 11-1709
Banbury Tarts, 1-142
Banbury Tarts, Rich, 8-1308
Bannocks, Drop, 1-142
Bannock, Trapper's Sweet, 1-62
Bárány Pörkölt Árpakásával (Lamb and
    Barley Stew), 6-918
Barbados Barbecue Sauce, 10-1623
Barbecue Menus, 1-144; 4-644, 645

Barbecue Sauce(s), 1-146; **10**-1614, 1623
    Apricot, 1-147
    Barbados, 10-1623
    Chili, 5-725
    Curry, 10-1623
    Fresh-Lemon, 7-1053
    Greek, 1-146
    Herb, 10-1623
    Honey, 10-1623
    Hot, Deep South, 10-1623
    Lemon, Savory, 1-146
    Molasses, 8-1184
    Orange, 1-146
    Pineapple-Chili, 10-1623
    Piquant, 5-726
    Red-Hot, 10-1623
    Relish, Chuck's, 10-1543
    Sherry, 10-1624
    (for Shrimps), 3-403
    Smoky, 10-1624
    Soppin' Sauce, 11-1731
    Texas Hot, 1-146
    Wine, 5-726
Bareh Pello, 8-1215

Barley, 1-147
    Casserole, 1-147
    and Chicken Livers, 3-391
    Flour, 5-707
    and Lamb Soup, 11-1695
    Mushroom-Barley Casserole, 8-1200
    Mushroom Barley Soup, 6-987
    -Onion Soup with Beef Balls, 7-1122
    Pudding, Finnish, 1-62
    Soup (Gerstensuppe), 1-121
    Soup (Krupnik), 9-1421
    Water, 1-147
Barmbrack, 6-949
Barquettes, 2-280

C

G

H

Limpa Bread, 2-229
Limu Niu (Coconut Spinach), 9-1435
Lindströmin Pihvi (Beef à la Lindstrom), 5-680
Lindy's Strawberry-Glazed Cheesecake, 3-367
Lingonberries with Cabbage Salad (Kålsallad med Lingon), 11-1791
Linguado Recheado (Ana of Povoa's Stuffed Sole), 9-1455
Linzer Torte, 4-635

Liqueur, 7-1069
Soufflé, 11-1688
Liquids, To Measure, 7-1117
Lisbon Turkey Stuffing (Recheio a Moda de Lisboa Para Peru), 9-1457

Litchi or **Lichee Nut,** 7-1071
Gelatin Dessert, 7-1072
and Peach Dessert, Jellied, 7-1072
Salad, 7-1072
Litsong Baboy (Barbecued Suckling Pig), 9-1369

Liver, 7-1072
Beef
and Bacon, Broiled, 2-192
French-Fried, 7-1073
and Limas, Creole, 7-1073
Liver Dumpling Soup (Leberknödelsuppe), 5-793
and Noodles, Italian Style, 7-1073
and Onions, Smothered, 7-1073
with Onions, Venetian, 2-192
Panfried, 2-192
Potted, Danish Style, 2-192
Pudding, 1-49
and Sausage Loaf, 10-1636
-and-Sausage Ring, Savory, 7-1073
Sautéed, Bernese (Berner Leberli), 11-1802
and Vegetables, Piquant, 7-1073
and Brown-Rice Ring, 7-1073
Calf's Liver (Veal)
Baked, 9-1351
Deviled (Athae Chin Gyaw), 11-1717
Dumplings, Delicate, 7-1074
Loaf, 7-1128
Pirozhki, 10-1568
Sautéed (Geröstete Kalbsleber), 1-122
Steak Béarnaise, 7-1073; 12-1897
Swiss, 7-1073
Chicken
-and-Bacon Sandwiches, 7-1076
with Carrots and Peas, 7-1075
Chopped, 6-987; 7-1075
Cutlets, 9-1470
and Green Beans, Sautéed, 7-1075
Omelet, 7-1075
Pâté, 7-1075
Pâté, Ruby-Glazed, 6-979
with Rice Soup, Italian, 7-1075
with Sage, 10-1578
with Sage (Fegatini di Pollo alla Salvia), 6-955
Sauce, 7-1076
in Sour Cream, 7-1076
Terrine, Quick and Easy, 8-1312
in Curry-Tomato Sauce, Braised, 7-1072
Deviled in Croustades, 7-1073
Dumplings, 4-586; 7-1147
Goose
and Greben, Chopped, 7-1075
To Cook, see Pâté de Foie Gras, 5-708
Truffled, 5-708
Lamb
Balls and Noodles, 7-1074
Creole, 7-1074
Pot Roast with Noodles, 7-1074
with Rice, 7-1040
Savory Baked, 7-1074
and Mushrooms, 7-1072; 8-1198
Pâté (Leverpostej), 4-536

Pork
with Barbecue Sauce, 7-1074
in Mustard Sour-Cream Sauce, 11-1698
with Onions, French, 7-1075
Pâté, Danish, 7-1074
Pot-Roasted, with Barbecue Sauce, 9-1476
Pudding, Old-Fashioned, 9-1448
Sauce, 9-1369
and Vegetable Pie, Savory, 7-1075
and Vegetables, 7-1074
Pudding (Maksalaatikko), 5-680
Sausage, see Liverwurst
Sliced, with Spleen Sauce (Iscas), 9-1456
Steaks, 11-1771

Liverwurst or **Liver Sausage,** 7-1076
Appetizer Salad, 10-1635
with Creole Sauce, 7-1076
Filling, 4-662
Masked Liver Mold, 10-1635
Mushroom Liver Pâté, 7-1076; 8-1197
Patties, 7-1076
Potato, and Egg Salad, 7-1076
Sandwiches, 7-1076
Spread, 2-280
Lizzies, 3-435
Llapingachos (Potato and Cheese Patties), 11-1708

Lobster, 7-1076
-Avocado Sandwiches, 7-1081
Bisque, 7-1077
Bordelaise, 2-213
au Brandy, 7-1078
Broiled, 1-146
Butter, 10-1615, 1624
Cantonese (Ch'ao Lung Hsia), 3-399
Casserole à la Costa, 7-1080
Chowder, 3-419
Chowder, Fish, Jamaican, 6-967
Crab-Stuffed, 7-1080
Egg-Lobster Salad, Molded, 7-1080
Fried (Gebratener Hummer), 5-793
Liguanea, 7-1081
Lobsterburgers, 10-1602
Macaroni, and Artichoke Salad, 7-1092
Macaroni, and Orange Salad, 7-1092
Marinade for, Uncooked, 7-1110
-Muffin Sandwiches, 11-1722
and Mushrooms Parmesan, 8-1198
Newburg, 7-1078; 8-1218
-Noodle Casserole, 2-321
and Orange Cocktail, 7-1077
Pie (Quiche de Langouste), 5-740
Pilaf, 2-321
Quiche, 10-1529
Rabbit, 7-1081
Ring, Jellied, 7-1080
Salad, 10-1583
Salad, English Style, 4-621
Salad Tropicale, 10-1581
Sauce, 5-695; 7-1150
Sauce (Hummersaus), 8-1236
and Shell Chowder, 7-1091
Soufflé, 7-1078
Spread, 2-280
Stew, 7-1078
Stew, Wiscasset, 1-45

Lobster, Rock-Lobster Tails
in Almond Sauce, 7-1078
Boiled, 9-1384
and Chicken, Costa Brava, 7-1080
Chowder, 7-1078
Curried, 7-1078
Deviled, South African, 7-1080
and Fillet of Cod Sarapico, 7-1080
French-Fried Butterfly, 7-1078
Salad, Curried, 10-1582
Steamed, 7-1078
Stuffed, 7-1081

Loganberry(ies), 7-1081
-Cheese Tarts, 7-1081
Ice, 7-1082

Jam, 6-965; 7-1082
Pie, 7-1081
Loggers' Flapjacks, 5-703
Løksaus (Onion Sauce), 8-1240

Lokshen Kugel (Noodle Pudding), 6-993
Lomi Lomi Salmon (Hawaiian Salad), 1-34
London Broil, see Beef, Flank Steak

Loquat(s), 7-1082
Jam, 7-1082
Spiced, 7-1082
Lord Baltimore Cake, 1-46
Lord Baltimore Cake, Golden, 7-1045
Lorenzo à la Filipini, 2-281
Lorraine Salad, 9-1469
Losoś do Sosów Goracych i Zimnych (Poached Salmon), 9-1422
Lotus Ice Cream, 8-1276
Louis Dressing, 10-1614, 1622
Louisiana Pancakes, 11-1797
Louisiana Pecan Cake, 4-513

Low Calorie, 7-1082
Angel Cake Lemon Delight, 7-1088
Apricot Whip, Baked, 7-1087
Banana Slim Shake, 7-1088
Beef Patties, Barbecued, 7-1084
Blueberry-Topped Cheesecake, 7-1087
Buttermilk Dressing (salad), 2-254
Canapé, Cheese Mushroom, 3-355
Cheese-Tomato Grill, 7-1085
Chicken, Fried, 3-383
Chicken, Glazed Roast, 7-1085
Chocolate Mousse, 3-415
Chocolate Sauce, 3-416
Cod Fillets, Creole, 7-1084
Coffee Sponge, 7-1087
Cottage Beef and Eggs, 7-1084
Cottage Cheese and Cucumber Salad, 7-1085
Crab-Cheese Dip, 7-1083
Cucumber Sauce, 7-1086
Curried Lamb Mold, 7-1084
Eggs, Swiss, 7-1085
Fruit-Cocktail Whip, 7-1088
Green-Bean and Carrot Salad, 7-1085
Green Beans, Cape Cod Style, 7-1086
Green Peppers, Sautéed, 7-1086
Lemon Custard, Frozen, 7-1054
Lemon Topping, 7-1088
Lime-Grape Dessert, 7-1088
Mocha Molds, 7-1167
Mushrooms, Stuffed, 7-1083
Onions and Cucumber, Curried, 7-1086
Orange Cake, 7-1087
Orange-Milk Starter, 7-1088
Peach Sherbet, 7-1087
Pineapple Sherbet, 9-1410
Radishes, Braised, 7-1087
Radish Salad, Panama, 7-1086
Salad Dressing, Cooked, 7-1086
Salad Dressing, Piquant, 7-1086
Salad, Patio, 7-1085
Salad, Silhouette, 7-1086
Seasonings for Fish, Meat, and Poultry, 7-1084
Seasonings for Vegetables, 7-1086
Shrimps and Vegetables, Skewered, 7-1084
Slick Chick Soup, 7-1083
Strawberry Fluff, 7-1087
Tomatoes and Cabbage, Simmered, 7-1087
Tomato Salad Dressing, 7-1086
Tuna Salad, Jellied, 7-1085
Tuna, Scalloped, 7-1084
Vegetable Soup, Creole, 7-1084
Luau, Chicken, 1-34

Luncheon Menus
Buffet Luncheon, 7-1089
Intimate Luncheon, 4-632
Parisian Luncheon, 4-633
Salad Luncheon, 7-1089
Spring Luncheon, 4-632
Lusitanian Oysters (Ostras Lusitanas), 9-1456
Lutfisk, see Cod, Codfish

M

N

O

S

Salad(s), Fruit, continued
Cottage-Cheese and Blueberry, **10**-1587
Cranberry-Cream, **10**-1587
Cranberry and Orange, Jellied (QC),
10-1523
Crenshaw Fruit Salad Supreme, **3**-495
Five-Fruit Salad Plate, **5**-754
Fresh Grape and Plum, **5**-812
Fresh-Pear Cactus, **8**-1330
Fresh-Pear, Cheese, and Anchovy, **8**-1330
Fresh Pineapple and Avocado, **9**-1408
Fresh Tangerine and Apple, **11**-1809
Fresno, **10**-1588
Fruit, with Coconut Dressing, **3**-456
Fruit Plate with Pistachio Cheese, **5**-755
Fruit Salad Bowl, **1**-33
Grape and Cheese, **5**-812
Grape, Pear, and Celery, **10**-1588
Guava, **1**-33; **5**-829
Golden-Apple, **1**-77
Lemon and Orange, **7**-1052
October, **10**-1587
Orange, Banana, and Walnut, **10**-1588
Orange and Date, **10**-1588
Patio, **7**-1085
Peach, Four, **8**-1316
Peanut-Butter, **8**-1325
Pear-Cheese, **8**-1330
Persimmon, Grapefruit, and
Pomegranate, **9**-1364
Pineapple-Orange, **9**-1408
Pineapple-Strawberry, **5**-758; **7**-1089
Pineapple, Two-Tone, **9**-1408
Prune-Plum and Grape, **9**-1415
Seafoam, **10**-1587
Southwestern, **11**-1727
Virginia City, **1**-56
Waldorf, **1**-60; **10**-1588
Waldorf, Pineapple, **10**-1588

Salad(s), Jellied
Avocado, **1**-130
Avocado Ring with Strawberries, **11**-1776
Cabbage, **10**-1583
Cheese Ring, **10**-1588
Cheese and Strawberry, **11**-1776
Cider, **1**-103; **3**-446
Cinnamon-Apple, **10**-1587
Clam-Aspic, **6**-979
Cottage-Cheese and Tomato, Jellied,
6-980
Cottage Pear, **3**-361
Crabmeat, **10**-1583
Crabmeat, Molded, **6**-979
Crabmeat Ring, Jellied, **7**-1080
Cranberry, **4**-632
Cranberry-Cream, **10**-1587
Cranberry Fruit Ring, **3**-424
Cranberry, Jellied, **8**-1225
Cranberry and Orange (QC), **10**-1523
Cucumber, **8**-1225
Deviled-Egg, **5**-788
Egg-Lobster, Molded, **7**-1080
Egg and Olive Mold, **4**-606
Fish Ring, Jellied, **7**-1080
Fresh Blueberry and Lime Mold, **2**-208
Fresh Grape and Chicken Mold, **5**-812
Fresh-Grapefruit and Apple, Molded,
5-814
Fresh-Pear and Cucumber Aspic, **8**-1330
Fresh-Plum, Jellied, **9**-1417
Fruit-Cocktail Loaf, **5**-788
Ginger-Ale Fruit Mold, **5**-803
Ginger Peach Mold, **8**-1317
Grapefruit, Jellied, **5**-814
Ham, Molded, **6**-858
July Day Salad, **1**-14
Lemon-Orange-Cottage-Cheese Mold,
7-1052
Lemon, Spiced Prunes in, **11**-1754
Lime and Blueberry, Molded, **7**-1067
Lime and Cheese, Jellied, **7**-1067
Lime-Pear, **8**-1330
Litchi, **7**-1072
Liver, Tomato, and Cream-Cheese
Loaf, **5**-787

Lobster, **10**-1583
Lobster Ring, Jellied, **7**-1080
October, **10**-1587
Orange Cottage-Cheese Cups, **8**-1268
Orange-Ginger-Ale Mold, **5**-803
Orange-Pineapple, **5**-788
Pâté de Foie Gras in Aspic, **5**-708
Pear and Blue-Cheese, **5**-788
Pear and Cream-Cheese, Jellied, **6**-980
Pear de Menthe, **8**-1330
Pecan and Apple, Jellied, **8**-1334
Pineapple Blue-Cheese Ring, **7**-1153
Pineapple Cheese Mold, **5**-788
Pineapple, Two-Tone, **9**-1408
Potato, Jellied, **5**-787
Salmon Loaf, Curried, **10**-1595
Salmon Salad Ring, Molded, with
Cucumbers in Sour Cream, **5**-786
Seafoam, **10**-1587
Seafood Cocktail, **5**-786
Shrimp Mold, Savory, **6**-979
Shrimp Ring, Jellied, **7**-1080
Silhouette, **7**-1086
Spinach Mold with Ham, **5**-787
Tomato-Ham, **10**-1583
Tomato-Juice Squares (QC), **10**-1523
Tomato, Masked, **7**-1115
Tuna and Avocado, Molded, **5**-787
Tuna, Jellied, **7**-1085
Tuna and Salmon Mold, **10**-1583
Tuna-Vegetable Mold, **12**-1866
Vegetable, **5**-787
Vegetable Ring, Jellied, **6**-980
Vegetable Salad, Jellied, **3**-424
Waldorf, Jellied, **1**-100
Watermelon, Molded, **12**-1920
Western Perfection, **2**-258
Winter Fruit, Molded, **5**-755

Salad(s), Main-Dish Salads
Albacore, Pickled, **1**-8
Almond-Chicken, **1**-14
Apple-Tuna, **12**-1867
Artichoke and Shrimp, **1**-112
Avocado Crabmeat, à la Ritz, **1**-130
Avocado Halves with Spiced Shrimps,
10-1581
Avocado Shrimp Boats, Puerto Rican,
1-130
Bean and Cheese, **10**-1582
Beef, French, **10**-1580
Brain, **8**-1211
Cantaloupe and Shrimp Luncheon Salad,
Fresh, **2**-296
Celery and Crabmeat, **10**-1582
Cheese-and-Bacon Rice, **10**-1550
Cheese (Käsesalat), **11**-1804
Cheese-Potato, Hot, **10**-1582
Chef's, Brussels, **10**-1580
Chef's, California, **5**-825; **7**-1063
Chef's, Classic, **10**-1580
Chef's, Orange, **10**-1580
Chicken, **3**-391
Chicken-Avocado, **1**-130
Chicken, Chinese, **10**-1582
Chicken-Macaroni, Baked, **7**-1094
Chicken, Perfect, **10**-1582
Chicken (QC), **10**-1522
Chicken and Rice, with Cashews, **2**-314
Crab, Curried, **3**-488
Crab, Dressed, **4**-621
Crab and Grapefruit, with Avocado
Mayonnaise, **12**-1934
Crab, Hot, **12**-1928
Crab Louis, **3**-488
Crabmeat, **10**-1583
Duck, Alaska, **1**-23
Dungeness Crab Louis, **1**-76
Egg, Ham, and Macaroni, **4**-607
Egg-Macaroni, **7**-1095
Egg, Mexican, **4**-523
Egg, Piquant, **4**-606
Egg-Salad-Stuffed Tomatoes, **10**-1582
Egg, Savory, **4**-606
Fish, in Clamshells, **10**-1665
Fish and Macaroni, **7**-1092

Frankfurter and Potato, Hot, **5**-722
Frankfurters and Hot-Potato, **10**-1580
Fresh-Grapefruit and Crab, **5**-814
Fresh-Grapefruit and Salmon, **5**-814
Fresh-Grapefruit Shrimp, **10**-1581
Fresh-Pear and Crabmeat, **8**-1330
Grape-Turkey, **5**-812
Green-Bean, with Potatoes, Hot (Salade
Liègeoise), **2**-200
Green-Bean and Potato (Insalata di
Fagiolini e Patate), **6**-960
Ham, **1**-38; **6**-858
Ham, Broiled, **6**-858
Ham and Egg, **6**-864
Ham Fruit Salad, **6**-858
Ham and Macaroni, Hot, **7**-1094
Herring, **6**-913
Herring and Ham (Sill och Skinksallad),
11-1787
Herring (Haringsla), **4**-590
Herring, Salmagundi, **9**-1383
Honeydew Rings with Shrimp Salad,
6-911
Kidney-Bean, **1**-159
Lamb, Cucumber, and Tomato, **10**-1580
Lamb and Potato, Minted, **10**-1580
Liver-Sausage Appetizer, **10**-1635
Liverwurst, Potato, and Egg, **7**-1076
Lobster, **10**-1583
Lobster, English Style, **4**-621
Lobster, Tropicale, **10**-1581
Macaroni, Bean, and Egg, **7**-1095
Macaroni and Cheese, **7**-1095
Macaroni, Cheese, and Sour-Cream,
10-1582
Macaroni, Lobster, and Artichoke, **7**-1092
Macaroni, Lobster, and Orange, **7**-1092
Macaroni, Shrimp, and Orange, **7**-1092
Macaroni, Tuna, and Orange, **7**-1092
Meat (Kjøttsalat), **8**-1235
Meat and Vegetable, **10**-1580
Mock Lobster, **5**-689
Mussel, **8**-1203
Nham, **11**-1717
Olivier (Salat Olivier), **10**-1566
Orange Chicken, **8**-1268
Oyster, **8**-1290
Peanut-Butter Potato, **8**-1325
Pineapple-Ham, **9**-1408
Pineapple, Tuna, and Rice, **9**-1408
Potato, with Ham and Cherries (Karto-
felnii Salat s Vechinoi i Vishniami),
10-1566
Rockfish, Curried, **10**-1558
Rock-Lobster, Curried, **10**-1582
Salade Niçoise, **9**-1384; **10**-1582
Salade Parisienne, **10**-1580
Salade Russe, **10**-1587
Salami-Carrot, **10**-1589
Salmagundi, **7**-1039
Salmagundi, with Salami and Liverwurst,
10-1580
Salmon, **10**-1582
Salmon Louis, **10**-1597
Salmon-Potato, **10**-1597
Salt-Herring, **10**-1665
Sardine and Cheese, **10**-1612
Sauerkraut and Bean, Hot, **10**-1632
Seafood, **10**-1665
Seafood (Nuta), **6**-972
Shellfish Plate, **10**-1652
Shrimp, **6**-911; **10**-1580
Shrimp and Celery, **10**-1662
Shrimp-Crab, Hot, **10**-1652
Shrimp and Egg, Japanese, **10**-1580
Shrimp, Exotic, **10**-1662
Shrimp-Grapefruit, **10**-1662
Shrimp Macaroni, **10**-1662
Smoked-Sturgeon Deviled Eggs, **11**-1782
Supper Salad, **5**-775
Sweetbread and Cucumber, **11**-1794;
12-1897
Tomato-Ham, Jellied, **10**-1583
Tuna-Fish, **10**-1582
Tuna, Marinated, **12**-1867
Tuna Plate (Thon en Salade), **11**-1802

T

U

V

W

Y

Z

ACKNOWLEDGEMENTS

The editors and publisher of *Woman's Day* wish to thank the authors, publishers, and copyright owners listed below for their permission to reprint special material.

Six recipes in **Austrian Cookery, Volume 1,** from *The Viennese Cookbook* by Irma Rhode, copyright 1951 by Hill and Wang, Inc., and reprinted by permission of Hill and Wang.

Eight recipes in **Belgian Cookery, Volume 2,** from *A Belgian Cookbook* by Juliette Elkon, copyright © 1958 by Farrar, Straus & Giroux, Inc., and reprinted by permission of Farrar, Straus and Cudahy, Inc.

Seven recipes in the **Bread** entry, **Volume 2,** from *The Pepperidge Farm Cookbook* by Margaret Rudkin, copyright © 1963 by Margaret Rudkin, and reprinted by permission of Atheneum Publishers; registered trade mark ® Pepperidge Farm, Inc.

The Art of Chinese Cookery in **Volume 3,** from *The Art of Chinese Cooking* by Mimi Ouei, copyright © 1960 by Mimi Ouei, and published by Random House, Inc.

The Twelve Days Before Christmas in **Volume 3,** originally published in *Woman's Day,* December, 1962, and incorporated in *A Sense of Seasons* by Jean Hersey, copyright © 1964 by Jean Hersey; used by permission of Dodd, Mead & Co., Inc.

Six recipes in **Czechoslovakian Cookery, Volume 4,** from the *Bohemian-American Cook Book* by Marie Rosicky, and reprinted by permission of Automatic Printing Co.

Dutch Cookery in **Volume 4,** from *The Art of Dutch Cooking* by C. Countess van Limburg Stirum, copyright © 1961 by C. Countess van Limburg Stirum, and reprinted by permission of Doubleday & Company, Inc.

Thirteen recipes in the **Game** entry, **Volume 5,** from *The Wild Game Wild Fowl Cook Book* by Martin Rywell, copyright © 1952 by Martin Rywell, and published by Pioneer Press, Harriman, Tennessee.

Irish Cookery in **Volume 6,** from *Feasting Galore* by Maura Laverty, copyright 1952, 1955, © 1957, 1961 by Maura Laverty, and reprinted by permission of Holt, Rinehart and Winston, Inc.

Norwegian Cookery in **Volume 8** and **Swedish Cookery** in **Volume 11,** from *The Art of Scandinavian Cooking,* copyright © 1965 by Nika Standen Hazelton and published by The Macmillan Company, New York, and Collier-Macmillan Canada, Ltd., Toronto, Ontario.

Puerto Rican Cookery in **Volume 9,** from *The Art of Caribbean Cookery* by Carmen Aboy Valldejuli, copyright © 1957, 1963 by Carmen Aboy Valldejuli, and published by Doubleday & Company, Inc.

Russian Cookery in **Volume 10,** from *The Best of Russian Cookery* by Alexandra Kropotkin, copyright © 1964 by Alexandra Kropotkin and published by Charles Scribner's Sons.